X-Planes of Europe

X-Planes of Europe

Secret Research Aircraft from the Golden Age 1946-1974

Tony Buttler and
Jean-Louis Delezenne

X-PLANES OF EUROPE

Published in 2012 by Hikoki Publications

©Tony Buttler and Jean-Louis Delezenne 2010

ISBN 9 781902 109213

All rights reserved. Apart from any fair dealing for the purpose of private study, research, criticism or review, as permitted under the Copyright, Design and Patents Act 1988, no part of this publication may be reproduced, stored in a retrieval system, or transmitted in any form or by any means, electronic, electrical, chemical, mechanical, optical, photocopying, recording or otherwise, without prior written permission. All enquiries should be directed to the publisher.

Printed in China

Hikoki
1a Ringway Trading Estate, Shadowmoss Rd,
Manchester M22 5LH
www.crecy.co.uk

Contents

Acknowledgments	7
Introduction	9
de Havilland DH.108 Swallow (1946)	15
Sud-Ouest SO 6000 Triton (1946)	22
Armstrong Whitworth AW.52 (1947)	27
Saunders-Roe SR.A/1 (1947)	36
Leduc 010, 016, 021 and 022 (1947-1956)	42
Arsenal VG 70 (1948)	52
Sud-Ouest SO M.2 (1949)	55
Avro 707 (1949)	58
Nord 1601 (1950)	70
Boulton Paul P.111 (1950)	73
Boulton Paul P.120 (1950)	82
Sud-Est SE 2410 Grognard I and SE 2415 Grognard II (1950-1951)	86
FAF (F + W) N-20-2 Arbalète (1951)	92
Fairey Delta 1 (1951)	98
Handley Page HP.88 (1951)	104
SAAB 210 (1952)	111
Short S.B.5 (1952)	115
Short S.B.1 and S.B.4 Sherpa (1953)	126
Sud-Est SE 5000 Baroudeur (1953)	134
Sud-Ouest SO 9000 Trident I and SO 9050 Trident II (1953-1955)	143
Rolls-Royce 'Flying Bedstead' (1953)	154
Nord 1402 Gerfaut I and 1405 Gerfaut II (1954-1955)	161
ONERA Deltaviex (1954)	168
Payen PA 49 Delta (1954)	171
Fairey Delta 2 (1954)	173
Nord 1500 Griffon I (1955) and Griffon II (1957)	184
SNECMA C.400 Atar Volant and C.450 Coléoptère (1955-1959)	196
Saunders-Roe SR.53 (1957)	206
Short S.C.1 (1957)	214
Hawker P.1127 (1960)	225
Handley Page HP.115 (1961)	234
Bristol 188 (1962)	238
Dassault Balzac (1962)	250
EWR VJ 101C (1963)	258
Hunting H.126 (1963)	266
BAC.221 (1964)	272
Dassault Mirage G (1967)	280
VFW VAK 191B (1971)	286
The Musée de l'Air et de l'Espace, Paris le Bourget	293
Surviving airframes	294
Glossary	295
Bibliography and Source Notes	297
Index	299

Dedication

To those who dreamed the impossible dream – the many devoted European aircraft designers and builders who created the rare and exotic aircraft you see on the following pages, and the courageous test pilots who, in too many cases, sacrificed their own lives in pursuit of aeronautical progress. The knowledge gained from their efforts allows modern military airmen to survive in hostile skies, and commercial air travellers to fly in comfort and safety at near-sonic speed to the four corners of the globe.

Acknowledgments

Great and sincere thanks must go to the following for their help in researching this book, and many apologies if anyone has been left out: British National Archives; Michel Benichou; Ken Ellis; Peter Green; Barry Guess and Mike Fielding (BAE Systems, Farnborough Archive); Bill Harrison; George Jenks and members of the BAE Woodford Heritage Centre; Harry Fraser-Mitchell (Handley Page Association); Henry Matthews; the late Eric Morgan; Wolfgang Muehlbauer; RAF Museum; Thomas Mueller; Brian Riddle (Royal Aeronautical Society); Alexis Rocher Clive Rustin; Peter Twiss; and Ray Williams. Also, mention must be made of the membership of the 'Secret Projects' web forum (which can be found on http://www.secretprojects.co.uk), who have supplied some important pieces of information.

Extra-special thanks must go to the following individuals: Phil Butler, for supplying many photos, for making the text of his articles in *Aeromilitaria* available, and for much other help; Chris Farara, for checking the accuracy and editing the text of several chapters; John Farley, for similar treatment to many of the English subjects, and for clarifying numerous technical points (so vital for a book of this nature); and to Mike Kirk, for his overall help with all matters relating to the Swiss aircraft.

Initially this book was contracted by Specialty Press in American, but in 2011 various policy decisions brought a switch to Crécy Publishing, with the final book to be produced under the Hikoki banner. My great appreciation goes to Mike Machat and the team at Specialty Press for all of their help during the early phase of the book's production, then to Jeremy Pratt, Gill Richardson and the team at Crécy for bringing it to fruition. It has been a pleasure to work with you all.

Tony Buttler
Bretforton, United Kingdom
February 2012

I would like to thank the many individuals responsible for their outstanding assistance in the production of this book, and to acknowledge the foresight of Specialty Press in recognising the importance of this subject matter, which covers a lesser-known but still very important chapter of aviation history.

In addition, I would like to express my deepest gratitude to the Musée de l'Air et de l'Espace du Bourget for allowing access to its photographic archives. I hope that through the words and photographs on these pages, I can bring back to life, even for a few moments, the magnificent pioneering aircraft now preserved forever in the proud air museum located at the historic Le Bourget Airport near Paris, France.

Finally, thanks to my wife, Suzie, who through the years has allowed for so much of my aviation material to occupy more space in our home each day.

Jean-Louis Delezenne
Sherman Oaks, California
February 2012

Introduction

The design of many of today's famous aircraft, both military and civilian, is still influenced by the achievements of research aircraft that first flew more than half a century ago. Their development and flight testing, often deep into unknown territory, could be thrilling and fascinating and, at times, very dangerous. In fact, many pilots lost their lives during this period because, although most of these aircraft carried no military load, just recording equipment, in some cases their performance was often in advance of the combat aircraft then in service. A striking example of how their work benefits us today is the Lockheed Martin F-35 Lightning II Joint Strike Fighter, which is being built in partnership with BAE Systems in the UK, the corporate outgrowth of many of the English companies mentioned here. The F-35's ingenious lift-fan and vectored-thrust system was first explored on aircraft such as the Short S.C.1 in 1957, the Hawker P.1127 of 1960, and the French Dassault Balzac in 1962. Indeed, there is a strong vein of vertical take-off study running throughout this entire volume.

A number of world aviation firsts, most of which are taken for granted in today's digital world, occurred at secluded flight test facilities in England and France, including development of the world's first jet airliner, the first rear-mounted jet engine transport, again the first VTOL jet fighter, and the first supersonic airliner. All utilised technological advances pioneered by the rare and exotic X-Planes of Europe. Some of the types featured are fortunately now proudly displayed in the permanent collections of aviation museums, and a comprehensive listing of these venues is found on page 294. The profusion of types described here also illustrates just how many new designs could appear over a relatively short period of time – difficult to imagine now in these days of very long-term development programmes. During the period spent writing this book, however, the Russian Sukhoi organisation flew its T-50 fighter, the first maiden flight of a major new combat aircraft to be seen anywhere in the world for many years. Just about a year later the Chinese flew the large Chengdu J 20 fighter and in the process indicated that the centre of development for new military aircraft is perhaps no longer now in America and Europe, but in Asia.

Selecting what to put in and leave out has been difficult, but the parameters have generally been aircraft for pure research only, with types that were really prototypes for combat aircraft left out. However, such a demarcation line can be extremely difficult when you get a type such as the Saunders-Roe SR.53, which in many respects fulfilled both roles, having first been ordered as a fighter prototype but later used purely for research. The same applies to Saro's SR.A/1, but each of these aircraft broke new ground (for the UK) in the field of rocket power and flying boats, respectively. In France the Dassault Mirage G series were in many respects fighter prototypes, but they were also the first French aircraft to have swing wings, so they must be included. Aircraft such as the Hawker P.1052 and Supermarine 510, however, were both built to gain experience with swept wings, but others before them (like the de Havilland DH.108) had already looked at that particular feature and each of these types was based on an existing fuselage (the Sea Hawk and Attacker jet fighters respectively), so they did not qualify. Likewise, the delta wing on the Dassault Mirage I prototype was preceded by another delta-winged aircraft, the Nord Gerfaut. The Handley Page HP.88, of course, also used an Attacker-type fuselage, but that aircraft looked at a new wing shape altogether. No doubt some readers will be disappointed that certain aircraft have been omitted, but that also means that debate about the subject is still ongoing after all of this time – not a bad thing in our modern age.

We must say how delighted we were to be asked to co-write this book, which has been a most enjoyable task. The list contains some of our all-time favourite aeroplanes, but in fact all of the types covered here are full of interest to the aviation historian. We hope you receive just as much enjoyment in reading about them.

Many of the aircraft types produced in the United Kingdom included here have been featured previously both in books specifically covering research aircraft and in individual magazine articles. Consequently, much of the information may well be familiar to some readers, but the author has delved deep into the National Archives at Kew and other collections to provide what is hoped to be a good amount of new information as well. Some explanations are required for the background to the testing of these aeroplanes.

In the text you will find countless references to the Society of British Aircraft Constructors (SBAC) Show, which was held initially at Radlett, then at Farnborough in September of each year. This body was the British aircraft industry's national trade association and as such represented companies that manufactured and supplied all manner of aircraft and equipment to customers. It covered the civil, military and space sectors, and pretty well every aircraft and engine manufacturer, and their subcontractors such as metal alloy suppliers, was a member. British readers know what a high-profile and high-value event Farnborough was, and the Paris Show was, of course, just as important to the French aircraft industry. These were trade shows and a shop window where the two national industries could show off their new products, usually vital for any new aircraft, and they were also some of the few occasions where the public could see these usually secret aeroplanes.

The first two post-war SBAC Shows at Radlett took place in 1946 and 1947 and were private events open by invitation only; at that stage most of the exhibits were still propeller-driven. In 1948 the Show moved to Farnborough where it has been ever since, and the public has been admitted on certain days. From 1962 it went biennial (like Paris Le Bourget), and the exhibition of foreign aircraft was sanctioned in 1966 (although at that stage only if they used a British engine or major components). Big sales efforts were made before and during the shows, backed up with plenty of publicity photographs and material. As a consequence, the best images of many research aircraft were made just prior to and during these shows, although sadly a few did not last very long, and pictures of some of them are few.

There are also plenty of references to the Royal Aircraft Establishment (RAE), both at Farnborough in Hampshire and Bedford, and to the Aeroplane & Armament Experimental Establishment (A&AEE) at Boscombe Down near Salisbury in Wiltshire. Farnborough is one of the great names of British aviation history. Apart from analysing aircraft, the RAE undertook all manner of general aviation research for which an immensely impressive collection of test facilities (including wind tunnels) was gradually put together. Indeed, some of the most important research in aviation history was carried out at the various RAE sites, but particularly at

With the SR.A/1 Saunders-Roe became specialists in the category of flying boat jet fighters and in 1951 it produced this advertisement for possible future developments.

INTRODUCTION

Farnborough. RAE Bedford, in the county town of Bedfordshire, was in 1946 established at the RAF airfield at Thurleigh; it subsequently became an important research and experiment facility and saw a considerable amount of aircraft development test flying.

Boscombe Down was (and is) the facility where new British military aircraft were checked and cleared for service use, but the Establishment's long concrete runway also made it ideal for the first flights of many research aircraft. A&AEE Boscombe Down was opened in 1939 after the organisation had moved from its previous home at Martlesham Heath in Suffolk. A lack of space usually prevents anything more than a passing mention for the test pilots, but in the UK during the 1950s many of them were as famous as today's top sportsmen and women.

By comparison with the UK, French experimental programmes did not receive the same archival coverage or preservation of information. Indeed, since most of these aircraft were tested in complete secrecy the amount of archival material available sometimes remains limited. Perhaps the most graphic example of this disparity is seen in the number of European X-Planes still in existence and preserved for posterity today. For instance, of the nineteen basic types of research aircraft tested in Great Britain from 1946 to 1964, thirteen actual airframes remain in various museums located throughout the United Kingdom. Of the fifteen different types of French research aircraft flown from 1946 to 1962, only six aeroplanes can be found, and they are all in the same museum near Paris.

Also, unlike the equally vital and pioneering aviation industry of Great Britain, the thriving French aviation industry of the 1920s and 1930s came to an abrupt halt during the German occupation of France during the Second World War. Although the last two years of that war witnessed the introduction of the first turbojet engines used in combat fighter aircraft, in late 1945 the French aviation industry found itself with no experience in adapting this new powerplant to existing airframe designs. Although several French test pilots had the unique opportunity of flying the first Allied jet aircraft in England after the war, the rare jets captured from the German Luftwaffe had not yet reached France for testing. Hence, in 1945 the French aeronautical industry had literally to start from a clean sheet of paper. Indeed, France faced the virtual rebuilding of her aircraft industry.

A host of problems and other rather significant challenges loomed large for the development of post-war French aviation. For one thing, most of the remaining aircraft factories had been forced into producing machinery and general goods for the occupying Germans and were thus, rather ironically, bombed into oblivion by Allied forces. A great deal of the mechanical tooling involved was either secretly transferred to Germany or simply lost during the war. In addition, by 1945 about 90% of productive capacity had been destroyed, technicians were dispersed and there were no full-scale design offices in existence. To further complicate matters, raw materials for manufacturing of any sort were also very scarce.

Around the world, engineers in the field of aerodynamic research were becoming quite active in the refinement of aircraft design for an entirely new generation of aeroplanes capable of reaching near-sonic speeds. This was in the interest of bolstering an air force's ability to intercept rapidly approaching enemy bombers as fast as possible. France, however, was in a very limited financial position in 1945, and was thus unable to create a large national aviation design and manufacturing industry. The interim government therefore decided to reorganise the industry into a grouping of manufacturing activities arranged by their geographical location within five distinctive sectors of the country. In a textbook example of seeking to achieve excellence through competition, this new policy was formulated to encourage each of the national design centres to develop its own independent avenues of research and design.

This new regionalised French industry soon learned to adapt during the enactment of a five-year master plan that defined, in very specific terms, all the requirements needed for machines that would serve the armed forces. Aeronautical factories could now work under licence and at the same time produce some exciting and innovative new French aircraft designs. In fact it did not take long for a strong start to be made, and in 1947 there were thirty-three prototypes of different types built, although the quality was admittedly somewhat variable. Two years later thirty-eight prototypes were constructed and it was by then clear that, whatever might be lacking in resources, the ideas were there in plenty. The next stage was to begin a rationalisation of the facilities in order to produce aircraft of international repute that would stand alongside the products of other nations, and if possible make them even better. Hence another decision was made to nationalise the industry to make it stable but also to keep a thriving section (about 26%) under free enterprise. As such both portions worked

X-PLANES OF EUROPE

remarkably well, and by 1957 the development of the French aircraft industry had reached a stage where it had entered European and world markets with a selection of well-designed and well-made aircraft of all kinds. And this was backed by active research in many fields.

In the 1950s designs for an entirely new generation of high-performance jet-powered aircraft were begun, which resulted in lighter and faster aeroplanes intended to intercept any high-altitude foreign aerial threat. Most of the fighter designs assessed in France during the 1950s were developed towards the same goal; in addition, rocket and ramjet powerplants, used either by themselves or in combination with turbojet engines, were tested extensively during this time.

Listed below are the names of the major regional manufacturing centres (Sociétés Nationales), with brief descriptions of the major projects for which they were responsible. It should be noted at this point that much has been written about the French aviation industry over the years, and it appears that no two examples contain exactly the same nomenclature when describing certain aircraft types. Specifically, the use of full stops within company names or aircraft designations seems quite random at first glance, with an aircraft like the famed Sud-Est Caravelle referred to as the 'SE-210', 'SE. 210', or even 'S.E. 210'. Likewise, the acronym used for French engine manufacturer SNECMA has also been written as 'S.N.E.C.M.A'. For the purpose of consistency within this book, the names of French aircraft companies and aircraft designations are written without full stops.

Also, for completeness it is worth recording some other background history. The former l'Arsenal de l'Aéronautique company was established back in 1936 in an old Breguet factory at Villacoublay. In 1947 Arsenal was privatised and at the end of 1952 the organisation became SFECMAS (Société Française d'Étude et de Construction de Matériels Aéronautiques Special). Then in 1955 SFECMAS was merged with SNCAN as SNCAN Nord. In addition SNCAC, the Société Nationale de Constructions Aéronautiques du Centre, and also known at times as Aérocentre, had been formed in 1936 by the nationalisation of the Farman Aviation Works and the Hanriot company. This organisation was liquidated after the end of the Second World War and in 1949 its assets were distributed between SNCAN, SNCASO and SNECMA. The Farman brothers had gone on to re-establish their firm in 1941 as the Société Anonyme des Usines Farman, or SAUF, but this new company was absorbed by SNCASO in 1944. A further attempt was made

The most ardent example of the successful application of research data accumulated from the great aircraft shown in this book is the incomparable Aérospatiale-BAC Concorde, seen here in an artist's rendering. Capable of carrying 100 passengers in luxurious comfort while cruising at twice the speed of sound at 60,000 feet (18,288m), Concorde entered commercial service in 1976 and flew for nearly three decades. The world's only successful supersonic airliner, the Anglo-French SST was retired in 2003, almost six decades after the first flights of pioneering British and French X-Planes. *Mike Machat*

to reform SAUF in 1952, but again the effort proved unsuccessful and the company was finally dissolved in 1956. It is also important to note that at the beginning of 1957 a total of fifteen airframe companies and six aero-engine companies (including big concerns like Sud-Aviation down to small light aeroplane companies) belonged to the Union Syndicale des Industries Aéronautiques, an equivalent to the British SBAC.

SNCASE (Société Nationale de Constructions Aéronautiques du Sud-Est): This company was commonly known as Sud-Est ('South East'). Sud-Est manufactured the Sea Venom carrier-based jet fighter under licence from de Havilland, conducted maintenance of French Air Force Republic F-84G Thunderjets, and developed a new concept aircraft called the SE 5000 Baroudeur. This company also worked on a civil aviation project, the twin-engine SE 210, soon to be called the Caravelle. The Caravelle was the world's first jet-powered transport aircraft to have its engines mounted on the aft fuselage and, with 282 built, was also Europe's most successful and most produced commercial airliner of the period.

SNCAN (Société Nationale de Constructions Aéronautiques du Nord): This company was commonly known as Nord ('North'). Nord had several different projects in development at the same time, including the Mach 1 Gerfaut interceptor and a prototype twin-engine piston-powered transport aircraft called the N 2500, predecessor to the N 2501 Noratlas. That aircraft closely resembled the American Fairchild C-119 Flying Boxcar with its blunt nose section, high wing and twin-tailboom configuration. Nord also conducted pioneering research work in the field of military weaponry with the rocket-powered SS 10 and SS 11 guided missiles.

SNCASO (Société Nationale de Constructions Aéronautiques du Sud-Ouest): This company was commonly known as Sud-Ouest ('South West'). Sud-Ouest designed and developed France's first turbojet-powered aircraft, the two-place straight-wing SO 6000 Triton, as well as the futuristic hybrid turbojet/rocket SO 9000 Trident series of high-performance interceptors.

SNECMA (Société Nationale d'Étude et de Construction de Moteurs d'Aviation): This was the French national company for the design and construction of aviation engines, and was responsible for the new high-performance ATAR turbojet engines. (The name ATAR comes from Atelier Aéronautiques de Reichenbach, an aeronautical workshop in the city of Reichenbach, Germany, located near Lake Constance, and the site of the Zeppelinwerks.) This is where German turbojet technicians and engineers captured by Allied Forces at the end of the Second World War produced a derivative of the BMW 003 centrifugal-flow jet engine.

On 1 March 1957 Sud-Est SNCASE and Sud-Ouest SNCASO were merged to form Société Sud Aviation. Soon afterwards it started the design of the Super Caravelle supersonic airliner, which, once the company had joined forces in 1962 with the British Aircraft Corporation, was turned into the Concorde SST. Aérospatiale, originally known as Société Nationale d'Industrie Aérospatiale (SNIAS), was created in 1970 by the merger of Sud Aviation, Nord Aviation and the Société d'Études et de Réalisation d'Engins Balistiques, or SÉREB. Finally, a merger was made on 10 July 2000 of Aerospatiale Matra S.A. with the Spanish company Construcciones Aeronáuticas S.A. (CASA) and the German Daimler Chrysler Aerospace AG (Dasa) to create Europe's largest aerospace company – the European Aeronautic Defence & Space Company, or EADS.

The visionary Marcel Dassault (formerly Marcel Bloch), founder and owner of Bloch Aircraft, decided after the war to adopt his resistance nickname 'd'assault', and went on to produce what became the most prolific aircraft type ever built in France. The adaptation of his MD550 Mirage 1 prototype design to utilise the powerful ATAR 9 turbojet engine from SNECMA resulted in Dassault's operational Mirage III jet fighter and interceptor, which became one of the most successful Mach 2 designs of the 1960s.

In terms of organisation and planning, in 1957 the French Air Ministry controlled several organisations, the most important of which was the DTIA, which in terms of air matters was the equivalent to the British Ministry of Supply. DTIA stood for Direction Technique et Industrielle de l'Aéronautique de Secrétariat d'Etat à l'Air and as such was the managing organisation for the SMPA (Service de Marchés et de la Production Aéronautique) contracts division; the STA (Service Technique de l'Aéronautique) developments division; the CEV (Centre d'Essais en Vol – the French equivalent of A&AEE Boscombe Down) flight test centre at Bretigny-sur-Orge – with annexes at Marignane, Istres near Marseille, Villacoublay and Toulouse – which was responsible for testing prototype aircraft, giving official

X-PLANES OF EUROPE

guidance, running a test pilots' school and had at its disposal more than 200 aeroplanes; the CEMH (Centre d'Essais des Moteurs et des Hélices), a similar organisation to CEV but covering engines and propellers; and the STTA (Service Technique de Télécommunication de l'Air) for radio and RADAR. This was all backed up by the ONERA organisation (the Office Nationale d'Étude et de Recherches Aéronautiques), which was in charge of research needs and the general advancement of aeronautics, its work programme each year being decided in agreement with the DTIA. ONERA's central office was based at Châtillon-sous-Bagneux with other test and research establishments at Chalias-Meudon, Palaiseau, Modane and Alger.

During the early 1950s there were wry comments made at Paris Air Shows and other events about the French nation's 'industrie des prototypes'. While the production of small prototypes was indeed plentiful, this policy had proved to be a necessary part of the post-war build-up of the industry. The French domestic market for aircraft was not large and aircraft production had to be related to the national economy as a whole. Wisely, France for some time did not attempt the development and production of very large aircraft, particularly on the military side, which meant that the industry was not handicapped by the drain on resources and man-hours that projects comparable to the British or American heavy jet bomber programmes would have entailed. Instead the emphasis during this period was on lighter aircraft to meet the tactical needs of the French Air Force and on advanced projects calling for ingenuity in design and conception. Some of the resulting projects are featured in this book.

And of course during this exciting time exceptional pilots risked their lives on a daily basis to test various experimental prototypes to their limits, and in so doing took calculated risks to ensure the safety of pilots of future production aircraft. Many of these courageous pioneers lost their lives while testing French prototype aircraft in the quest for aviation progress, including test pilots like Constantin Rozanoff and Charles Goujon. Others like André Turcat expanded the flight envelopes to break world records in the 1960s and tested new aircraft that would ultimately lead to the pinnacle of the French aviation industry, the incomparable Concorde, the world's only successful supersonic airliner. And indeed it was André Turcat who was at the controls of that revolutionary Anglo-French aircraft when it made its maiden flight in March 1969.

While not an X-Plane itself, the French Dassault Mirage IV epitomised all of the design and performance features seen in the French experimental aircraft included in this book. Perhaps the most successful European Cold War strategic bomber, the Mirage IV utilised nearly every design innovation first tested in experimental French research aircraft during the 1950s. Essentially a larger twin-engine iteration of the classic Mirage III fighter, this two-man, delta-wing jet bomber served the French Air Force from 1964 until 2005 and possessed a top speed of Mach 2.2, or 1,454mph (2,340km/h). *Copyright Musée de l'Air et de l'Espace, Paris/Le Bourget*

1 de Havilland DH.108 Swallow (1946)

de Havilland DH.108

Span: 39ft 0in (11.89m)

Length: TG283: 25ft 10in (7.87m); TG306: 24ft 6in (7.47m); VW120: 26ft 9.5in (8.17m)

Gross wing area: 328.0sq ft (30.50sq m)

Gross weight: TG283: 8,800lb (3,992kg); TG306: 8,960lb (4,064kg); VW120: c9,200lb (4,173kg)

Powerplant: TG283: 1 x DH Goblin 2 (D.Gn.2), 3,100lb (13.8kN); TG306: 1 x DH Goblin 4 (D.Gn.4), 3,500lb (15.6kN); VW120: 1 x DH Goblin 5 (D.Gn.5), 3,600lb (16.0kN)

Max speed/height: TG283: 300mph (483km/h); TG306: 633mph (1,018km/h) at sea level and Mach 1.02 at 30,000ft (9,144m)

Ceiling: Above 40,000ft (12,192m)

One of the best-known of all British research aircraft is the swept-wing de Havilland DH.108. This aeroplane was the first 'high-speed' type built in this country to feature swept wings, and three examples were constructed. Most tragically, however, it is best known for killing three pilots because each of the airframes was lost in a crash. Such events have tended to overshadow the fact that the DH.108 was the first British aeroplane to fly supersonically, and it gathered a lot of important data.

Civil programme

Towards the end of the Second World War steps were taken to ensure that the British aircraft industry would still have a good supply of work once the conflict was over. The Brabazon Committee was responsible for establishing a series of specifications for various civil aircraft types, by far the most advanced of which would be the world's first jet airliner, the DH.106 Comet from de Havilland at Hatfield. This featured a swept wing and tailplane, but in its earliest forms the DH.106 was to have been a tailless aircraft. As such it was really so advanced that a scale-model aeroplane was ordered to find some of the potential problems and to learn some of the techniques required for high-speed jet-powered flight. The result was the DH.108, an aircraft that was given the unofficial name Swallow.

De Havilland was experienced in jet aircraft design, having produced Britain's second jet fighter, the DH.100 Vampire. The DH.108 was a development of the Vampire and the new aeroplane was covered by Specification E.18/45 of January 1946. This requested two DH.108 airframes and stated: 'The aircraft is required as a means for conducting full-scale experiments into the possibilities of high-speed flight using swept-back wings, obtaining qualitative measurements of aerodynamic and structural phenomena under such conditions, and to act as an approximately half-scale version of the projected multi-engined jet propelled transport aircraft [the Comet]'.

After the DH.106 had been redesigned with a tailplane the DH.108 became a pure research aircraft. It made use of the fuselage and powerplant (single de Havilland Goblin) of the Mk 1 version of the Vampire – the fighter's tailbooms and wings were removed and special swept-back wings were introduced set at an angle of 43° 47' at the leading edge. It was hoped that using Vampire fuselages would save time and money, but it was desired to keep the similarity of the Comet and DH.108 as close as possible, for

X-PLANES OF EUROPE

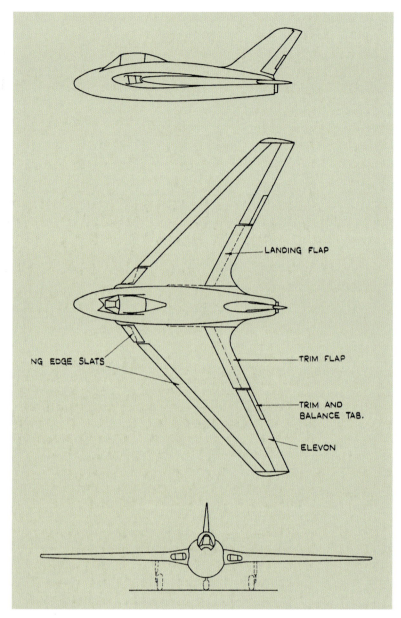

Drawing of DH.108 TG283 with full span slats. *British National Archives*

example in using similar skin thicknesses. Later, a third example (VW120) was built, which used a Vampire Mk 5 forward fuselage.

The DH.108 was a single-seat aircraft and had the original Vampire fuselage pod extended rearwards to make room for the fin. The pod had been built in wood, but the new additions to the airframe – rear fuselage, fin and wings – were all made in light alloy. The swept wing used a main spar plus auxiliary front and rear spars and housed extra tanks to supplement the standard fuel in the fuselage. For its planned low-speed role, the first aircraft (TG283) had wooden full-span fixed Handley Page slats extending along the wing leading edge and over the air intakes, a feature that restricted its speed to 351mph (565km/h). The second aircraft (TG306) introduced retractable slats to permit it to fly at higher speeds. Inboard on the trailing edge were trim/landing flaps, and outboard right to the wingtips were the elevons.

VW120 introduced an ejection seat (which the first two had lacked) and there were differences in the cockpit canopy on all three airframes. VW120 also had a more pointed nose, a stronger airframe, a more powerful engine, power operation on the wing surfaces only (the earlier aircraft had manual operation), and fully automatic slats. The new Servodyne power-operated controls incorporated variable 'feel-back'. TG283 and TG306 had retained their Vampire serials, but when first ordered in 1945 they had been allocated VN856 and VN860. These were cancelled in February 1946, and the retention of the Vampire serials may have been due to the fact that these were classed as modified or refurbished airframes. VW120 was a new serial but was allocated only two weeks before the aircraft flew. TG283 and TG306 were built as Vampires by English Electric, and Vampire undercarriages were used on all three DH.108s.

Lethal flying career

After delivery to Hatfield on 24 September 1945, work on converting TG283 was rapid, and the aircraft began its taxi trials in early May 1946. Geoffrey de Havilland Jr first flew it as a DH.108 on 15 May, not from Hatfield but from Woodbridge. The aircraft was taken to Woodbridge by road because it had a longer runway and was surrounded by woods, which made it a far better venue to maintain security. On 19 May TG283 was flown to Hatfield to open the type's manufacturer's trials.

Between 5 October 1948 and May 1950 TG283 undertook a programme of low-speed test flying from Farnborough. The RAE's subsequent report revealed that a lift coefficient of 0.7 (essentially the lifting effectiveness of the wing) gave general handling characteristics not unlike those of an orthodox aircraft. But at values of between 0.7 and 1.21 flaps up and 1.23 flaps down (the maximum for the respective conditions), the effectiveness and response of all controls deteriorated, making the control of the aircraft very tiring for the pilot in all but calm weather. In calm conditions the minimum approach speed with the original undercarriage was 1.23 Vs (1.23 x Vampire stalling speed), but this was reduced to 1.12 Vs after a long-stroke Sea Vampire undercarriage had been fitted. This modification provided increased ground clearance, which permitted a larger incidence at touchdown. When taxiing,

The first DH.108, TG283, photographed outside a hangar at Hatfield. Unusually, de Havilland wrote the serial number on the aircraft's rear fuselage as TG/283. *BAE Systems*

the DH.108 proved to be very similar to the Vampire, and the view from the cockpit was described as excellent, but having the aircraft so close to the ground meant that care was needed to avoid obstacles.

On 1 May 1950 TG283 crashed during stalling trials. After performing a stall at 15,000 feet (4,572m) with the flaps down, the aircraft went out of control and entered an inverted spin. The anti-spin parachutes failed to function properly as TG283 descended. The pilot (Sqn Ldr George Genders of RAE Aero Flight) prepared to evacuate, but at around 2,000 feet (610m) a partial recovery was achieved. Then the aircraft entered a normal spin and crashed near Hartley Wintney. Even with no ejection seat Genders still managed to get out, but he was killed when his parachute failed to stream in the height available. TG283 had completed 135 hours flying as a DH.108.

TG306 flew as a DH.108 in June 1946, having flown to Hatfield as a Vampire on 11 February with just two hours time-in-air. This airframe was used to assess the swept wing's high-speed characteristics and progress was rapid, but the pilot soon encountered compressibility at a height of 35,000 feet (10,668m) and around 340mph (547km/h) EAS. Its effect was a nose-down pitching tendency, which had been predicted by the designers but was found to be much less violent than had been anticipated. It had also been calculated, however, that if compressibility phenomena were encountered at low altitude the amount of this nose-down tendency would be appreciably increased. There was also some pilot-induced oscillation, and not having a tailplane reduced the available damping in pitch. In September 1946 TG306 attended the first post-war SBAC Show at Radlett.

The aircraft's performance was such that a decision was made to try to break the World Air Speed Record, currently held by a Gloster Meteor at 616mph (991km/h), and for this purpose TG306 had its cockpit modified with additional framing. However, on the evening of 27 September, during one of the trials flights made in preparation for the attempt (Flight 8 in the series), the pilot (Geoffrey de Havilland Jr) lost control and was killed when TG306 began

A similar official view of VW120, which shows some of the changes introduced on the later aircraft after the loss of TG306. *BAE Systems*

The second DH.108 was TG306, which in this side-angle air-to-air view shows most of the surviving features left over from its short-lived days as a de Havilland Vampire fighter. It also has the cockpit modified in readiness for the ill-fated attempt at the world speed record. *BAE Systems*

A manufacturer's model photograph dated 1947, which shows VW120, the first DH.108 to receive a new serial. *Author's collection*

a powerful pitching oscillation and broke up over Egypt Bay near Gravesend. TG306 had started a dive at 10,000 feet (3,048m) above the Thames Estuary but eventually went into a violent outside loop, which made both wings fail under download. It was calculated that before the disaster happened TG306 had reached around 580mph (933km/h) EAS (Mach 0.87) in a shallow dive at about 7,000 feet (2,134m), a combination of Mach and EAS higher than anything previously obtained. Earlier, on Flight 6 (26 September) TG306 had achieved Mach 0.86 (595mph [957km/h] EAS at 5,000 feet [1,524 m]), and on Flight 7 (27 September) Mach 0.855 (630mph [1,014km/h] at 1,500 feet [457m]). Subsequent tunnel testing showed that at high Mach numbers the DH.108 suffered a loss of elevon effect in the pitching plane, which later changed to a reversal of control, and this was accompanied by a nose-down change in trim and reduced longitudinal control. The aircraft's total time-in-air as a DH.108 to the time of take-off on Flight 8 was just 13 hours. Geoffrey de Havilland Jr was the son of Geoffrey de Havilland Sr, the man who had founded the famous company.

Despite such a terrible loss, the value of the DH.108 had been established and a third airframe was ordered. VW120 first flew on 24 July 1947 with the various modifications and

Rather more photos appear to have been made of VW120 than of the two earlier aircraft, which with its longer nose was certainly the more graceful of the three DH.108s. This pair of images was taken during a publicity flight. *BAE Systems*

A rare picture of VW120 on display at the SBAC Show at Radlett in September 1947. Note how the short undercarriage left the fuselage very close to the ground. *Author's collection*

VW120 makes a dramatic low-level pass during a public show. Sqn Ldr John Derry became famous when he made the first British supersonic flight in this particular aircraft. *BAE Systems*

Striking rear view of VW120 taken at Hatfield in August 1947. *Phil Butler Collection*

improvements outlined above, which were an attempt to counter the weaknesses that had been established by analysing TG306's crash. In September 1947 VW120 attended the SBAC Show at Radlett, and on 12 April 1948, flown by Sqn Ldr John Derry, it set a new 100km closed-circuit speed record at an average 605.23mph (973.8km/h). However, flights at high speed and altitude revealed a loss of roll control at Mach 0.99 and insufficient pitch control at Mach 0.97, so Mach number limits were now placed on the aircraft. On 6 September 1948, in a dive from 45,000 feet (13,716m), VW120 entered a steep dive and Derry lost control until the aircraft reached 23,500 feet (7,163m), where he was able to get it back into level flight. During the descent a speed of Mach 1.04 indicated was recorded (calculations for instrument error corrected this to Mach 1.02), so in the process the DH.108 had become the first British aircraft to break the sound barrier (albeit while out of control). VW120 was also the world's first supersonic aircraft that could take off and land under its own power, and Mach 1 was achieved in another dive on 1 March 1949. On 11 and 12 September 1948 the record-breaking VW120 was displayed to the public at the Farnborough Show by de Havilland test pilot Gp Capt John Cunningham.

VW120 went to RAE Farnborough on 28 June 1949 to begin a trials programme in stability and control. During the summer it was released for a few days to take part in the National Air Races at Elmdon on 1 August, but on 15 February 1950 it crashed at Brickhill near Bletchley after the pilot (Sqn Ldr Stewart Muller-Rowland, another RAE Aero Flight pilot) had lost control. In fact, the aircraft disintegrated in the air below 10,000 feet (3,048m) as the result of a descent at high speed from about 27,000 feet

A beautiful image of the third de Havilland DH.108, VW120. *BAE Systems via Phil Butler collection*

(8,230m), but the reasons for the crash and why Muller-Rowland never ejected have not been fully established. However, it was found that VW120's port wing had failed in upload. When test pilot Capt Eric Brown had handed over charge of Aero Flight to Stewart Muller-Rowland, he described the DH.108 as a 'killer', with a nasty stall and 'vicious undamped longitudinal oscillation at speed in bumps'. His comments proved to be prophetic. VW120 had flown for 122 hours and 25 minutes.

A tragic record with three deaths in three aeroplanes can cloud any judgement made on the series of DH.108s. The losses were terrible, but they happened in an era when many test pilots died while trying to push the boundaries of aviation – the risks were always great! Overall the DH.108s could be described as partially successful in that they achieved advances in swept-wing and supersonic knowledge but without providing all of the answers. They also showed that 1940s technology was not ready for tailless high-speed aircraft. At the start of its career the Comet also proved to be an ill-fated aeroplane. After entering revenue service with the British Overseas Airways Corporation two examples broke up in mid-air. Fatigue failure in the outer seam of an aerial hatch on the top of the fuselage was found to be the cause, something that the DH.108 design studies could never have foretold. The Comet programme was delayed substantially while the airliner was redesigned but, by the time it was ready to return, the Americans, with the Boeing 707 and Douglas DC-8, had grabbed much of the world market for the first jet airliners. In general the later Comets had long and successful careers, but sometimes the people who break new ground are not the ones who reap the full benefits. De Havilland's sad experiences with the early Comets and the DH.108 are a perfect case in point.

2 Sud-Ouest SO 6000 Triton (1946)

Sud-Ouest Triton (SO 6000-04)

Registration: F-WFDH
Span: 30ft 0.5in (9.16m)
Length: 34ft 5in (10.48m)
Wing area: 45sq ft (14sq m)
Max gross take-off weight: 8,400lb (3,810kg)
Powerplant: 1 x RR Nene 100, 5,005lb (22.2kN)
Max speed/height: 600mph (965km/h) at sea level
Ceiling: 39,370ft (12,000m)

The Sud-Ouest SO 6000 Triton (Newt) was officially the first French turbojet-powered aircraft. Studies for the SO 6000 began in 1943 as a clandestine project secreted away in a small city apartment during the German occupation, and were conducted under the guidance of aeronautical engineer Lucien Servanty. Small models were even tested in secret wind tunnels. The Triton was envisioned as an all-metal low-wing aircraft to be powered initially by a yet-to-be-produced Rateau turbine engine, thereby making the aircraft an all-French project. Unlike conventional military designs on the drawing board at that time, this aeroplane would feature a fully enclosed cabin with dual controls and side-by-side seating for the pilot and co-pilot, which resulted in a rather bulky fuselage, the duct for the engine air passing between the two crew members and the exhaust exiting through a tailpipe. Modern features introduced on this research aircraft, which was designed really as a jet training aeroplane, included a tricycle undercarriage and ejection seats (although these were not installed at the start). However, the side car-door style of access was not what one might associate with the latest jet aircraft, but in truth the Triton presented an appearance that was more like a small airliner or an executive jet rather than a military aeroplane. It had an all-metal structure with stressed metal skin and a single wing spar, and the wing was fitted with trailing-edge flaps between the ailerons and fuselage.

Shortly after the war the French government requested that five prototypes together with one static test unit were to be built. Construction of the first airframe began in the original First World War-era Nieuport factory in Issy-le-Moulineaux outside Paris, but was later transferred to the old Farman aircraft factories in Suresnes, also near Paris. As was typical with many turbojet aircraft of that period, airframe development exceeded that of the respective aircraft's powerplant. Work on the fuselage went faster than projected, while development of the 3,250lb (14.4kN)-thrust French Rateau SRA-1 engine lagged behind. Consequently the decision was made to equip the Triton for its first flight with a single German wartime 1,980lb (8.8kN)-thrust Jumo 004B jet engine. Since France had acquired control of the German sector where BMW had been producing Jumo engines during the war, the designation of the first aircraft became SO 6000 Triton J (J for Jumo).

Although the Jumo was indeed a huge step forward in aircraft propulsion, this first-generation centrifugal-flow turbine engine was notoriously unreliable during its service in the Luftwaffe. The Triton's test pilot, Daniel Rastel, experienced this trait first-hand when he acquired his first jet engine experience in a captured Messerschmitt Me 262, which was powered by two Jumo 004Bs – the aircraft suffered an engine failure during its 20-minute flight. The first two prototype Tritons flew with Junkers Jumo engines, but another decision was taken to equip the next three with British Rolls-Royce Derwent turbojets. France had finally entered the Jet Age behind Germany, Great Britain, the United States and Russia.

The Triton's inaugural flight took place on 11 November 1946 in the hands of Daniel Rastel. This event occurred only three days before the opening of the Paris Air Exhibit held in central Paris near the Champs-Élysées under the famed glass ceiling of the Grand Palais. The third Triton prototype was proudly displayed there for the public (although minus its engine) and soon became the star of the show after the widespread circulation of some very enthusiastic press releases. The glowing promotional text predicted Triton flights with then unheard-of speeds of 540mph (900km/h), or nearly Mach 0.8. On another occasion publicity photos were taken showing the first prototype (01) standing alongside a Panhard Dynavia car; at that time both represented the height of technology in aviation and motoring.

The first flight of the Triton 1 actually lasted 10 minutes and the aircraft flew at less than 180mph (296km/h), barely the minimum take-off speed, and at an altitude of only 1,000 feet (305m) while being forced to fly around the airfield perimeter of Orléans Bricy; the altitude was reached with some difficulty. French aviation history had, however, still been made that day, and the French aviation industry's progress with turbine-powered flight would soon start to grow.

After the achievement of its first test flight, the Triton test aircraft were all grounded for more than six months while engineers and mechanics tried to solve a series of problems identified in the initial series of sorties. Unfortunately, the reality of the Triton programme was far from the press headlines of the Paris Air Exhibit. Subsequent test flights following the type's return to fly test on 26 April 1947, when it achieved 220mph (354km/h), showed some minor improvement and recorded airspeeds slowly moved beyond 250mph (400km/h). However, several new aerodynamic problems began to appear such as airframe vibration and inherent instability characteristics in several different flight regimes. The decision was thus made to wait for an improved Rolls-Royce

The interior of the hangar at the French Mélun-Villaroche test facility showing the Triton I on the right, and two Sud-Ouest SO 6020 Espadon fighters on the left. The Triton's single Rolls-Royce Nene turbojet produced 5,016lb (22.3kN) of thrust. The empty weight was a diminutive 5,382lb (2,639kg). *Musée de l'Air et de l'Espace, Paris/Le Bourget*

The SO 6000 Triton 03 was registered F-WFXY. All French prototype aircraft are registered with the national prefix 'F' for France, then with a 'W' as the first or second letter of the following four to denote its special flight test status. Note the solid nose, a feature of this airframe only, other Tritons having a nose intake. *Copyright Musée de l'Air et de l'Espace, Paris/Le Bourget*

Nene engine (rather than the Derwent) before continuing with the flight test programme. The new power unit would address the serious problem of a lack of power, and Hispano-Suiza had just begun the manufacture of Nenes under licence to equip the French Air Force's de Havilland Vampire fighters, which were built by Sud-Est as the SE 530 Mistral. Aircraft 04 first flew with the Nene installed on 19 March 1949 from Bricy, and a few days later pilot Jean Sarrail took it to a very satisfactory Mach 0.75 – 555mph (893km/h). The stability was apparently also now improved and subsequently a speed of 593mph (954km/h) and a ceiling of 39,000 feet (11,887m) were recorded.

Triton test flying continued into the early 1950s, mostly with airframe 04, which allowed pilots and flight test engineers alike to familiarise themselves with a turbine-powered aircraft that could approach high subsonic speeds. After more than four years of research and development work with the Triton, the manufacturer claimed a modicum of success in that it had created the first French jet aircraft to fly. When compared to the jet aircraft of other nations at that time, however, the Triton's achievements were modest at best, with a top speed of just Mach 0.75. Perhaps the most significant point,

An overhead view of the Triton 03 showing the small shoulder-mounted air intakes to best advantage. Like other first attempts at harnessing turbojet power to conventional airframes, the Triton's post-Second World War design lineage is quite evident in this photo. This aircraft was the first jet-powered prototype developed in Europe with side-by-side seating for pilot and co-pilot. Note the unique overhead cockpit window configuration. *Musée de l'Air et de l'Espace, Paris/Le Bourget*

however, is that many French pilots received their first experience flying a jet-powered aircraft with the Triton, but once the aeroplane had reached its maximum potential flight capabilities SNCASO decided to focus its effort on a concurrent but more advanced design, which it called the Espadon, and which eventually became France's first jet fighter – and as such does not qualify for this book. By the way, the Triton's designer, Lucien Servanty, was subsequently to head the French design team on the Aérospatiale-BAC Concorde supersonic airliner.

Survey of the six Triton airframes

Triton 01: As France's first turbojet-powered aeroplane, the first Triton prototype was historically a most significant aircraft. However, after a series of only eight test flights, which accumulated a total flight time of 1 hour and 30 minutes, the first Triton prototype was retired in November 1947. In due course Triton 01 was replaced by airframe 04 equipped with a more powerful Rolls-Royce Nene 100 turbojet engine producing 4,850lb (21.56kN) of static thrust. Hispano-Suiza built this engine under license.

Triton 02: The second Triton prototype was identical in dimensions and specifications and was built to full flight standards, but was never flown. This airframe was most certainly kept aside to await the French Rateau SRA-1 engine, which sadly was never to become available.

Triton 03: Airframe 03 (serial F-WFXY) was initially to be powered by a Rolls-Royce Derwent engine (in which form it never flew), and was then refitted with the Nene turbojet. This was the first Triton aircraft to be equipped with a Heinkel-designed ejection seat for emergency escape at high speed. Retired after only two flights, the fuselage had been modified from the initial design by deleting the 'shark-mouth' air intake and moving the cockpit windows further forward for better pilot visibility. The aircraft experienced a 'failure to retract' the undercarriage on its first flight on 4 April 1950, and the second flight made on 3 May met with a similar problem. The aircraft never flew again and is now an exhibit at Le Musée de l'Air et de l'Espace (MAE).

Triton 04: This Triton (serial F-WFDH) achieved its inaugural flight on 19 March 1948 and completed a total of 189 test flights; it also achieved the highest speed recorded during the programme, Mach 0.75. This aircraft differed from the initial design in having the 'shark-mouth' air intake supplemented by additional air scoops located directly behind the cockpit and above the wing roots, a modification that was necessary to provide enough air for the more powerful Nene engine. In fact 04 was the first Triton to fly with this power unit. It made its final flight on 3 November 1950 at Bricy, and it was an engine overheat and seizure problem that brought a close to the flight programme.

Triton 05: Airframe 05 was first flown from Bricy by Daniel Rastel on 23 May 1949 but was retired after making only eight flights, accumulating a total of 2 hours and 45 minutes. This airframe was damaged beyond repair on flight eight on 21 July 1949 after having to make a forced landing when the aircraft ran out of fuel. As a result the Triton 03 airframe was then brought back into service to continue the test flight programme, but made only two more flights in that role.

Triton 06: Airframe 06 was built to flight specifications but was never flown. It was used strictly as a static test article.

3 Armstrong Whitworth AW.52 (1947)

Armstrong Whitworth AW.52

Span: 90ft 11in (27.71m)

Length: 37ft 3.5in (11.37m)

Gross wing area: 1,314.0sq ft (122.20sq m)

Gross weight: TS363: 34,154lb (15,492kg); TS368: 33,305lb (15,107kg)

Powerplant: TS363: 2 x RR Nene 2 (R.N.2), 5,000lb (22.2kN); TS368: 2 x RR Derwent 5 (R.D.7), 3,500lb (15.6kN)

Max speed/height: TS363: 500mph (805km/h) at sea level; 480mph (772km/h) at 36,000ft (10,973m). TS368: 449mph (722) at sea level

Ceiling: TS363: 50,000ft (15,240m); TS368: 45,000ft (13,716m)

Since the development of powered flight there have been numerous efforts to produce pure flying wing aeroplanes. Of course the definition of a flying wing can be as broad or narrow as one might wish, but here we are talking about aircraft with little or no fuselage, a large-span wing, and no conventional horizontal tailplane. During the 1940s the highest-profile attempts to produce such a type were made by the American Northrop company, work that culminated in the XB-35 piston and YB-49 jet bomber programmes. However, the British Armstrong Whitworth Aircraft (AWA) company also experimented in some depth with flying wings, and the AW.52 represents the most important result of that work. It was a jet-propelled, tailless experimental aircraft with large-chord, low-drag wings and was preceded by a research glider called the AW.52G. The DH.108 already described was of course another flying-wing project from this period.

A beautiful wing

Armstrong Whitworth's work on flying wings got going in 1943 when the design of the AW.52G glider project began. In fact AWA referred to the AW.52 and AW.52G as tailless types, but they both came very close to being all-wing aeroplanes. One objective of the research was the provision of stick-free stability, but to maintain fore and aft stability was a major problem with any tailless aircraft and entailed the fitting of devices to prevent early stalling. In this respect the AW.52 used the boundary layer to ensure that laminar flow was maintained, which was achieved by a series of narrow slots, 0.25 inch (6.35mm) wide, placed span-wise along the wing surface and connected via ducts and chambers to the compressor intake ducts. In practice this boundary-layer suction arrangement worked quite well.

Longitudinal and lateral control were both achieved by one control surface (referred to as the Controller) on each wing, which functioned like the normal elevator and aileron. This was partly balanced by a shrouded forward surface sealed at the hinge, the balance chambers being suitably vented to ensure good stick-free stability for the aircraft. Further balance was provided by a geared spring tab. The Controller was carried behind a Dowty hydraulically operated surface known as the Corrector, the main function of which was to provide a powerful trimming device without impairing the lightness of the manually operated small-chord Controller. This was used to counteract major changes of longitudinal trim such as would occur when the landing flap was lowered.

Armstrong Whitworth drawing of the AW.52 which was prepared before the first example had flown. *British National Archives*

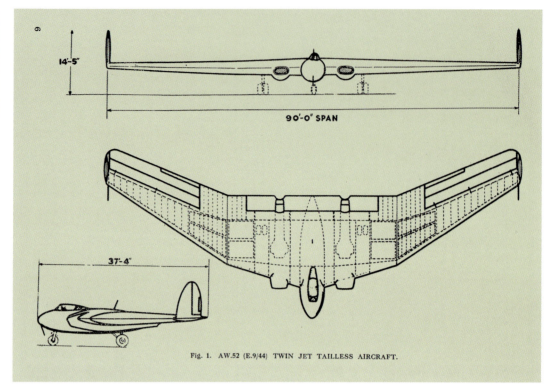

Fig. 1. AW.52 (E.9/44) TWIN JET TAILLESS AIRCRAFT.

Another key problem in the design of high-speed tailless aircraft, or indeed any swept-back wing, was the provision of adequate flexural and torsional stiffness to prevent aileron reversal and wing-aileron flutter. The bending stiffness of a swept wing was vitally important since pure bending distortions produced changes in incidence, something that did not occur in a normal unswept wing.

A low level of drag was another possibility offered by this type of aircraft, although for the AW.52 no attempt was made to provide a thin wing; in fact, the thickness/chord ratio was 18% from the root to the knuckle joint and 15% at the tip. The fuselage was kept as small as possible, the engine nacelles were almost completely buried in the wing, and large fins and rudders were mounted at the wingtips, their size being determined by reasons of stability and control with one engine out. There was a large landing flap beneath the centre wing, and the aircraft had eight fuel tanks and a tricycle undercarriage. Light alloy stressed skin construction was used throughout, and like the AW.52G this was a two-seat aircraft with an observer's position behind the pilot. However, the observer had no ejection seat, so after the loss of TS363 the aeroplane was flown with only the pilot aboard.

In late January 1945 the Ministry issued Specification E.9/44 to cover the project and two AW.52s were ordered with the serials TS363 and TS368. In fact, for some time the aircraft was described as a mail plane, a cover that was often used to justify the development of an advanced aeroplane like this, but the long-term objectives included flying-wing bombers and airliners.

The AW.52G glider

The AW.52G was not an exact replica of the full-size jet, but the general layout of the two types was very similar. It was given the military serial RG324 and was towed into the air for the first time on 2 March 1945 from AWA's Baginton facility by a tug version of Armstrong Whitworth's Whitley bomber. Charles Turner-Hughes was the pilot, but later Frederick Ronald Midgley and Eric Franklin shared the flying programme. The objective was to operate the AW.52G from a height of 16,000 feet (4,877m) over a speed range of around 50 to 250mph (80 to 400km/h), but on occasion the glider was taken to 20,000 feet (6,096m), which gave a flight time of around 35 minutes. RG324 was built entirely in wood and had a D-type spar with one main girder and a structurally stiff nose skin of metal-faced ply, which was used to obtain a smooth surface to give laminar flow on the lower drag sections. A fixed tricycle undercarriage was fitted.

By late September RG324 had completed thirty-two flights. Some of its later flying was made from Bitteswell, and in September 1946 the AW.52G formed a static exhibit at the first

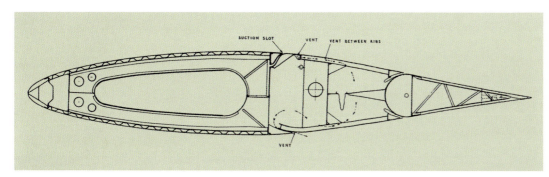

Cross-section detail of the AW.52's wing. *British National Archives*

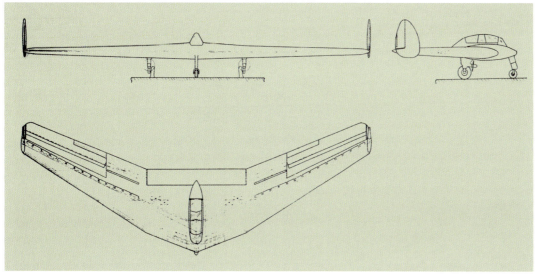

Three-view drawing of the AW.52G. *British National Archives*

post-war SBAC Show, held at Radlett. Further test flying with AWA, using an Avro Lancaster as tug, included drag trials and also some lateral and directional control tests laid down by the RAE. On 1 June 1950 RG324 joined the Airborne Forces Experimental Establishment at Beaulieu for handling trials, then on 6 September it was towed to Boscombe Down. The AW.52G returned to the air on 27 June 1953 when it was towed back to Baginton to become a car park 'guard' at the AWA factory, a position it still occupied in April 1957. However, deterioration of its wood structure through exposure to the weather ensured that

Armstrong Whitworth AW.52 G Glider used for testing and development of flying wing concept, first flight on 2nd March 1945, towed by an Armstrong Whitworth Whitley. *Chris Sandham-Bailey www.inkworm.com*

Photographs showing the AW.52G glider on the ground and during an aerotow. *Phil Butler collection*

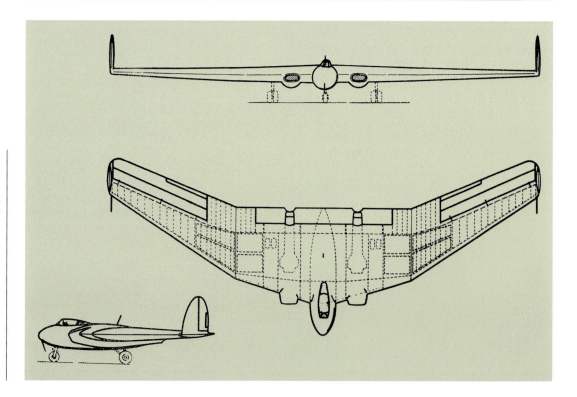

A three-view drawing of the AW.52. The outer wing trailing edges show the Corrector and Controller flight control surfaces. The latter forms the trailing edge itself and the former is placed ahead of it. During flight these surfaces operate together. *British National Archives*

The first AW.52 was TS363, seen here at Baginton. *Ray Williams collection*

it was eventually broken up. The AW.52G had a span of 53ft 4in (16.25m), a length of 14ft 7.5in (4.46m), a wing area of 445sq ft (41.39sq m), and a weight of 6,000lb (2,722kg).

The AW.52 jet

The two AW.52 research aircraft were assembled at the Baginton factory and proved to be quite difficult to build, primarily because of the need for a very even surface. In fact, the smoothness of the wing surface and the freedom from wrinkles were described as 'amazing', but this smoothness was essential to provide the desired laminar flow. Taxi trials commenced in April 1947 and eventually TS363 was dismantled and taken by road to Farnborough to go on static display at the September SBAC Show. It was then moved to A&AEE Boscombe Down to begin its flight testing. More taxi trials were made in October, and on 13 November, powered by Rolls-Royce Nene engines, TS363 flew for the first time with AWA chief test pilot Sqn Ldr Eric Franklin in the cockpit. The first public performance was made at AWA's Bitteswell airfield on 16 December and it was noted how quiet the '52' was compared to other jet aircraft. W. H. 'Bill' Else joined the flying programme in April 1948, and 'Jo' Lancaster became part of the team in May 1949.

During the first twenty-five flights the Corrector system functioned satisfactorily, but when trimmed in the accepted manner the aircraft became statically unstable stick-free at speeds between 230 and 345mph (370 and 555km/h). On the approach for landing the AW.52 lost its speed very slowly. By October 1948 a self-generated vibration of the wing was being experienced at a speed of around 288mph (463km/h), which took the form of a wing flexure (with a considerable amplitude at the wingtip), and on some occasions in gusty weather a short-period oscillation was also encountered. In fact, there was a general lack of

TS363 is seen over a snow-covered central-England landscape on 31 December 1947 during the first air-to-air publicity flight made by the aircraft. On one or two of these images the snowy background and white colour scheme make TS363 a little indistinct. *Ray Williams collection*

For comparison these images show the second Derwent-powered AW.52 TS368, which had smaller intakes to feed the less powerful engines. The shots were taken in September 1948, on or around the date of the aircraft's first flight. *Peter Green collection*

harmony between the pitch and roll controls.

In September 1948 TS363 made its appearance at the Farnborough Show, then in December it was dismantled at Baginton to permit several major modifications to be made. This included some substantial stiffening of the Corrector for high-speed flight. Until then TS363 had been limited to a maximum speed of 350mph (563km/h) and Mach 0.65. Back in the air, flight testing still showed problems with vibration, but by May 1949 trimming and stability tests were giving results that were close to predictions. The aircraft was, however, very sensitive in pitch, and because of this the pilots never used a sharp elevator motion to initiate any oscillation. Then, during a test flight on 30 May 1949, TS363 was lost after entering an oscillation. At about 5,000 feet (1,524m), while descending, the aircraft entered turbulent air conditions and a fore and aft oscillation began. This became worse and the pilot, Flt Lt J. O. 'Jo' Lancaster, was unable to regain control. He was forced to eject (in the process making the first emergency ejection with a Martin-Baker seat in the UK), and the aircraft crashed a few miles from Leamington Spa. Lancaster was only slightly injured, but TS363 was wrecked after breaking up completely as it struck the ground at a shallow angle; the trail of wreckage was nearly half a mile long. TS363 had made sixty-five flights and flown for 37 hours, and overall its performance had proved to be disappointing. It was found that the degree of laminar flow achieved did not match expectations, while a high level of drag was

Armstrong Whitworth AW.52 Experimental flying wing, powered by two Rolls-Royce Nene turbojets. *Chris Sandham-Bailey www.inkworm.com*

experienced during manoeuvring.

The second AW.52 had a less powerful Rolls-Royce Derwent powerplant because it was intended to explore the lower end of the speed range and investigate airframe vibration. TS368 made its maiden flight from Bitteswell on 1 September 1948. In the air its general flying characteristics were much the same as TS363, but the take-off performance was far inferior with very poor acceleration both on the ground and immediately after take-off. The only occasion where both AW.52s were seen in the air together was during a demonstration for Ministry officials held on 26 October 1948. After the loss of TS363, the second machine, having at that stage completed thirty-eight flights, was grounded while the entire airframe underwent ground vibration tests. By December it had flown another six times and by mid-March 1950 significant progress was being made with the troublesome problem of longitudinal oscillation; however, the aircraft was usually limited to a maximum speed of 276mph (444km/h).

This image, another from the December 1947 publicity sortie that was flown by Eric Franklin, presents good underside detail and shows the two Nene jetpipes. *Ray Williams collection*

On 25 October 1950 TS368 joined RAE Farnborough and during the first months of 1951 there were further reports of oscillation problems in flight. For a new series of airflow tests, some portions of the wings were painted black to permit observations to be made as the airflow exerted its influence on a thin chemical film deposited on the wing (the black covering

TS363 in low-speed condition with flaps and undercarriage deployed. Both AW.52s carried the standard 'P' for prototype on their noses, but no RAF roundels or national insignia were ever painted on either of the carefully polished white airframes. *Ray Williams collection*

The AW.52 sported a large landing flap beneath the centre wing trailing edge, which curved beneath the jetpipes. *Author's collection*

This photograph of TS363 was taken at Bitteswell, possibly on 16 December 1947 during the type's first public performance. *Ray Williams collection*

TS363 shows that wing shape again, this time while thrilling the crowds at the September 1948 Farnborough Show. *Peter Green collection*

was required because the evaporated chemical left a white deposit that was not visible on the original white surface). Unfortunately, it was calculated that only a relatively small area of the wing, in fact as little as 5%, was experiencing laminar flow. This programme ended in September 1953 and the second AW.52 was Struck Off Charge on 10 March 1954. Sadly, TS368 was not preserved and from June 1954 was used as a weapons target at Shoeburyness.

At the start both AW.52s were painted white. Film of one of them flying at the Farnborough Show or for publicity purposes shows an incredibly graceful and elegant machine, which perhaps presented too much of an advance in airframe design for the technology of that time to handle. One wonders what could have been achieved had these aircraft had fly-by-wire available to them. In the end the AW.52s suffered from problems with control and stability that were never cured completely. The laminar flow results were a disappointment, and as a result there was never any hope of a large airliner being built with this wing form. That said, the AW.52 was a remarkable achievement, perhaps more so than one might first imagine because during the 1940s AWA had acquired a great deal of its trade through building other people's aeroplanes – the flying wing was by far the most advanced all-new aircraft to be built and flown by the company.

Later in its career RAE Farnborough used TS368 on airflow trials, for which sections of the wing were painted black. *Peter Green collection*

The Northrop YB-49 bomber was a contemporary of the AW.52 and made its maiden flight on 21 October 1947. This aircraft was perhaps more of a true flying wing in that there was no fuselage ahead of the wing leading edge. *Terry Panopalis collection*

3 Saunders-Roe SR.A/1 (1947)

Saunders-Roe SR.A/1

Span: 46ft 0in (14.02m)

Length: 50ft 0in (15.24m)

Gross wing area: 415.0sq ft (38.60sq m)

Gross weight: 19,033lb (8,633kg)

Powerplant: 2 x Metrovick Beryl. TG263: M.V.B.1, 3,230lb (14.4kN); TG267: M.V.B.2, 3,500lb (15.6kN); TG271: M.V.B.2, 3,850lb (17.1kN)

Max speed/height: TG271: 495mph (796km/h) at sea level, 497mph (800km/h) at 20,000ft (6,096m)

Ceiling: TG271: 43,000ft (13,106m)

During the 1930s the flying boat was looked upon as a rather exotic way to travel to distant parts of the world, and during the Second World War such aircraft filled a crucial role on maritime patrol and anti-submarine duties. However, little attention was paid to producing a flying boat fighter, even though flying boats offered virtually unlimited runway lengths (with no need for tarmac surfaces) and, as the Schneider Trophy seaplanes had demonstrated in the 1920s and 1930s, potentially high speeds. After the war several countries looked at the idea of a boat fighter, but in the UK the work came together with the SR.A/1 prototypes from Saunders-Roe. Based on the Isle of Wight, this company was a flying boat specialist and the resulting SR.A/1s were true fighter prototypes, but since no other British company was to build anything like them, the three examples also served as research aircraft. Indeed, they were covered by a specification with the Experimental 'E' prefix, namely E.6/44.

A unique capability

Proposals for conventional piston-powered boat fighters were few and far between, in part because of the high drag produced by the high engine position that was necessary to keep the propellers clear of the water surface. However, the application of jet propulsion to a small boat fighter was far more attractive since the engines could be housed inside the fuselage, thereby reducing drag and offering a performance much closer to that of a land plane. The main problem was ensuring that the tailpipe had adequate water clearance. In July 1943 Saunders-Roe (Saro) presented some proposals for a jet-powered flying boat fighter, which it called the SR.44. In April 1944 E.6/44 was written around the project and three prototypes, TG263, TG267 and TG271, were ordered. E.6/44 stated that the fighter should be able to operate from enclosed waters and relatively calm seas, and – importantly – from any part of the world. This final point was significant because the impetus for the new aircraft came from a need for such a type in the Pacific war against Japan, where airstrips in the battle areas were in short supply, but sheltered lagoons were plentiful. The versatility of such an aircraft had been recognised, but the war ended before the boat fighter was ready.

The SR.44 was subsequently named SR.A/1 and was powered by two Metropolitan-Vickers (Metrovick) F.2/4 Beryl axial turbojets. The SR.A/1's structure was made of conventional light alloy with formers and stringers, the fin was built integral with the fuselage, there was a two-spar tailplane, and the wings were built around main and auxiliary spars. Retractable wingtip floats were fitted, the ailerons were placed outboard of the float storage bay, and the aircraft had dive recovery flaps on the inner wing underside. The

The first Saunders-Roe SR.A/1 prototype, TG263, is seen on a test flight in the Isle of Wight area in March or April 1951. *Saunders-Roe Archive*

hull was subdivided by watertight bulkheads in such a way that when fully loaded the aircraft should not sink if any compartment was open to water. The engines were placed side by side in the centre fuselage with the exhausts on the fuselage sides aft of the wings and all of the fuel (426 gallons [1,937 litres]) held in four wing tanks. Armament was four 20mm cannon mounted across the upper nose (this was never fitted), and there was a capability to carry bombs or rockets or underwing auxiliary tanks.

The initial design work, the mock-up and much of the construction was undertaken by Saro's Anglesey facility, but the first airframe was moved in sections to Cowes on the Isle of Wight for final assembly. By the end of 1945 the first prototype's hull structure was nearly complete, but by then Saro had become occupied with its SR.45 project, a huge passenger flying boat later called the Princess, which eventually flew in 1952. As a result of this extra workload the SR.A/1 began to fall behind schedule.

Off the water

The first prototype TG263 eventually flew with Geoffrey Tyson in the cockpit during the evening of 16 July 1947, just after he had completed taxi trials in the mouth of the River Medina. On the sea the aircraft had a tail-down attitude to ensure that the air intake was always clear of the water. It took only 12 seconds to get airborne and climbed quickly. Tyson and Flt Lt J. O. 'Jo' Lancaster, both Saro test pilots, shared the early flight testing, but in 1949 Sqn Ldr John Booth replaced Lancaster when he joined Armstrong Whitworth. After five flights TG263 was grounded while a tendency for Dutch rolling was dealt with by the introduction of a bullet fairing in the tail/fin junction, and metal strips were added to the rudder's trailing edge to improve lateral stability. The flying resumed on 30 August, but a few weeks later both engines stopped during a test flight and Tyson was forced to make a 'dead-stick' landing in the Solent. Troubles were subsequently experienced

TG263 is pictured moored outside the Saro main hangar at Cowes in July 1947, around the time of its first flight. *Author's collection*

An original Saro photograph showing TG263 taking off. The noise and the spray thrown out behind the aircraft must have made it a splendid sight. *Saunders-Roe Archive*

with the fuel system and tanks, and the future of the Beryl engine was made uncertain by the forthcoming take-over of the project by Armstrong-Siddeley Motors (in fact the engine was abandoned in mid-1948). Then winter weather and other problems restricted flying so much that during 1948 only one flight was possible before mid-March.

However, on 30 April 1948 the second prototype, TG267, made its maiden flight, and on 25 May TG263 took part in a display at West Raynham with other types of prototype aircraft. On 11 June the first SR.A/1 went to the Marine Aircraft Experimental Establishment (MAEE) at Felixstowe, a facility that performed the same tasks for water-based aircraft that Boscombe Down had done for land-based types. Unfortunately, due to the end of the Beryl programme and some speed and height restrictions placed on the SR.A/1 by the Ministry of Supply (MoS), MAEE was rather limited in the trials that it could perform with the aircraft.

The third prototype, TG271, fitted with uprated Beryls, was flown for the first time by Geoffrey Tyson on 17 August 1948, and he was the pilot when this aircraft was first displayed at the 1948 Farnborough Show. One section of his routine involved a long low-level inverted pass at an altitude of less than 100 feet (31m), which for a flying boat was most unusual, then, still inverted, the aircraft climbed into cloud. TG271 showed superb handling and manoeuvrability, and during the winter of 1948/49 was used in an in-depth hydrodynamic and aerodynamic research programme. Besides Farnborough, during September TG271 also appeared at several Battle of Britain displays where once again this unusual jet fighter was a showstopper. It was found, however, that the SR.A/1 suffered from premature tip stalling, a problem that

TG263 is now fitted with the metal cockpit canopy, which the machine kept to the end of its career. The metal canopy was fitted after TG263 lost its Perspex version on 27 May 1948 during a high-speed dive from 35,000 feet (10,668 m). *Author's collection*

This lovely picture shows TG263 banking towards the camera – a very early view because the aircraft does not yet have the fin/tail junction bullet, which was one of the few modifications introduced to the SR.A/1 in the light of flight testing. Note the gun ports spread across the upper nose. *MetroVick via High Duty Alloys*

This underside view of TG263 shows detail of the carefully shaped flying boat hull. *Author's collection*

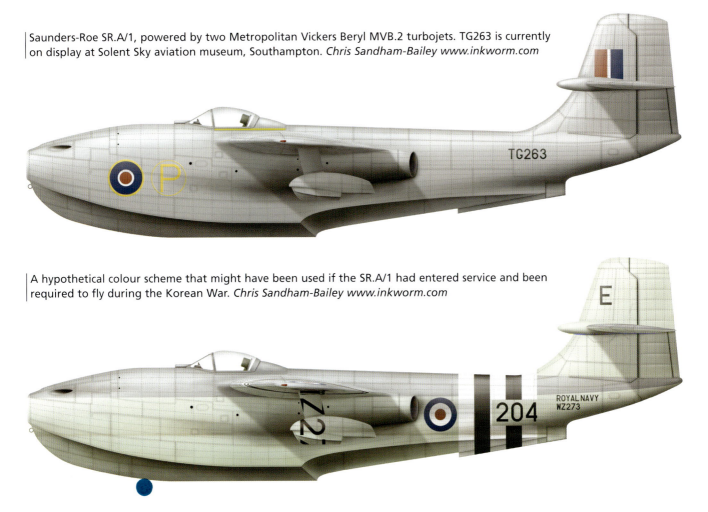

Saunders-Roe SR.A/1, powered by two Metropolitan Vickers Beryl MVB.2 turbojets. TG263 is currently on display at Solent Sky aviation museum, Southampton. *Chris Sandham-Bailey www.inkworm.com*

A hypothetical colour scheme that might have been used if the SR.A/1 had entered service and been required to fly during the Korean War. *Chris Sandham-Bailey www.inkworm.com*

The third example, TG271, is seen here outside the famous Saunders-Roe hangar at Cowes in late 1948. Unlike the other SR.A/1s, TG271 had 'pen-nib' exhaust fairings between the fuselage skin and jetpipe. *J. C. Hamon via Eric Morgan*

needed sorting out. Eventually TG267 had its outer wing modified, which produced a substantial improvement, but on 16 December 1948, after it had been grounded for a long period, Tyson was forced to land this aircraft with the starboard float in the up position. At the end of the year TG267 joined the first prototype at MAEE.

On 12 August 1949 TG271 was lost when it hit an object in the water just after landing at Cowes. This tore a hole in the starboard side planing surface, broke off the starboard wing float, and made the aircraft turn over. The pilot was Lt Cdr Eric Brown, one of the most famous test pilots of all time. Brown was able to escape, but the aircraft sank and has never been found since the water depth and strong currents experienced at the spot where it

disappeared made it very difficult to carry out a search. Prior to the crash, however, Brown had found the SR.A/1 to be a good aircraft and in it he had reached a speed of 0.82 Indicated Mach Number (IMN), which he described as 'a remarkable performance for a flying boat [that] compared favourably with contemporary straight-wing fighters'.

After this accident, on 17 September TG267 dived into the sea with its pilot Sqn Ldr 'Pete' Major during practice for a display at MAEE Felixstowe. Major, who was to have displayed the aircraft to the public that afternoon, was killed. Around 50% of TG267's airframe was recovered. Again, the aircraft was not at fault, but the SR.A/1's future was now bleak and, indeed, the flight test programme was closed. However, with the changing political situation

TG271, is seen inside Saro's Columbine hangar in early spring 1949 with Princess flying boat G-ALUN to the left. *Saunders-Roe Archive*

This image, taken after TG263 had become a museum piece, shows the detachable undercarriage fitted to the SR.A/1s to enable them to be manoeuvred on land. *Author's collection*

and news of hydro-ski research now under way in the United States, the surviving aircraft flew again in 1950. John Booth made the first sorties in mid-May, and although TG263 did not fly again until 10 October, by 19 December it had completed another fourteen flights in a short hydrodynamic programme for the MoS. It was during this period that Saro proposed a hydro-ski jet fighter called the P.121, which was to be capable of high subsonic speeds, but the project was not taken up.

This was not quite the end, however. On 17 June 1951, and with the Class B registration G-12-1, TG263 flew to Greenwich Reach in readiness to be towed up the River Thames into London for exhibition at the Festival of Britain, the SR.A/1's last public appearance. The return to Cowes on 24 June was the final flight and on retirement the aircraft went to Cranfield College of Aeronautics for use in ground instruction. From 1955 the individual Beryl engines were used at different times in Donald Campbell's record-breaking speedboat *Bluebird* (which broke several world records before the Beryl was replaced by a Bristol Siddeley Orpheus), and during 1966 TG267 became an exhibit of the Skyfame Museum at Staverton. Today it resides at Southampton. There were no production orders for the SR.A/1, in part because the Beryl was not in production for very long and a new engine would have required some redesign to the fuselage (not many types of slim axial jets were then in existence). The worldwide availability of wartime-built concrete runways and the fact that the boat fighter was always going to lose some performance against a ground-based fighter, were also factors working against Saro's aircraft. The SR.A/1 really lost its opportunity with the end of the war in Japan in 1945, but it remains a unique and fascinating exercise in fighter development.

This colour view of SR.A/1 TG263, thought to have been taken in July 1947, appeared in the journal *Aeronautics*.

A less well-known picture showing the surviving SR.A/1 TG263 beached outside the famous Saro hanger. The image is dated 21 August 1950, which falls into a period when the aircraft was apparently not flying.

5 Leduc 010, 016, 021 and 022 (1947-1956)

Leduc 010

Span: 34ft 6in (10.52m)
Length: 33ft 7in (10.25m)
Max gross take-off weight: 6,614lb (3,000kg)
Powerplant: 1 x Leduc Ramjet, 3,520lb (15.6kN)
Max speed/height: Mach 0.82 (limited to Mach 0.84)
Ceiling: 39,370ft (12,000m)

Leduc 016

(third Leduc 010 built with additional wingtip engines)
Span: 34ft 5.5in (10.50m)
Length: 33ft 7in (10.25m)
Max gross take-off weight: 7,165lb (3,250kg)
Powerplant: 1 x Leduc Ramjet, 3,520lb (15.6kN) (4,400lb [19.6kN] thrust at Mach 0.84)
2 x Turboméca Marboré 1 turbojets on wingtips, 551lb (2.45kN); these engines later removed and replaced by wingtip fuel tanks to become 010

Leduc 021

Span: 38ft 0.5in (11.595m)
Length: 41ft 0in (12.50m)
Wing area: 237sq ft (22.0sq m)
Max gross take-off weight: 13,228lb (6,000kg)
Powerplant: 1 x Leduc Ramjet, 14,300lb (63.7kN) sea level thrust at 620mph (1,000km/h)
Max speed: Mach 0.87
Ceiling: 66,000ft (20,117m)

Leduc 022

Span: 32ft 8in (9.95m)
Length: 59ft 9in (18.21m)
Wing area: 226.9sq ft (21.1sq m)
Max gross take-off weight: 19,786lb (8,975kg)
Powerplant: 1 x Leduc Ramjet, 14,300lb (63.6kN) sea level thrust at 620mph (1,000km/h)
1 x SNECMA Atar 101-D 3, 7,040lb (31.3kN)
Max speed/height: Mach 1 at 19,685ft (6,000m); Mach 1.15; (Mach 2 at 45,932ft [14,000 m] planned)
Ceiling (achieved): 28,870ft (8,800m)

By as early as 1913 French engineer René Lorin had presented in an article the first plausible theory for what could be described as a ramjet, expressing the concept that exhaust gases from internal combustion engines could be directed into nozzles to create jet propulsion; this was published in the journal l'Aérophile. However, at the time it was impossible for him to use his idea for an aeroplane because there was no aircraft capable of going fast enough to allow a ramjet to function properly. Later Lorin tested a primitive power unit on a speeding car, but sadly, when he died in 1933, he had been unable to get much scientific support for his ideas.

French aeronautical engineer René Leduc worked for many years on the development of a ramjet engine for aircraft propulsion. Known technically as an athodyd duct (Aero-thermo-dynamic-duct – a thermo-propulsive fuselage duct) this advanced-technology engine had no major rotating components. A thermo-propulsor engine (the early name for a ramjet) relies upon air being forced into an intake, which is designed to make the air lose kinetic energy but gain pressure as it passes through a diverging duct and directly into a combustion chamber. There, burning fuel dispensed by several concentric rings of injectors increases the total energy causing the expanding gasses to accelerate out into the atmosphere via an exhaust outlet shaped like a venturi ring. When Leduc applied for a patent in 1933 to cover his ramjet design he discovered the published works of his countryman René Lorin and tried to contact him, only to hear of his recent death. As a result Leduc would pay homage to Lorin's achievements in his own work. For many years the history behind Leduc's work was actually little known outside France. He had to work for years in the laboratory and wind tunnel to establish the basic theories for his propulsive duct, and the design of his aeroplane had to use the best of the then-existing high-speed aerodynamic knowledge. However, Leduc also had very considerable practical experience in structures, which proved to be of great benefit when preparing his design.

Leduc gained his first success in 1935 with a small but practical engine developing 9.7lb (0.043kN) of thrust. The French government was sufficiently impressed by the test data collected on the wind tunnel model to establish a project for a two-seat aircraft with a maximum speed of 550mph (910km/h) and capable of flying continuously for 3 hours. Further testing of a 1/10th-scale model of the Leduc 010 was conducted in the Eiffel wind tunnel. The first structural components of the real aircraft were built in the Breguet factory in Villacoublay near Paris, while a model of the 010 was also exhibited by Leduc at the Paris Salon of 1938. Here, when the official world speed record stood at 380mph (611km/h) and the unofficial record at around 450mph (724km/h), Leduc's claims of more than 600mph (965km/h) and a ceiling of 80,000 feet (24,375m) were received with polite and sometimes not so polite scepticism.

Leduc 010

When the Germans invaded Northern France in 1940, however, all of the components manufactured up to that point had to be shipped secretly to the Free (unoccupied) Zone in

The ramjet-powered Leduc 010 mounted atop a Sud-Est SE 161 Languedoc mother ship makes for an interesting contrast in old and new aircraft propulsion technologies. *Copyright Musée de l'Air et de l'Espace, Paris/Le Bourget)*

X-PLANES OF EUROPE

The 010 seen aboard its Languedoc carrier plane.

Montauban. Most of the airframe was apparently virtually complete and some work was continued on it, although the majority of the parts were dispersed in order to hide them from the Germans. During the war years work on the thermo-propulsor did continue in secret until in April 1944 the allies bombed the factory where the aircraft parts were kept; although the wing assembly suffered the most damage, thankfully the thermo-propulsor system was unharmed. When liberation came in August 1944 the hidden parts were brought out, assembly was restarted and the aircraft was completed in December 1945. The Leduc 010 had a tubular double-skinned fuselage 7 feet (2.13m) in diameter, the inner shell of which contained the pilot's cockpit and was surrounded by an outer shell that formed the inlet duct to the ramjet engine aft of the cockpit. Each of the Leduc test vehicles was essentially a metal tube housing a ramjet, with the wings, tail and fin fitted outside, while the cockpit pod, mounted on the nose, acted as a cone for the annular intake.

The first composite flight of the Leduc, mounted above the fuselage of a specially modified four-engine piston-powered Sud-Est SE 161 Languedoc mother plane, was made from the small airfield at Blagnac on 19 November 1946. Veteran French test pilot Jean Gonord, who had joined Leduc Aircraft in 1946, was in the 010 and the Languedoc's pilot for the historic first flight was Jean Perrin, who subsequently was to become something of a specialist in 'mother plane' flying. The Languedoc transport was a development of the Bloch 160 and was first flown in 1939.

Intended for use during the war years as a commercial airliner, this aeroplane served more aptly as a military transport for both the French Air Force and Navy well into the 1950s. Serving among other roles as an engine and radar systems test bed, the Languedoc was a natural candidate for the Leduc's air-launching duties. Even the aircraft's large twin vertical stabilisers were ideal for efficient aerodynamics, allowing the Leduc's wake turbulence to flow between the transport's fins when the mated aircraft were airborne. The SE 161 was powered by four 1,200hp Pratt & Whitney R-1830 Twin Wasp engines and weighed 28,000lb (12,700kg) empty, which made for a very efficient payload capability – yet another positive factor in its selection as the Leduc launch aircraft (in fact Leduc had to wait some time before he was able to get his hands on a Languedoc, and this brought delays to the 010's first flight). Additionally, the aircraft's top speed of 273mph (445km/h) provided sufficient speed to fire the Leduc's ramjet engine in flight. The SE 161 was 80 feet (24m) in length and had a wingspan of 96ft 5in (29.4m).

Since a ramjet is unable to provide any usable thrust at slow airspeeds, the Leduc needed the momentum provided by the launch aircraft to start its ramjet powerplant in flight. First tested as an unpowered glider on 21 October 1947, the Leduc 010 was carried high above the fuselage of its Languedoc mother ship, which then released it at an appropriate altitude. Aboard the transport the research aircraft was mounted on trunnion fittings and there was also a steadying jack beneath its tail. On its first two free flights the separations were successful and the unorthodox-looking test aircraft flew well as a glider, but the first dead-stick landing resulted in two burst tyres. Having proved the aircraft, the same configuration was used in another twenty-four flights to test both the systems and the combustion, and it was said that when the duct was first lit Leduc (who was in the Languedoc) involuntarily asked the pilot to stop because the flames appeared so alarming.

The Leduc's maiden free powered flight was made on 21 April 1949 with the Languedoc accelerating the Leduc 010 to the required minimum airspeed of 200mph (320km/h) to achieve sufficient aerodynamic pressure for the ramjet to be able to ignite. The 010 was then released over Blagnac and Jean Gonord put it into a climb in what was the world's first solely ramjet-powered aeroplane flight, and the first flight of an integrated airframe/engine. It was achieved through having both aircraft enter a dive while still joined and, when sufficient speed had been reached, the tail attachment would be retracted and the two underwing clamps released thereby permitting the 010 to pitch upwards and fly away. Once ignited, the ramjet could sustain power with fuel flowing through its circular array of 500 injectors and burners. During this first flight, which lasted all of 12 minutes, a maximum speed of 465mph (755km/h) was attained at only half power; indeed, the aircraft was subsequently flown at 50% power to a speed of 510mph (815km/h).

The 010 possessed an extraordinary rate of climb and early flights were extremely tough on the pilot, since heights of 36,100 feet (11,000m) were reached without using pressurisation; although dynamic pressure provided a small ram effect, once the flame had been extinguished this made the cabin very uncomfortable. On another sortie Gonord took the aircraft to Mach 0.85, at which point he first encountered the sometimes violent effects of compressibility, thereby also making the 010 the first aeroplane built in France to experience this phenomenon. However, the 010 powered flight test programme moved forward rather slowly, with just five sorties in 1949 and only three in the summer of 1950.

Two more examples of the original Leduc aircraft were built, the first the 010-02 of identical configuration, which was rolled out of the Toulouse factory in March 1950. During the winter of 1950/51 both the first and second 010s were moved to Istres in the hands of CEV to continue their testing, and now the programme began to move forward more quickly. The second aircraft flew a total of forty-four flights, including eleven powered by the ramjet, while the first machine continued its flight tests with thirty-eight flights successfully concluded, including thirty-five with the ramjet. However, during the following year both airframes were unfortunately destroyed.

On 27 November 1951 the second Leduc 010's nose cone separated on impact during a hard landing on rough ground, seriously injuring CEV test pilot Jean Sarrail, although he later recovered. The problem was a fuel valve, which caused a complete engine cut, Sarrail being unable to reach the airfield. The second mishap occurred on 25 July 1952 when 010-01, flown by Yvan Littolf, touched the carrier aeroplane while separating and suffered a broken pitot and jammed ailerons. The pilot recovered from the ensuing spin and made a belly landing on the rough stones of the Crau. Once again the jettisonable cabin broke from its fittings and the pilot suffered injuries but fortunately survived. Littolf was now the assistant pilot to Gonord. In all the first two 010s completed fifty-one free flights out of a total of 166 test flights with the carrier aircraft.

In 1951 the third aircraft, Leduc 016, made its debut; it had completed at the new Leduc factory at Argenteuil, Leduc having by now set up his own company. This aircraft differed from the 010 in having two wingtip-mounted Turbomeca Marboré 1 turbojet engines that were intended to accelerate the 016 to sufficient speed for proper ignition of the ramjets, and to allow it to cruise and land on jet power alone. This aircraft was first flown by Gonord on 8 February 1951 but the twin turbojet engines were removed after the aircraft suffered three serious landing accidents; the alteration essentially returned the third airframe to 010 standard. In fact, the 016 had proved difficult to handle when the Marborés were in place because the pilot now had to control the ramjet, the pump turbine and the two auxiliary jets. The pump turbine was a key element of the powerplant since it had to pump fuel at the colossal rate required by the ramjet, Leduc having designed a small gas turbine to do this task. And fuel not only provided a weight problem – there was also the one of stowage in a relatively small airframe. This aircraft completed eighty-three test flights, twenty-five of which were 'free' from the mother ship.

Development continued with two examples of the larger and more advanced Leduc 021 and the supersonic 022. The revised 016 continued to fly until 19 January 1954 when it was retired to Le Musée de l'Air, the arrival of the 021 series removing any further need to use the 016 since the new aircraft were equipped for the high-altitude phase of the programme. Although at the beginning the 010 family had been intended to reach a planned 1,000km/h (621mph) speed target, with their comparatively low performance they primarily became test beds to check the functioning of the elements of the control system.

Bigger and better

Each Leduc design brought an increase in size and power, and it had originally been planned to fit Marboré jets on the wingtips of the new 021, but the troubles with this arrangement on

Looks can be deceiving, as the side view of Leduc 021 shows an entirely different aerodynamic shape from the Leduc 010 and 016 series. The rather conventional vertical stabiliser was carried over, but the aft fuselage is now quite altered both in shape and proportion from the previous configuration. Note the aircraft's unique two-wheel tandem main landing gear. *Tony Buttler collection*

the 016 led to the idea being abandoned. Again, however, the two 021s were built mainly to serve as test beds, in this case to assess the 'motor' and also to reach much higher altitudes in the region of 20,000m (65,600 feet). Neither the new 021 nor the 010 series had been designed for high speed, and the limiting Mach numbers for the 010 and 021 were respectively 0.75 and 0.85; it was to be the 022 that would move into the supersonic regime. The reason behind this, according to Leduc himself, was that at this stage he had more than enough problems without including those of transonic flight, and also, since the airflow in the duct was

A ramp shot of the mated Leduc 021 and SE 161 Languedoc mother ship. The tall boarding stairs for the Leduc pilot are visible above the SE 161's forward fuselage, but these were removed before flight. Note the outrigger landing gear in the extended position, which was also retracted before flight. The tall, robust A-frame struts not only supported the Leduc but also ensured a safe distance for separation of the two aircraft in flight. *Musée de l'Air et de l'Espace, Paris/Le Bourget*

Both Leduc 021s are atop twin Sud-Est SE 161 Languedocs. The people and cars in the picture give a proper sense of scale to this unique pair of tall composite aircraft. *Musée de l'Air et de l'Espace, Paris/Le Bourget*

This excellent study of the Leduc 021 in its hangar shows the unique aircraft's clear conical cockpit in good detail. While overall pilot visibility was superb, the cockpit's vulnerable location directly ahead of the circular air intake made emergency jettison for bailout a dicey proposition. *Musée de l'Air et de l'Espace, Paris/Le Bourget*

The Leduc 021.

always subsonic, most full-scale testing could be done subsonically. He had therefore designed the simplest possible aeroplanes to achieve this purpose, the Leduc ramjet aircrafts' fuselage duct and conical entry giving a futuristic appearance that was purely coincidental. The sleek nose, with its submerged cockpit, was chosen less for performance than to ensure a symmetrical flow into the duct.

The 021's new Plexiglas cockpit fairing was a striking ultra-modern design feature with the pilot in a nosecone cockpit now well ahead of the intake. Although the wings appeared quite small, in fact the wing area was considerable and the small weight of the ramjet gave – by mid-1950s standards – a remarkably low wing loading. The wing was tapered, but by having all of the taper on the leading edge this actually gave a slight degree of sweepback. Such was the skill of the Leduc team that an integrally machined wing made of ribs and skin panels as a torsion box was made for the 021 as early as 1952/53. Plain ailerons and camber flaps occupied the entire trailing edge and the t/c ratio was 10% at the root and 8% at the tip. Wingtip nacelles were fitted that, having originally been designed to house the turbojets, contained the balancer wheels of the landing gear while also functioning as end plates to effectively increase the aspect ratio. The two main tandem wheels retracted

From the looks of this machine the future has arrived. A front view of the radical Leduc .21 reveals the perfectly circular cross-section and slight dihedral of the wings. Retractable outrigger 'pogo' landing gears keep the wings level while the aircraft is on the ground. *Musée de l'Air et de l'Espace, Paris/Le Bourget*

upwards, forward and aft of a single shock absorber, and there was a small tail wheel. The fuselage was built in double-skinned light alloy and the tail unit had simple control surfaces, which, like the ailerons, had slightly inset hinges and horn mass-balances. For the powerplant air entered the annular opening surrounding the pilot's cockpit and passed to the centre of the fuselage, where it entered a series of six internal cylindrical ducts of increasing size, the leading edge of each duct being ringed with fuel ejectors. The resulting mixture was ejected from the fuselage rear end as a high-velocity jet. On the 021 the ramjet engine was lit by the exhaust from a Turboméca Artouste turbine mounted at the rear end of the central nacelle.

The first 021 made its initial flight on 16 May 1953 as the world's second type of ramjet aircraft to fly. For its first launching from the Languedoc the 021's ramjet was lit before release, with the joined aeroplanes diving at 240mph (386km/h), but later in the programme the 021 was released 'cold' and then had the ramjet lit while in a dive, which permitted it to be flown under its own power for longer. This new configuration proved to be very successful, allowing the aircraft to achieve a maximum speed of Mach 0.87 and attain an impressive altitude of 66,000 feet (20,000m). The 021's test flight programme comprised 385 flights (248 'free') made between August 1954 and December 1956 and totalling 517 flight hours, all flown in the hands of two very capable test pilots, Yvan Littolf and Jean Sarrail.

The flight envelope was explored at various altitudes between 32,800 and 65,600 feet (10,000 and 20,000m) with flights lasting anywhere from 15 minutes to 1 hour on the aircraft's 630-gallon (2,864-litre) fuel load. The Leduc 021's rate of climb was nothing short of spectacular, with a rate of 39,300 feet per minute (11,980m/min) immediately after take-off, then falling off to 2,900 feet per minute (884m/min) in the more rarefied air at 49,000 feet (14,935m). The aircraft's acceleration was so terrific that the de Havilland Vampire and Gloster Meteor chase planes, when flying on full power, were unable to keep up with it. Like the 010, the 021 was also assessed (in 1955) by CEV, where it was flown by Bernard Witt.

Both Leduc 021s appeared at the Paris Air Show at Le Bourget Airport in 1955. The crowd was astonished to witness a most impressive flight display that included one separation of the Leduc from its Languedoc launch aircraft at an altitude of only 1,200 feet (366m) right in front of the crowd. Igniting its engine with a roar, the 021 made two high-speed passes directly in front of the show crowd, then landed with its drag chutes fully deployed. Company colour films of the 021 screened to a journalist showed flames pouring out of the orifice under static and semi-static conditions, but in free flight, as speed increased, only a reflected glow was to be seen, and rarely was there a trace of the smoke of incomplete combustion.

A close-up of the engine exhaust reveals clearly the concentric array of fuel burners, sometimes known as the stratoreactor (the ramjet). *Musée de l'Air et de l'Espace, Paris/Le Bourget*

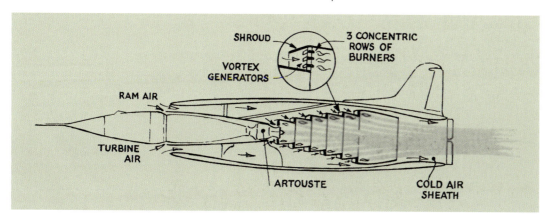

Section drawing through the Leduc 021 showing the arrangement for the ramjet powerplant. The 021 had six shrouds, whereas the 010 had only five and the later 0.22 seven.

Supersonic

Leduc was fully aware of the limits involved in using a propeller-driven launch aircraft in operational air force service. The 021 was of course purely a test vehicle (although it was built with provision in its wing roots for two 30mm cannon to be fitted), but work was also started on the high-speed 022 Mach 2 interceptor development, which incorporated a SNECMA Atar 101 D3 turbojet installed within the athodyd ring. Supersonic flight had always been Leduc's ultimate target and he had no illusions about the problems of ramjet fuel consumption without the help of compressibility. (Because of the relationship of thrust to the square of the speed, a ramjet aeroplane must climb supersonically, for that is the only way to keep down the fuel consumption.) This more conventional turbine powerplant permitted the 022 to take off independently (without the need of a mother plane) and cruise under its own power, then accelerate to a speed where the ramjet could be ignited. Although flown on turbojet power for the first time on 26 December 1956, after having been taken by road to the airfield at Istres for its maiden flight, it was not until the aircraft's thirty-fourth flight on 18 May 1957 that the ramjet was lit successfully for the very first time.

The model 022 was double the weight of the model 010 and, when flying at a speed of 620mph (1,020km/h), its ramjet powerplant produced 14,300lb (63.6kN) of thrust. Fuel was housed in the wings and also between the double walls of the fuselage duct. The wing had 30° of sweepback and a thinner aerofoil than the 021, and a tricycle undercarriage was fitted. The level of integral design went much further with the whole skin form milled as a series of panels. Its streamlined nacelle consisted of a light alloy monocoque structure, to the front of which was attached a tubular framework that held the pilot's seat in a transparent cabin shell. Again a Turboméca Artouste was mounted in the tail of the nacelle to act as an accessory drive unit.

On its 141st flight on 21 December 1957 the first 022 reached a speed of Mach 1.15. On the Leduc the controls were easier to operate than on some other research aeroplanes because there were six different stages of afterburner instead of only two on types like the Nord Griffon II. Estimates made in 1955 for the 022 indicated that it would achieve Mach 2 in the climb and reach 80,000 feet (24,375m) in less than 5 minutes. About 30% of the aircraft's all-up weight was to be accounted for by approximately 600 gallons (2,728 litres) of fuel, which would permit around 60 minutes cruising on the Atar turbojet with something less than 10 minutes at full speed and power on the ramjet.

Unfortunately, in late 1957 Leduc 022-1 caught fire on take-off and was badly damaged, although the pilot was able to operate the brake chutes and jump out of the aircraft. In fact, the entire Leduc programme was finally terminated in 1958 after the 022 had made 141 flights

This rear-three-quarter view shows the Leduc 022's spindly but adequate landing gear structure. Streamlined spears at the extremities of the tailplane control surfaces were external counterbalances, while external fuel tanks were mounted on the wingtips. The aircraft had obvious limited range for rotation on landing with the main gear mounted so low and so far forward on the fuselage. *Musée de l'Air et de l'Espace, Paris/Le Bourget*

This bird's-eye view of the final Leduc model, the swept-wing 022, reveals the unusual proportions of the barrel-like fuselage and extended nose section. The vertical stabiliser is enlarged and swept back as well; note also the raised bubble cockpit for improved pilot visibility. *Musée de l'Air et de l'Espace, Paris/Le Bourget*

(eighty-one powered). Cancellation of the project came primarily as a result of severe military budget cuts, the French government making the decision to procure the more conventional turbojet-powered delta-wing Dassault Mirage III fighter since great progress had also been made with jet engines fitted with afterburners. A second Leduc 022 prototype was at the time under construction and work on this was halted, and one half of the staff at Leduc was dismissed as the company ended its work as an aircraft manufacturer (the company does still exist). Both 021 and 022 were developed to the order of the French Air Ministry, but this official support was withdrawn as part of major cutbacks in military contracts and spending made during 1957 due to the cost of the Algerian War (which had broken out in 1954). Indeed, the cost of this conflict contributed to the end of several French prototype aircraft programmes at this time.

It is interesting to note that the Mach 1 Nord 1402/1405 Gerfaut, the Mach 2 Nord 1500 Griffon II, and the Leduc 022 were all competing under the same French Air Force requirement, finally won by the more conventional, more reliable, and ultimately easier to operate Mirage III. Leduc also had on his drawing board several paper projects including a delta-wing aircraft and a twin-fuselage, twin-ramjet-powered interceptor. The different Leduc aeroplanes, sometimes known as 'Flying Blowlamps', made a total of well over 700 test flights, which may seem like a rather high number for such a radical aircraft. However, like the air-launched rocket-powered American X-Planes, many of these flights were 'captive' or mated missions where both the Leduc and Languedoc were airborne, but where the Leduc was not launched into free-flight from its mother ship. These captive flights included all combinations of having the Leduc pilot onboard or not, and the aircraft's onboard systems operating or not.

Le Musée de l'Air et de l'Espace near Paris has one Leduc 010 on display, the only survivor of the three examples built. This facility also houses an example of the Leduc 022, the second airframe, which was never flown, the Leduc family having presented this extremely rare aircraft to the Museum in 1979, 11 years after René Leduc had passed away.

This in-flight view of the Leduc 022 shows the extreme aerodynamic cleanliness of the airframe. The 022 made a total of 141 test flights, eighty-one of which were powered by the ramjet, and reached a top speed of 750mph (1,200km/h). *Musée de l'Air et de l'Espace, Paris/Le Bourget*

6 Arsenal VG 70 (1948)

Arsenal VG 70

Span: 29ft 10in (9.10m)
Length: 31ft 10 in (9.70m)
Wing area: 182.8sq ft (17sq m)
Max gross take-off weight: 7,275lb (3,300kg)
Powerplant: 1 x Junkers Jumo 004B-2 turbojet engine, 1,980lb (8.80kN)
Max speed/height: 497mph (800km/h) at altitude

Just after the opening of the Second World War in October 1939 the designer at Arsenal, Jean Galtier, started work on a piston-powered fighter aircraft called the VG 60. This was revised in 1942, and again in 1944, on the second occasion with the new effort looking at ways of fitting a jet engine, the German Junkers Jumo 004. Then, after acquiring data gathered by Messerschmitt engineers from wind tunnel testing on swept-wing designs (primarily, it is understood, for the Messerschmitt P.1092), in the autumn of 1945 Galtier decided to build a new research aircraft fitted with a swept wing called the VG 70. Like the SNCAN 1601 (qv), the VG 70 was a private-venture aircraft dedicated in general to the study of swept wings, but in particular with future high-speed fighter aircraft in mind.

The design of the VG 70 was begun soon after France's liberation when the only available engine of the required class was the 004. Because of the lack of power provided by this unit it was necessary for Galtier to keep the aircraft's dimensions as small as possible. Consequently, some imaginative features were incorporated within the airframe – for example, as the fuselage diameter was little greater than that of the jetpipe, it was necessary to build integral fuselage frames and tailplane spars of steel and, of course, to give the spars sweepback. In addition, the main high-pressure wheels of the retractable tricycle undercarriage had to be turned during their retraction into the wing, and it was also necessary to collapse the nosewheel strut before it was raised.

The single-seat VG 70's fuselage was built in metal while the wings and low-position tail were manufactured in wood. The two-spar cantilever wing was mounted at a relatively high position; it had 6° of dihedral, a leading-edge sweep angle of about 43°, and elliptical tips. Seven fuel tanks were housed in the wings, 'pillar-box'-type slots were fitted (which pre-first flight testing suggested were not actually required), and there were dive brakes on the top of the wing. To feed the Jumo 004B-2 turbojet there was a rather crude-looking air intake in the lower forward fuselage, but tests at Chalais-Meudon made before October 1947 also indicated that this ventral intake was not so favourably located as had been first thought. The engine itself was housed in the rear fuselage together with three more fuel tanks. Tunnel tests indicated the potential for a top speed on the level of more than 560mph (901km/h) at 23,000 feet (7,010m), and, in a 10° dive, Mach numbers of around 0.9 representing speeds of the order of 680mph (1,094km/h). A British anti-spin parachute was fitted.

Photographs of the Arsenal VG 70 are rare but this one shows the unusual ventral air intake very well.

The brief flight test programme

In the autumn of 1947 the attractive little VG 70 was reviewed at Villacoublay by representatives of the British magazine *Flight*, the statically displayed, near-complete airframe having already graced the Paris Aero Show in mid-November 1946. The single VG 70 was completed in 1947 and by mid-October had performed its taxi tests (at which point the first flight was expected in November). However, the start of the flight test programme was substantially delayed after wind tunnel testing had revealed some potential aerodynamic problems. The VG 70's maiden flight finally took place from Melun-Villaroche on 23 June 1948 when the aircraft was piloted by Modeste Vonner, chief test pilot at Arsenal. As such it became the second French jet aircraft to fly, following the Triton (see above). No significant problems were experienced during the limited flight testing that was completed and, despite the lack of thrust provided by the Jumo 004, some quite high speeds were recorded. The intention was to re-engine the VG 70 eventually with a 3,500lb (15.6kN) Rolls-Royce Derwent 5

This view of the follow-on Arsenal VG 90 fighter shows the various changes made from the VG 70. The VG 90 was a bigger aircraft and was powered by a Rolls-Royce Nene jet.

Nose angle photo of the VG 70.

engine to provide more thrust – predictions indicating a maximum speed at altitude of 600mph (965km/h) with the new powerplant. As such it was to be re-titled VG 71.

In fact, this plan never came to fruition and VG 70 testing was terminated after just five flights, in part through the lack of availability of an experienced jet pilot. In addition it was clear that the relatively low level of power made available by the Jumo had made necessary certain limits for flying the aircraft, which were quite tight. Another problem was that the centrifugal Derwent was fatter than the axial Jumo jet and therefore its installation would have necessitated a redesign of the VG 70's fuselage, so that idea was also dropped. The flight test programme was discontinued in early 1949 and work moved on to the follow-on VG 90 naval strike fighter, which benefited considerably from Arsenal's experience in producing the VG 70 and which first flew on 27 September 1949 before taking part in a naval fighter competition. There was also a proposed development called the VG 80 with a single more powerful RR Nene turbojet engine, but this too did not proceed. The VG 70 itself does not survive.

Picture showing maintenance work being undertaken on the sole VG 70 to be built.

7 Sud-Ouest SO M.2 (1949)

Sud-Ouest SO M.2
Registration: F-WFDK
Span: 29ft 9.5in (9.08m) without tip tanks
Length: 32ft 6in (9.90m)
Wing area: 189.8sq ft (17.65sq m)
Max gross take-off weight: 11,861lb (5,380kg)
Powerplant: 1 x RR Derwent 5, 3,220lb (14.3kN)
Max speed/height: 590mph (950km/h) and Mach 0.9 at 29,530ft (9,000m)
Ceiling: Unknown

The very similar Sud-Ouest SO M.1 and M.2 were scale-model proof-of-concept test aeroplanes built to assess the aerodynamics of and to acquire data for the construction of the planned Sud-Ouest SO 4000 jet bomber.

Glider to start

The M.1 glider, which was shown at the Paris Salon in 1946, had an all-metal structure with a pressurised cabin and tiny teardrop canopy – in an emergency the pilot would evacuate the aircraft through a ventral hatch. It had swept horizontal surfaces with a rounded fin and rudder and was one of the first French aeroplanes to employ lateral control by the use of a combination of small ailerons interconnected with spoilers and leading-edge slats. To land, the glider had a retractable central skid undercarriage with wingtip stabilising skids. The M.1's span was 29ft 3in (8.91m) and length 29ft 6in (8.99m).

Under civil registration F-WFDJ, the SO M.1 made its first captive flight on 6 April 1948. A dozen of these were completed before, after taking off from Orléans-Bricy, the M.1 left its Languedoc carrier aircraft to make its first free flight on 26 September 1949. Jacques

The Sud-Ouest SO M.1 glider F-WFDJ seen mounted above its carrier aircraft, a Heinkel He 274.

X-PLANES OF EUROPE

Early photographs of the SO M.2 in its original condition with no markings. Note the three central main wheels placed one behind the other.

Guignard was in the cockpit, the release was made at an altitude of 13,125 feet (4,000m), and after a smooth flight he was able to land a few minutes later without problems. A second flight was made on 30 September and a third on 5 October, the latter with a release from 23,620 feet (7,200m). To increase the flight time a Heinkel He 274 was used for these sorties, since this could take the M.1 to higher altitudes than the Languedoc, which automatically provided gliding flights of longer duration. The M.1's tenth and final glide took place on 30 August 1950, and during its flying programme it achieved speeds in excess of 373mph (600km/h). The flying qualities were good but there were problems with the aileron controls being too strong at high speed and with the roll performance.

(It should be noted that another scale-model glider built to represent a future bomber was the Aérocentre NC 271-01, first revealed to the public at the November 1946 Paris Show and first flown free from its carrier aircraft on 28 January 1949. The follow-on rocket-powered NC 271-02 aerodynamic model was in May 1949 being prepared for its first flight from the He 274 when the project was abandoned. Consequently both NC 271s, together with the well-advanced NC 270 bomber prototype, were scrapped. Had the rocket-powered NC 271-02 flown it would have qualified for full inclusion in this book.)

Powered test aircraft

The little M.2 was a half-scale model of the bomber. Its single Rolls-Royce Derwent 5 was fed by laterally disposed air intakes, which stood proud on the fuselage sides, and the central efflux was flanked by two small outlets for turbine-cooling air. The main undercarriage had an unusual arrangement of three tandem retractable wheels stowed in the central fuselage together with a relatively large nosewheel, and for take-off there were also small jettisonable wheels attached to the retractable wingtip skids. A skin 0.12 inches (3mm) thick was used to provide what was described by *Flight* magazine as 'a remarkably smooth wing' – both the M.1 and the M.2 had a mid-position laminar flow wing swept 31° at the mainspar. For take-off and landing the pilot could raise his seat and improve his vision by means of a retractable windscreen, and *Flight* added that 'the cockpit roof, embodying this screen, is a brilliant piece of work in Perspex'. The internal fuel load totalled 1,430lb (649kg).

The SO M.2 was displayed nearly complete at the Paris Salon in May 1949, photographs showing the retractable windscreen in the stowed position. One would have assumed that the SO M.1 glider would have flown first, but in fact it was the M.2 that became the first to fly, on 13 April 1949; again it was crewed by Sud-Ouest chief test pilot Jacques Guignard. Later, during a flight flown by Daniel Rastel on 9 May 1950, the M.2 reached a speed of 621mph (1,000km/h) in a shallow dive (although some sources state that this was achieved on the level, making it the first French jet to exceed 1,000km/h in level flight). The indicated Mach number was apparently 0.93.

In April 1951 the M.2 began to receive some significant modifications, the most important of which was the installation of servo-controls. In addition it was given a more powerful Derwent 8 engine, wingtip fuel tanks and a modified undercarriage retraction system, as well as provision for powder rockets to be fitted to provide more thrust at high altitudes. Phase two of the SO M.2's test flying programme opened during the following October after these changes had been completed, the maximum weight having risen from the previous 9,370lb (4,250kg) to 11,861lb (5,380kg). This later programme analysed the effects of the servo-control system in the Mach 0.9 to 0.93 speed range at high altitudes, at the time a new technology for France. It is understood that the SO M.2 possessed good flying qualities (except at high speeds) but suffered from a lack of power.

The SO 4000 bomber (registered F-WBBL) was powered by two Nene engines made by Hispano-Suiza and first flew on 15 March 1951 from Orléans-Bricy airfield. It should have flown in 1950, but during taxi trials on 23 April 1950 the undercarriage collapsed, causing severe damage. The aircraft's flying characteristics were also found to be quite poor and it was seriously underpowered, with the result that no further flights were made and the project was abandoned.

Later the serial number F-WFDK was applied to the M.2's rear fuselage. This picture appears to have been made after the aircraft was modified in 1951.

The SO M.2 was a scale model test aircraft for the Sud-Ouest SO 4000 bomber F-WBBL.

8 Avro 707 (1949)

Avro 707
Span: 33ft 0in (10.01m)
Length: 40ft 2.25in (12.25m) with probe
Gross wing area: 366.5sq ft (34.08sq m)
Gross weight: 8,600lb (3,901kg)
Powerplant: 1 x RR Derwent 5 (R.D.7), 3,500lb (15.6kN)
Max speed/height: Unknown
Ceiling: Unknown

Avro 707B
Span: 33ft 0in (10.01m)
Length: 41ft 3.5in (12.59m) with probe
Gross wing area: 366.5sq ft (34.08sq m)
Gross weight: 9,500lb (4,309kg)
Powerplant: 1 x RR Derwent 5lb (R.D.7), 3,500lb (15.6kN)
Max speed: 461mph (742km/h)
Ceiling: Unknown

Avro 707A
Span: 34ft 2in (10.41m)
Length: 42ft 4in (12.90m) with probe
Gross wing area: 408.0sq ft (37.94sq m)
Gross weight: 9,800lb (4,445kg)
Powerplant: 1 x RR Derwent 8 (R.D.7), 3,600lb (16.0kN)
Max speed/height: 478mph (769km/h), Mach 0.95 in slight dive
Ceiling: Unknown

Avro 707C
Span: 34ft 2in (10.41m)
Length: 42ft 4in (12.90m) with probe
Gross wing area: 408.0sq ft (37.94sq m)
Gross weight: 10,000lb (4,536kg)
Powerplant: 1 x RR Derwent 8 (R.D.7), 3,600lb (16.0kN)
Max speed/height: Unknown
Ceiling: Unknown

The development of the British V-bomber force from the late 1940s onwards was a huge achievement for the country's aircraft industry. Two of the V-bombers, the Avro Vulcan and Handley Page Victor, introduced for their time quite advanced (one might say even revolutionary) wing forms, respectively the delta and the crescent wing. Both types were also pretty big aeroplanes, so it was felt desirable to acquire flight test information on these wing shapes before the full-size machines were ready. This was achieved using smaller flying scale-model research aircraft, and the types ordered were the one-off HP.88 for the Victor (qv) and the 707 for the Vulcan. The Avro project eventually grew into a family of research aircraft.

An aerodynamic scale model

Two prototypes of the Avro 698 bomber were ordered in June 1948 (the 698 was named Vulcan in October 1952). In April of that year Avro had completed proposals for two single-seat flying models – a 1/3rd-scale Type 707 to investigate the problems surrounding the operation of the 698 at low speeds and altitudes,

The first Avro 707, VX784, used a Meteor fighter cockpit and nosewheel, and the resulting short nose gave the pilot a superb view. Here the underwing flaps are deployed for landing. *BAE Systems*

and the half-scale Type 710 to assess the delta's characteristics at high Mach numbers and altitudes. The British Ministry of Supply accepted the proposals, and on 22 June serials VX770 and VX777 were allocated to the 698 prototypes, VX784 and VX790 to the 707s, and VX799 and VX808 to the 710s. However, in February 1949 both 710s were abandoned because it was clear that they would absorb a substantial volume of the available development capacity. In contrast, the 707 would employ mostly wood construction and plenty of existing equipment, so this design was seen as a potentially quick supplier of data.

In due course, however, the 707's structure was altered to all-metal with a welded steel tubing assembly covered by unstressed aluminium alloy sheet panels, the wings and fin both having a two-spar structure. The Avro 707 had a single fin on the rear fuselage and a dorsal air intake positioned ahead of it. There were four control surfaces on the wing trailing edge, the inboard pair operating as the elevators with the outer pair acting as the ailerons. To save time a Gloster Meteor F.3 fighter cockpit and nosewheel were fitted, together with the main undercarriage from an Avro Athena trainer. Specification E.15/48 of October 1948 was written around the aircraft and one of the most important tasks was to examine flight at the high angles of incidence necessary for a delta wing at take-off and landing, although the testing was also expected to explore the flight envelope right up to about 500mph (805km/h). VX784 became airborne for the first time at Boscombe Down on 4 September 1949 in the hands of Avro's deputy chief test pilot Flt Lt Eric 'Red' Esler (having earlier completed taxi trials at its Woodford birthplace, together with a hop at Boscombe the previous day). Three more flights were

Left and top next page: Images of VX784 on display at the SBAC Farnborough Show in September 1949. Note the bifurcated ventral air intake. *Author's collection*

A rear-end view of VX784 shows the aircraft's circular fuselage and wing trailing-edge surfaces. *Avro Heritage*

swiftly completed to qualify the 707 for display at that month's Farnborough Air Show.

However, VX784 did little to explore the flight envelope for which it was designed because on 30 September Esler was killed when the aircraft went into the ground near Blackbushe Aerodrome. This accident occurred about 7 minutes into a handling check flight after some adjustments had been made to the ailerons. The aircraft completed its fall in a very slight tail-down attitude and the nose and centre fuselage were burned out. The cause of the accident is still not completely understood, but at the time of its loss the aircraft had been flying at a low speed and altitude and the fuselage-mounted air brakes (known as braking flaps) had been opened to about one-third of their range. When retracted these normally sat on top of the skin rather than flush with it; the high degree of extra drag could have resulted in a very high rate of descent with insufficient time to recover (VX784 had no ejection seat). The wing air brakes had also been fully lowered during the flight, and it was known that an adverse nose-up change of trim would occur when the air brakes were lowered. It was also known that flight with the ailerons was not pleasant, and that the weather conditions were worse than could have been anticipated from the ground, making for poor visibility. There was no failure of the aircraft's engine or structure, so it seemed likely that the wing brakes had contributed to the accident. After the enquiry, the 707s that followed were given a set of retractable and mechanically interconnected air brakes fitted to both the top and bottom wing surfaces.

The second prototype, VX790, was modified and subsequently became known as the 707B. VX790 introduced an all-monocoque-structure nose, which was made 2ft 6in (76.2cm) longer

The 707B VX790 was painted in a gloss blue livery. *Avro Heritage*

to improve the aerodynamics and the centre of gravity (c.g.). The cockpit was redesigned and there was now room for a Martin-Baker ejection seat, while a 12-inch (30.5cm) extension was made to the top of the fin. This second machine also had a modified Hawker Sea Hawk nose leg oleo extended by 9 inches (22.9cm) to provide a better angle of incidence at take-off. The first 707 had experienced a rather long take-off run since the lack of incidence meant that the elevators were ineffective until the aircraft was approaching the unstick speed (this extension was also introduced to the Vulcan nose leg). Apart from these changes, VX790 had almost the same wing structure and undercarriage as VX784. None of the 707s received a pressurised cockpit, and both of these early models had a single fuel tank in the rear fuselage.

VX790 made its first flight (from Boscombe) on 6 September 1950, piloted by Avro's superintendent of flying Wg Cdr R. J. 'Roly' Falk. After attending the SBAC Show at Farnborough it went to Dunsfold to begin a long period of research flying, before suffering a landing accident at Boscombe on 21 September 1951. The pilot, Wg Cdr Balmforth of the A&AEE, was injured when the 707, having touched down, became airborne again with a very high nose-up attitude, at which point a wing dropped and hit the ground, slewing the aircraft round and damaging the nose. It was repaired at Woodford and flew again in mid-1952, and was able to attend the September 1952 Farnborough Show. Immediately afterwards VX790 was transferred to RAE Farnborough for employment on delta-wing research. By this time it had shown that a tailless aeroplane, when airborne, could possess entirely satisfactory qualities across the speed range examined (from the stall at 94mph [152km/h] up to 438mph [704km/h]).

Bright blue 707B VX790 is seen in an Avro picture taken after the air intake had been altered in February 1951. Note the 'P' prototype marking and Hawker Siddeley logo on the extended nose. A small edition of the Avro logo is also painted on the fin. *Avro Heritage*

Here VX790 has the modified raised air intake. Gloster Aircraft's celebrated photographer Russell Adams took this picture. *Jet Age Museum*

VX790 lands at the September 1950 Farnborough Show. *Barry Jones via Terry Panopalis*

Two shots of VX790 taken between 7 and 9 July 1955 during RAE Farnborough's Golden Jubilee celebration event. A large number of aircraft were displayed on the ground and in the air, while various departments presented the work of the Establishment. For this exhibition the 707's wings were fitted with some of the equipment used for investigating the flow of air at low speeds. *Jet Age Museum*

Snowy scene showing the second 707A WZ736 (with the airbrakes deployed) and a Pickfords furniture removals van. *Avro Heritage*

During VX790's early test flights it was found that disturbed airflow produced by the cockpit canopy at higher speeds was impeding the air entering the intake. The result was partial starvation, and the structural modification that proved necessary to solve the problem introduced a substantial 'hump' to the 707's back. This work was undertaken in February 1951 and gave a much-improved airflow to the engine in all regimes but in particular at high angles of attack. However, this piece of development was not important to the Vulcan, so it slowed down the overall programme, although one benefit that did accrue was the tilting of the jet exhaust outwards and downwards, which was found to reduce the need for changes of trim on both the 707 and the Vulcan. VX790 went on, in January 1956, to join the Empire Test Pilots' School (ETPS) at Farnborough, but another landing accident on 25 September of that year brought an end to its flying career. In May 1957 the aircraft was transferred by road to RAE Bedford and was Struck Off Charge in November for use as a spares source. VX790 was scrapped in 1960.

Later versions

A 'high-speed' 707 in fact replaced the 'high-speed' 710. This was covered by Specification E.10/49 of July 1949, which stipulated a maximum speed of 576mph (926km/h) at 36,000 feet (10,973m). The new version was called the 707A and two (WD280 and WZ736) were built, the second for general research work at the request of the RAE. The forward fuselage ahead of the main spar attachment frame was identical to the 707B, but a new wing complete with non-bifurcated root intakes made this aeroplane far more representative of the full-scale bomber. Apart from a small section inboard, all of the wing

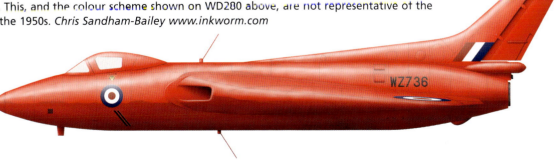

WD280, third 707 to be built, finished in natural metal, as preserved, and currently on display at the RAAF Museum, Point Cook, Australia. This aircraft has recently been repainted in a duck egg green colour scheme. *Chris Sandham-Bailey www.inkworm.com*

WZ736, second AVRO 707A built and finished in the high gloss red as preserved. Powered by one Rolls-Royce Derwent 8 turbojet. This is currently on display at the Museum of Science and Industry, Manchester, UK. This, and the colour scheme shown on WD280 above, are not representative of the liveries worn in the 1950s. *Chris Sandham-Bailey www.inkworm.com*

X-PLANES OF EUROPE

An underside view of the 'high-speed' Avro 707A WD280. *Avro Heritage*

The second 707A, WZ736. *Avro Heritage*

trailing edge was now swept just a little, the straight portion itself featuring a new and separate dive recovery flap; both fin and rudder were unaltered from VX790. This 707 would not be supersonic on the level, but it was hoped that a higher-power Derwent 8 jet would permit greater speeds than those achieved by the earlier 707s with the Derwent 5. At the start WD280 had manual controls, but power controls were eventually installed to deal with problems of stability. (The last three 707s each had powered controls retrofitted.)

Like the earlier 707s, WD280 was built at Woodford but, again, its first flight took place from Boscombe Down on 14 June 1951 with Roly Falk in the cockpit. The second 707A, WZ736, and the two-seat 707C, WZ744 (see below), were, however, assembled at Bracebridge Heath near Lincoln, which was the home of Avro's repair and overhaul organisation. By this stage the relevance of the 707 programme to the Vulcan had faded, and in many areas the development of the bomber had left the scale aircraft behind, which meant that these later 707s made little direct contribution to the bomber's progress. The Vulcan prototype first flew on 30 August 1952, so by mid-1951 much of its design had been frozen.

These views show the sleeker contours of WD280 compared to the earlier versions of the 707. *Barry Jones via Terry Panopalis*

However, experience with the 707A did influence one important area. When pulling 'g' at high altitude and high speed, a pronounced wing 'buzz' (a high-frequency vibration) was experienced. The addition of wing fences proved to be ineffective, but eventually a compound sweepback and a kink to the outer portion of the leading edge was introduced, which proved successful in eliminating the problem. The inner part of the outer wing received a reduction in sweep angle while the outermost portion was given more. The modification was done at Waddington (although only WD280 was so treated), and this particular problem does indeed stress the value of scale-model research aircraft, although in this case several production Vulcans with the original wing had to be retrofitted in an expensive modification programme.

On 30 June 1952 WD280 was cleared to take part in the Central Fighter Establishment's Annual Convention at RAF West Raynham, the event lasting until 4 July, and in September it was loaned back to Avro to perform at the Farnborough Show. In July 1953 the aircraft attended the Paris Air Show, then took part in various programmes of general research, initially with RAE Farnborough and, after 14 October 1953, with Avro at Woodford, where it was used for delta-wing experiments. After receiving its wing leading edge modification at Waddington, WD280 returned to Woodford in mid-February 1956. It was then delivered to Renfrew on 6 March for shipping to Australia aboard the carrier HMAS *Melbourne* in readiness to serve with the Commonwealth Aeronautical Advisory Research Council (CAARC), where it was employed until 1961 on low-speed tests to examine the flow of air over a delta wing. WD280 was based at RAAF Laverton and at one stage grit of varying coarseness was applied to the wing underside, which it was found improved the elevator and aileron's effectiveness and gave improved control. In July 1959 kerosene was poured over the port wing during flight to allow the path of the boundary layer to be traced, a porous coating of white china clay on the upper wing being made translucent by the fluid to reveal a layer of black shellac underneath. WD280 was finally Struck Off Charge in February 1967.

The second 707A, WZ736, did not fly until 20 February 1953, and both this aircraft and 707C WZ744 had to be towed by road from

X-PLANES OF EUROPE

WZ736 displays the type's wing root intakes and the three control surfaces along each wing trailing edge – from inboard to outboard are dive recovery flaps, elevators and ailerons. *Avro Heritage*

For comparison, this nose angle air-to-air shows the solitary 707C WZ744 with its wider two-seat side-by-side cockpit and the matte-black anti-glare panel in front of the canopy. The air brakes are fully deployed. *Avro Heritage*

| A later air-to-air view of WZ744. The new fairing on the fin leading edge housed a TV camera. *Clive Rustin collection*

| WZ744 taxis out for another flight. *Avro Heritage*

| The quartet of Avro 707s is seen taxiing at the 1953 Farnborough Show. *Barry Jones collection via Terry Panopalis*

X-PLANES OF EUROPE

WD280 was one of the 'high speed' 707As and was eventually coated in a bright red colour scheme. *Avro Heritage*

Bracebridge Heath to RAF Waddington to perform their maiden flights. WZ736 joined RAE Farnborough in June 1953 and was used by the Establishment for several projects. In September 1955 it joined the National Aeronautical Establishment (NAE) at Bedford to take part in 'automatic approach' trials. This work included automatic landing trials at the Armament & Instrument Experimental Unit (AIEU) at Martlesham Heath in November, and further control assessment trials were made at both venues during 1956. In July 1957 automatic throttle trials were continued at Bedford, and WZ736 was finally delivered to Farnborough in May 1962, where it was Struck Off Charge to serve as a source of spares for WZ744.

The two-seat 707

The final variant was the two-seat 707C with a side-by-side cockpit that was intended to provide delta training for the RAF. Specification E.10/49 Issue 2 was written for this dual-control aeroplane in November 1951, and four examples were planned, but only WZ744 was built. The only difference to the second 707A was the new cramped two-seat cockpit, which had insufficient room for ejection seats. Circular side windows also provided relatively poor lateral vision. On completion, WZ744 was moved to Waddington where Sqn Ldr T. B. Wales flew it for the first time on 1 July 1953. It then joined A&AEE Boscombe Down to provide pilot familiarisation of delta-winged aircraft. In September 1956 it went to Avro at Woodford to be kitted out with instrumentation for electrically controlled signalling (the normal control circuits were duplicated), which allowed it to be used by the RAE on some of the earliest work undertaken using fly-by-wire control systems.

The aircraft stayed with the RAE until June 1966.

The 707 series will always be remembered for its paint schemes, which followed a theme of non-standard brilliant colours. VX784 was never painted, but the 707B (VX790) introduced a gloss blue livery. Initially WD280 was salmon pink, but this was soon replaced by a bright red scheme, and WZ736 was coated in a glossy orange (later in its career WZ736 received a yellow paint scheme with a black trim). The two-seat 707C was painted silver with a matte-black anti-glare panel ahead of the cockpit. At the 1953 Farnborough Show the opportunity was taken to display the four surviving 707s with both of the Vulcan prototypes, and their combined flypast made a thrilling and memorable sight.

In the end, apart from the compound-sweep wing, the benefits provided by the 707 family to the Vulcan programme were not as substantial as would have been expected at the start. One problem was the failure to build the first examples as direct replicas of the aircraft for which they were to provide data – the dorsal intake, for example, had no relevance to the Vulcan and yet had to be modified before it would perform properly. The manual controls fitted to the 707s also gave problems, the solving of which consumed a good deal of time and effort, but since the bomber had powered controls this also did not help the larger aircraft. With hindsight, however, such criticisms are made all too easily. It must be remembered that, apart from the short-lived VX384, the Avro 707s all proved to be extremely useful research aeroplanes in providing data for the aircraft industry in general, both with regard to delta wings and many other important areas. Three examples still survive today.

WD280 subsequently received compound sweepback and a kink on the wing leading edge. The inner part of the outer wing had a reduced sweep angle while the outermost portion had more. This picture was probably taken soon after the job had been completed at Waddington. *Avro Heritage*

Contemporary Avro advertisement showing the gloss blue 707B VX790.

After being used as a spares supply the derelict carcass of 707A WZ736 is seen lying in the fire dump at Colerne on 9 April 1967, prior to being 'restored' and painted in red livery for museum display. *Roy Bonser-KEC*

9 Nord 1601 (1950)

Nord 1601
Registration: F-WFKK
Span: 40ft 10.5in (12.463m)
Length: 38ft 9.5in (11.823m)
Wing area: 324.95sq ft (30.22sq m)
Max gross take-off weight: 14,771lb (6,700kg)
Powerplant: 2 x RR Derwent 5, 3,530lb (15.7kN)
Max speed/height: 622mph (1,000km/h) at sea level
Service ceiling: 39,370ft (12,000m)

The single-seat Nord 1601 was a research aircraft designed and built to study and investigate the aerodynamics and behaviour of swept wings at high subsonic speeds, and the high-lift devices that went with them. A proposed Nord 1600 fighter to be powered by Rateau B-120 engines and tied in with the 1601 programme was not built. Versions of the 1600 were tunnel-tested with a T-tail and with a tailplane in the same lower position as the 1601, while the initial drawings for the 1601 had a more blended cockpit canopy than the version eventually employed, which was raised above the fuselage.

This aircraft was a cantilever mid-wing monoplane and had its wing swept 33° at one-quarter chord. The wing surface was fitted with ailerons, spoilers, leading-edge slats and trailing-edge flaps, and the horizontal tailplane and the fin were also swept. The metal fuselage employed a classic monocoque structure and the wings and control surfaces were also all manufactured in metal, the resulting smooth skin surfaces being blended beautifully around the fuselage and the engine nacelles. There was a retractable tricycle undercarriage and the aircraft had a powerplant comprising two Rolls-Royce Derwent jets mounted in underslung nacelles set closely against each side of the fuselage. Many French aircraft from this period had to be powered by British engines because of the lack of available French alternatives, and a British Martin-Baker ejection seat was installed for the 1601's pilot.

With the civil registration F-WFKK, the 1601 first flew on the 24 January 1950 with Claude Chautemps in the cockpit. Little information is available to the authors regarding the achievements of this attractive aeroplane, but it is understood that some important results and data were acquired from the flight test programme. A rate of climb of 115 feet per minute (35m/sec) was recorded and, with a limiting Mach number of 0.85, prior to the first flight it was known that a speed in the region of 625mph (1,005km/h) was expected. In March 1949 the 1601's estimated radius of action at 19,685 feet (6,000m) was given as 705 miles (1,135 km). Subsequent modifications made to the aircraft included the addition of a small dorsal fillet to the front of the fin. The sole example of the 1601 to be built was destroyed as a weapons target during the mid-1950s.

A series of walk-around photographs of the Nord 1601 research aircraft, two of which show it without the cockpit canopy in place. The wide track of the main undercarriage is apparent. *all Michel Benichou*

X-PLANES OF EUROPE

Picture of the Nord 1601 taken after the addition of a small dorsal fillet to the front of the fin. *Michel Benichou*

10 Boulton Paul P.111 (1950)

Boulton Paul P.111

Span: 25ft 8in (7.82m) with no tips; 29ft 9in (9.07m) or 33ft 6in (10.21m) with tips

Length: 26ft 1in (7.95m) as P.111; 31ft 6in (9.60m) as P.111A with probe

Gross wing area: 269.25sq ft (25.04sq m), 284.16sq ft (26.43sq m) or 290.13sq ft (26.98sq m)

Gross weight: 10,127lb (4,594kg) forward c.g.; 9,787lb (4,439kg) aft c.g. With ballast reduced

Powerplant: 1 x RR Nene 3 (R.N.2), 5,100lb (22.7kN)

Max speed/height: 649mph (1,044km/h) at sea level; 622mph (1,001km/h) at 35,000ft (10,668m). Maximum Mach 0.96 in dive

Normal ceiling: 35,000ft (10,668m)

A good number of the aircraft types described in these pages were designed to test new wing shapes – delta wings, swept wings, and/or other advanced ideas. The stubby-formed Boulton Paul P.111 and P.120 were the first British aircraft to be developed to test the delta wing, but the P.120 (see below) was lost in an accident very early in its life. The P.111 completed a good career of test flying with the RAF, but these aeroplanes never became involved in anything particularly controversial. Consequently, they tend to get rather overlooked in most accounts of 1950s and 1960s research aircraft against the more impressive supersonic aeroplanes or the new vertical take-off types.

The project began after German information had been reviewed, which stated that a delta was an attractive means of getting wing sweepback. Several of the 1940s research aircraft in this volume benefited to varying degrees from information found in German research institutes and facilities just after the end of the war. A major advantage of the delta was structural strength, and the RAE drew up the requirements for the project, Boulton Paul having been given the contract in the absence of a firm better able to undertake the work. However, by 1950 the programme had fallen well over a year behind schedule, the construction of the first airframe having started in 1947.

The P.111 was a pure delta with 45° leading edge sweepback, and its tips could be taken off in stages to reduce the aspect ratio and so influence tip stalling. It was specially designed for aerodynamic research at transonic speeds and was stressed to withstand Mach 1 at sea level. The wing had a constant wing thickness/chord ratio of 10% and used a two-spar structure. A nose intake fed a single Rolls-Royce Nene engine, which filled the P.111's wing centre section, so all of the 230 gallons (1,046 litres) of fuel had to be housed in the wings. The removable wingtips gave the opportunity to assess three different wing forms – the clipped delta as first flown (with the split elevons' surfaces stretching along the full span), and extensions with either a rounded tip or a near pointed tip. In the original layout (as built) there was a complete absence of flaps (no landing flaps or air brakes) and at a fairly late stage in the design work the anti-spin parachute was increased in strength so that it could be used for braking on landing. The fin was highly swept but had a straight trailing edge, and the aircraft had a wide-track tricycle undercarriage. The control system was described as 'rather advanced'. The elevons and rudder were power-operated, with pilot's feel provided in an entirely

X-PLANES OF EUROPE

This splendid photograph of the Boulton Paul P.111A VT935 was probably taken during its career with the RAE. *Author's collection*

artificial manner by the use of coil springs, which had nominally linear characteristics, i.e. the stick or pedal force was to be proportional to elevon or rudder displacement. Manual reversion was possible on all controls – the spring feel could be removed from the stick and manual trimming on the tabs was then available. Automatic trimming tabs were fitted to the elevons to ensure that the aircraft was always approximately in trim so that reversion to manual control, whether automatically or by selection, was always made without the introduction of large stick forces.

The specification covering the P.111 was E.27/46 of January 1947. Two aircraft (VT935 and VT951) were ordered against a contract placed in February 1947; however, in November 1946 they had been allocated the serials VT769 and VT784 – why these were changed is unknown. The first airframe was painted in an overall silver colour scheme with a black anti-glare panel around the cockpit canopy. In April 1950 VT935 was ready to taxi,

Opposite and Below: VT935 was photographed at Boulton Paul's Wolverhampton factory undergoing fuel-flow trials well before its maiden flight. In fact, the date is thought to be early February 1950. *Phil Butler collection*

by which time it had been decided to fit the second aircraft with a tailplane and rotatable wingtips. The first aircraft was so far advanced, however, that little could be done to alter it. In an MoS meeting held that month, the information that could be obtained by the Boulton Paul deltas was summarised as follows:

- Flight information to approximately Mach 1.0. The aircraft's maximum Mach numbers on the level would be between 0.85 and 0.90, but higher figures were expected in a dive.
- The effects of variation of aspect ratio from 2.3 to 4:1.
- The effects of changes in wing loading from 30 to 38lb/sq ft (146 to 186kg/sq m) – this would be accompanied by changes in aspect ratio.
- The effect of a tailplane at high speed and on landing (second airframe).
- The effectiveness of tip controllers at high and low speed (second airframe). This would be the first test of these items in flight on a modern aircraft.

A May 1950 picture of VT935 at Wolverhampton after the aircraft had received its silver paint scheme. *Phil Butler collection*

X-PLANES OF EUROPE

The P.111 is seen in flight early in its career, with the 'P' prototype letter painted on the nose. The wingtips are clipped (i.e. no tips are fitted); note also the large fairing on the port rear fuselage, which held the braking parachute. Pitot tubes were mounted on both wings. *Alec Brew, Boulton Paul Archive*

Flight test

The P.111 made its first flight on 6 October 1950 piloted by Sqn Ldr R. H. Smythe of the RAE's Aero Flight. This and subsequent contractor's flight trials were made from A&AEE Boscombe Down after the aircraft had been moved by road from its birthplace at Wolverhampton. VT935's public debut came at the SBAC Farnborough Show of September 1951 where Lt Elliot flew it. Relatively little information was released about the aircraft, but observers noted some quite tight turns and that, without flaps or dive brakes, the aircraft touched down rather 'hot'. Even with its 7-foot (2.13m) tail parachute, it required quite a lot of runway to slow down. In fact, the landing distance from an altitude of 500 feet (152m) was of the order of 1,200 to 1,300 yards (1,100 to 1,190m). VT935 then returned to Boscombe to continue its trials, but on 5 January 1952 the aircraft made a wheels-up landing after the undercarriage failed to lower. Following this it was returned to Boulton Paul at Wolverhampton for repairs.

A Boscombe Down report from July 1951 recorded the results of VT935's flight trials so far. Fifty sorties had been made occupying some 20 hours of flight time, most of which had been devoted to the development of a landing technique suitable for operating the aircraft from the main runway at Farnborough and reducing the length of the run overall. In fact, due to mechanical troubles, much of the flying had been done with the undercarriage down. There was a slight tendency for the aircraft to track to port

VT935 lands after another flight. The pronounced forward angle of the P.111's main undercarriage is well shown. *Phil Butler collection*

when taxiing on level ground in calm air, and a considerable amount of effort had been made to remove this rather undesirable feature before the first flight, but at this stage only small improvements had been made.

An early criticism of the aircraft in flight was that it had an abnormally high sensitivity in both roll and pitch. Much of the trouble was associated with the poor spring feel system, which allowed well over 1 degree of control movement for no force at all on the stick, in both roll and pitch. This also made flying at speeds above about 300 knots (345mph/555km/h) IAS very dangerous since at such speeds considerable normal accelerations and rates of roll could be initiated with negligible zero stick force. At speed the spring feel system was very sensitive and gave negligible resistance to pilot inputs at tiny deflections, but during landings it became quite the reverse and was too heavy. In other words, the controls felt heavy at low speeds when they needed to be light and were very light at high speeds when they had to be heavier. Eventually a Q-feel system based on hydraulic pressure was introduced, which proved to be far better and made the pilots feel more comfortable, but the initial problem highlighted the fact that the P.111 was one of the few aircraft at that time to use fully powered controls for which a simple spring feel system proved to be inadequate.

Boulton Paul P.111 powered by one Rolls-Royce Nene R3N2 turbojet. Currently on display at Midlands Air Museum, Coventry, UK. *Chris Sandham-Bailey www.inkworm.com*

X-PLANES OF EUROPE

These views show the nose of VT935 in its original P.111 form and after conversion to P.111A. The images reveal some of the changes made to the aircraft, including a new nose pitot mast and air brakes around the fuselage. *Phil Butler collection*

Above and left: The P.111A VT935 was repainted in yellow with a black flash on each side stretching to the wing roots. *Author's collection*

Below left and below: Although these photographs are of rather poor quality, they are valuable in showing very rarely seen angles of the aircraft. They show the P.111A at the RAE Farnborough Jubilee event on 8 July 1955. Note that the aircraft has the full tip extensions in place. *Author's collection*

X-PLANES OF EUROPE

It is thought that VT935 is seen here on display at Duxford in 1957. Note the deployed air brake petals. *Phil Butler collection*

In bumpy air both Dutch roll and snaking had been experienced, but neither had been severe. No measurements of rate of roll had yet been made, but the rolling power of the elevons was exceptionally high. A few complete rolls had been made in the aircraft and quite small stick deflections had produced abnormally high rates of roll. Apart from the pitch and roll problems, however, the P.111 was not considered unpleasant to fly, but it did show a very large change of trim when the undercarriage was lowered (equal to 4° of elevon at 180 knots [207mph/333km/h]). In early January 1952 the specification for the Fairey Delta 2 (qv) was amended to increase the maximum undercarriage retraction speed to 230mph (370km/h) after pilots had found that the P.111's 185mph (298km/h) limit had made retraction difficult to complete in the short time available.

While repairs from the belly landing were ongoing, the opportunity was taken to incorporate numerous modifications to the aircraft, including four petal air brakes around the fuselage aft of the cockpit and a long pitot head in the centre of the nose intake. As such VT935 was redesignated P.111A and featured a new bright yellow livery. Its first flight in this form, again from Boscombe after another road journey from Wolverhampton, was made by Boulton Paul chief test pilot A. E. 'Ben' Gunn on 2 July 1953. A Farnborough Show appearance followed two months later, the press highlighting one 'unbelievably rapid roll on one particular fast run' by Gunn as especially exciting. On 24 February 1954 the aircraft joined Aero Flight at RAE Farnborough to perform further delta-wing aerodynamic research, and on 16 February 1956 it was transferred to RAE Bedford. Trials flying during this period included sorties using the three different wingtip configurations. The P.111A also took part in the RAE Jubilee event at Farnborough in 1955 during which it performed a flypast in formation with two experimental Gloster Meteors (the jet deflection and prone-pilot airframes) and the vintage Westland-Hill Pterodactyl Mk IV flying wing aircraft. It was finally released from flying on 17 March 1957, and on 28 April 1959 was moved to the College of Aeronautics at Cranfield where it stayed until the 1970s.

A contemporary advertisement for Boulton Paul Aircraft Ltd that shows P.111 VT935. It appears to have been made using an original colour transparency.

11 Boulton Paul P.120 (1950)

Boulton Paul P.120

Span: 33ft 5.5in (10.20m)
Length: 29ft 7.5in (9.03m)
Gross wing area: 290.13sq ft (26.98sq m)
Gross weight: 12,580lb (5,706kg)
Powerplant: 1 x RR Nene 3 (R.N.2), 5,100lb (22.7kN)
Max speed/height: Maximum achieved c507mph (815km/h) at c4,000ft (1,219m)
Ceiling: Not established

Well before the P.111's construction was completed, by autumn 1948, additional information on control at high speeds, obtained from RAE tunnel testing, had made it clear that alternatives to the conventional aileron control must be investigated. By 1950 it appeared that a tail would be necessary for safe high-speed flight on a delta-winged aircraft (which in fact did not prove to be the case). In September 1948 it was agreed that all-moving wingtips should be fitted to the second machine for control purposes, although elevon control was to be maintained and the use of this or moving wingtips was to be an alternative at the discretion of the pilot. Demands to fit a tailplane had already been made, in part because the Gloster F.4/48 fighter (later called the Javelin) would have one, but they were not taken up straight away. Subsequent information, however, indicated a lack of damping on tailless designs at high speed, and this strengthened the desire to fit a tail.

A Ministry document of 19 July 1950 described how power-operated wingtip controllers were to be fitted to the second aircraft together with a power-operated variable-incidence trimming tailplane. As such the modified aircraft was renumbered P.120. It would keep the elevons and, by ground adjustment before flight, it should be possible to select the use of either the elevons or the tip controllers. When the elevons were used the tip controllers were to be locked central, but when the tip controllers were selected the elevons were to be used for trimming. Other differences were a new swept fin and rudder, which brought substantial changes to the rear fuselage, while dive brakes like those of the P.111A were fitted in four segments around the fuselage slightly behind the cockpit. The P.120's control system was very complex, but permitted all combinations of elevons, tips and tail. All of these additions (and some strengthening to the fin) resulted in a rise in all-up weight, and the wing itself was the full delta equivalent to the highest span tip extensions on the P.111.

Had the second aircraft been identical to the first, it would have followed about six months behind VT935, but the new features increased the time gap to 22 months. Ben Gunn made the silver-painted P.120's first flight on 6 August 1952, and the tailplane made a difference almost immediately – a very long take-off run was required because the tail had been set incorrectly! Unfortunately, on 29 August 1952, less than a month after the first flight, VT951 was lost. Over Southampton the pilot, Ben Gunn, decided to increase the speed to 450 knots (518mph/834km/h), the fastest the aircraft had yet reached. Suddenly there was a very loud bang and VT951 began a roll to port, but after the pilot had managed to level off he found that full starboard rudder allowed some control to be recovered. A look behind showed that about 2 feet (0.61m) of the port wing surface ahead of the outer port elevon had lifted. Gunn attempted to land but on the approach to Boscombe the aircraft became uncontrollable at about 3,000 feet (914m) in rough air, so he ejected. VT951 crashed at Cholderton in Hampshire and was destroyed, but Gunn was unhurt. When it was lost the P.120 had completed twenty flights for a total of 11 hours and 15 minutes flying. By then it had been painted black in readiness for the Farnborough Show. The crash reports revealed that when the flutter clearance of the P.120 was first discussed, the main wing and trailing edge control structures and mass distribution of the two aircraft were thought to be essentially the same. Earlier calculations had shown the P.111 to be free from wing-elevon flutter within the speed range for which it was intended, and later flight experience confirmed this up to 500 knots (576mph/926km/h).

The initial test programme for the P.120 did not require the use of the all-moving wingtip controls, so these were locked for the first flights. Flutter clearance of the P.120 would then be based on ground resonance tests conducted with this control locked. It was found, however, that certain measurements exhibited alarming resonances of the all-moving tips, which led to their being securely clamped to the main wing by means of 14-gauge sheet fully riveted around the profile. However, apart from the tip resonances, the other flutter modes to be measured appeared no more dangerous than those of the P.111, so the P.120 was cleared for wing flutter up to 500 knots (576mph/926km/h), flying with the tip control locked.

Consideration of the fuselage and tail unit modes led to flutter calculations suggesting that a near-flutter condition existed in the speed range 400 to 500 knots (461mph/741km/h to 576mph/926km/h), so at the start the aircraft flew with a speed restriction of 400 knots (461mph/741km/h). Increments of speed above this figure were then made in steps of 25 knots (29mph/46km/h). Flight tests were being conducted in relation to this suspected near-flutter condition of the tail unit when the aircraft, flying at about 440 knots (507mph/815km/h),

A rough drawing of the Boulton Paul P.120. *British National Archives*

Boulton Paul P.120 powered by one Rolls-Royce Nene RN.2. It was the last Boulton Paul design to fly. *Chris Sandham-Bailey www.inkworm.com*

X-PLANES OF EUROPE

Top and above: These two pictures of the P.120 were taken at Boscombe Down towards the end of its very short life, after it had been repainted for the forthcoming Farnborough Show in a black scheme with a yellow flash. However, the aircraft did not survive long enough to attend. *Phil Butler collection*

| The Boulton Paul P.120 VT951 is seen at Wolverhampton prior to painting and its first flight. *Alec Brew, Boulton Paul Archive*

lost the port elevon. The available evidence suggested that flutter involving the port powered-elevon controls and trimming tab played an important part in the accident, and the condition of the leading edge pitot tube (seen by the pilot before departing the aircraft to be damaged and bent) also suggested participation of the wing in the flutter. The investigations indicated very strongly that the elevon failure had been caused by flutter.

The crash prevented the P.120 from achieving very much in its short life and it is a pity that sufficient flying was not completed to provide some sort of comparison to the results obtained from the P.111. A report on their differing flutter characteristics, and their speed and handling performance, would have made interesting reading. During the 1950s the P.111 did go on to complete its contribution to the growing knowledge of advanced wing shapes and aerodynamics, but by the time it flew VT951's 45° sweep wing had become somewhat out of date when compared to the 60° of sweep now chosen for supersonic aircraft like the Fairey Delta 2. Although rather small aeroplanes, the P.111 and particularly the P.120 exhibited a certain degree of charm, and fortunately VT935 has survived into preservation.

12 Sud-Est SE 2410 Grognard I and SE 2415 Grognard II (1950-1951)

Sud-Est Grognard I (SE 2410)

Registration: F-ZWRJ ('J' on fuselage)
Span: 44ft 6.5in (13.58m)
Length: 50ft 7.5in (15.435m)
Wing area: 496.1sq ft (46.14sq m)
Max gross take-off weight: 32,518lb (14,750kg)
Powerplant: 2 x Hispano-Suiza licence-built RR Nene 102, 5,005lb (22.2kN)
Max speed/height: 645mph (1,038km/h) Mach 0.91 at 4,920ft
Ceiling: Unknown

Sud-Est Grognard II (SE 2415)

Registration: F-ZWRK ('K' on fuselage)
Span: 51ft 1.5in (15.58m)
Length: 55ft 3in (16.835m)
Wing area: 475.6sq ft (44.23sq m)
Max gross take-off weight: 31,966lb (14,500kg)
Powerplant: 2 x RR Nene 102, 5,005lb (22.2kN)
Max speed: 597mph (960km/h), Mach 0.835
Ceiling: Unknown

The Sud-Est SE 2410 Grognard I was the first French jet aircraft manufactured during the 1940s by SNCASE, and was ultimately one of the most innovative French aircraft ever flown. Although at the start intended to be a service aircraft, this never materialised. The design never went into long-term series production, but it did pioneer new aerodynamics and flight systems and other features never before flown on any other French aircraft, which makes it essential to include the type here. Its official name Grognard was idiomatic, and therefore difficult to translate, but in French it was used to refer to an old soldier and could mean 'grouser' or 'grumbler'. In fact, it was derived from the nickname of a soldier in Napoleon's Old Guard. Designed by noted French aeronautical engineer Pierre Sartre (who also designed the famed Caravelle twin-jet airliner, the world's first rear-engine jet aircraft, which established a design trend used by scores of airline and corporate jet transports to this day), the SE 2410 project was started in 1945 when Sud-Est proposed an aircraft that would incorporate a number of new, original concepts for achieving optimum aerodynamic efficiency.

To achieve the purest aerodynamic shape, all operational systems, landing gear and fuel tanks were integrated into the interior of the craft's rather bulky fuselage. The Grognard's most prominent visual feature resulted from the placement of the aircraft's two jet engines one ahead of, and slightly above, the other with individual exhausts in the rear fuselage. This configuration was similar to the British supersonic English Electric P1 Lightning interceptor, and by placing both engines on the aircraft's centre line the inherent problem of asymmetric thrust in the case of a loss of one engine was eliminated. The sight of a common streamlined air intake above the fuselage and aft of the cockpit earned the

SE 2410 the nickname of 'Hunchback' and, although aerodynamically efficient for parasitic drag reduction, this feature proved to be initially troublesome when, during excessive yaw movement, incoming ram air stalled when entering the engine duct. To cure this problem, internal baffles were added to control and prevent internal airflow separation. Ten years later the North American F-107A, built in the United States, also featured this somewhat radical air intake configuration, but with a large afterburning turbojet this aircraft was capable of flying at speeds of Mach 2.

Another novel design feature used on the Grognard was the incorporation of a special parachute to augment braking action after landing. With the new higher landing speeds for jet aircraft, it became readily apparent that wheel brakes alone were no longer adequate for decelerating an aircraft from more than 140mph (225km/h) to a stop on a 5,000 or 6,000-foot (1,500 or 1,800m) asphalt runway. This attempt at solving the problem of poor braking performance was another significant 'first' for a French aircraft, as drag chutes were employed as standard equipment on most of the world's Cold War-era high-performance jet aircraft, both fighters and bombers. The Grognard had a tricycle undercarriage with all wheels retracting into the fuselage.

The SE 2410 offered an aerodynamically 'pure' high-aspect-ratio shoulder-mounted wing with a radical 47° sweep at the leading edge. High-lift devices were fitted to the wing's leading edge in the form of a 'droop-snoot' thin-chord flap that extended outwards and downwards at slow speeds or when the aeroplane was flying at high angles of attack. This was the first use of both a swept wing and leading edge flaps on a French aircraft, and there were generous flaps on the wing trailing edge and small ailerons.

Another new feature was the low position of the horizontal tail, which placed it below the disturbed wake from the wing, the boundary layer over which tended to thicken and break away at the roots of the shock-waves. The only alternative way of getting the tailplane into a relatively undisturbed airflow was to put it high upon the fin – a less satisfactory solution and one more likely to lead to structural trouble.

Finally, one of the most innovative ideas used on the Grognard was the replacement in the cockpit of the traditional control column or stick with moveable seat armrests that allowed the pilot to control the aircraft with his elbows. While obviously an unorthodox method for flying an aeroplane, the primary advantage of this was better visibility of the instrument panel. This control method, while rather primitive, evolved into the side-stick controller, which was first flown in the North American F-107A; one was also later used in that company's rocket-powered hypersonic X-15 in the 1960s, and is now in common use throughout the world in everything from Airbus commercial airliners to homebuilt kit aircraft. The cockpit position also gave the pilot an excellent view.

Prior to the SE 2410's construction a scale model, 0.582 of full size, was completed for wind tunnel testing. The public had its first glimpse of this Grognard model at the 1949 Paris Air Show, where it was shown mounted on a stand. For maximum dramatic effect that model was 'flown' in a mock wind tunnel with an operator lying in the fuselage, activating the controls. At Chalais-Meudon this model was tested to very high angles of attack without the least sign of stalling at the air intake. Originally designed as a ground attack aircraft against French Air Force requirements, the Grognard was envisioned as a series of three different design variants:

Shown rolling out on landing with drag chute deployed, the SE 2410 Grognard I was a highly innovative aircraft for its time. Employing a high-mounted air intake allowed for a clean wing design, and optimised ram airflow for the two Hispano-Suiza licence-built Rolls-Royce Nene 100 engines, each of 5,000lb (22.2 kN) thrust, mounted one above and forward of the other in the rear fuselage. *Musée de l'Air et de l'Espace, Paris/Le Bourget*

X-PLANES OF EUROPE

The outlines in this ground view of the Grognard I have been enhanced by a technical artist, but give a good indication of the overall configuration. Oversize wheels and tyres were intended for soft or rough field operations. It is interesting to note that with an airframe as streamlined as this, a complex Second World War-style 'birdcage canopy' is still employed in such an advanced aircraft's design. *Tony Buttler collection*

- The SE 2400 was to be powered by two TGAR 1008 turbojet engines built by the newly formed SOCEMA (Company of Constructions and Mechanical Equipment for Aviation). This project was abandoned quite early on in favour of the SE 2410.

- The SE 2410 was powered by twin Rolls-Royce Nene turbojets built under licence by Hispano-Suiza. These engines, of 5,000lb (22.2kN) thrust, were the most powerful turbojets available at the time and this aircraft was unarmed and intended primarily to test the general configuration of the design. The first flight of the SE 2410 took place at Bretigny airfield on 30 April 1950 with test pilot Pierre Nadot at the controls, but initial testing revealed significant vibration problems at speeds in excess of 325mph (525km/h). This was only partially cured by the installation of exhaust orifice plates. Initially the aircraft had a nose probe in position.

- The SE 2411 was also powered by two Rolls-Royce Nenes built by Hispano-Suiza, but was equipped with an armament consisting of four 15mm guns and a complement of thirty-two air-to-ground rockets mounted in a retractable armament bay in the lower fuselage. This heavy strike bomber version was never built.

The only public showing of the SE 2410 Grognard I took place at the 1953 Paris Air Show at Le Bourget, where its existence was revealed after four years of secret testing and development. The Grognard I was also successfully used as the flying test bed aircraft for the first trials of the French Matra air-to-air guided missile. *Tony Buttler collection*

New and improved

In due course a further version, called the SE 2415, was built in the same general configuration as the SE 2410, but essentially this was a two-seat version of the Grognard I with a longer nose and a reduced wing sweep of 35° at the leading edge – the longer nose had brought the centre of gravity forward, necessitating the reduced sweep angle. The second crew position accommodated a radar operator to ease the flight workload for the pilot during a typical intercept mission. This two-man crew requirement mirrored exactly what was happening in the United States at that time, with single-pilot interceptors such as the North American F-86D Sabre being replaced by two-seat dedicated interceptor aircraft like the Northrop F-89 Scorpion and Lockheed F-94C Starfire, such was the complex state of in-flight electronics and radar systems in that era.

The SE 2415 was built and tested in parallel with the 2410 and was first flown on 14 February 1951, again with Pierre Nadot in the front cockpit. Despite its greater fuselage length, this aircraft still suffered the same vibration characteristics at high speed, and nearly seven months were spent trying to identify and solve the problem. Other troubles were encountered with the aircraft's tyres during high-speed ground runs, for which the solution was to replace the French tyres with those built by Dunlop for use on the British English Electric Canberra bomber. Tail flutter during the initial trials was also a problem, but was overcome after talks with British engineers at the 1951 Paris Show; the source was traced to over-balance, which was easily cured.

Although these solutions allowed the Grognard to meet and even exceed the original design specifications, they also caused the programme to pass its operational deadline by more than three months. Partly for this reason the French government changed its mind about a pending order for 360 Grognard aircraft to equip tactical fighter groups, which led to complete cancellation of the programme even before the flight trials had been completed. However, the whole ground attack requirement was in fact reviewed with the outcome that specialist warplanes in this category were deleted from the development programme. What counted against the Grognard here was that it had an unpressurised cockpit because the aircraft was intended for low-level operations, a feature that proved restrictive when looking for alternative roles. The order for a jet-powered ground attack aircraft subsequently went to the more promising Sud-Ouest SO 4050 Vautour fighter, first flown on 16 October 1952.

In flight, the SE 2415 Grognard II shows off its almost aquatic lines. The epitome of aerodynamic cleanliness in the early 1950s, this standard-configuration aircraft was one of the first French jets to feature leading-edge slats and the use of a drag chute for landing. *Tony Buttler collection*

The Grognard seen again on public display. Note the huge wheels and the large WW2-style heavily framed canopy. *Michel Benichou*

X-PLANES OF EUROPE

The first and only public presentation of the SE 2410 Grognard I took place at the Le Bourget Air Show in 1953, where it was revealed to the masses after more than four years of secret testing and development. Indeed, although first flown in April 1950, the French Air Ministry only made photographs of the SE 2410 available to the public press in January 1951, and details remained sparse for some time afterwards. However, after the cancellation the Grognard I was subsequently successfully employed as a trials airframe for its planned ventral snap-opening M-23 unguided rocket pack, then as the flying test bed aircraft for the first trials of the French Matra T-10 air-to-air guided missile (in the process becoming the first French aircraft to fire an air-to-air missile). The Grognard II was used for flight training at the Centre d'Essais en Vol (French Experimental Flight Centre), but exhibited underwhelming performance even in that role with a recorded top speed of only Mach 0.835 (580mph/953km/h) in a dive.

The final flight of the SE 2410 Grognard I took place when the aircraft made a belly landing in Toulouse and was damaged beyond repair. A Ministry pilot received a false fire-alarm warning in the air, which forced him to cut out his electrics, so that he had to make the belly landing. The SE 2415 Grognard II crashed one day less than a year after the SE 2410 accident, following the rupture of a flight control system cable and subsequent loss of hydraulic pressure. It too had to make a belly landing. Both prototypes, rather unceremoniously, ended their careers being demolished as ground targets at the French national military gunnery range in Cazaux.

The massive Grognards never exceeded Mach unity in level flight and never fulfilled their potential and so the type has, perhaps, never generated the interest that it does deserve. The two airframes eventually completed a great deal of flying with many different pilots, although flight testing of the two-seat SE 2415 was performed entirely with just the one pilot on board. The definitive version was to have been the SE 2418, powered by two Hispano-Suiza (Rolls-Royce) Tay 250 turbojets and fitted with the SE 2410's highly swept wings and the 2415's longer fuselage. This arrangement would have given a higher performance and limiting Mach number (up to 0.916 at 30,000 feet [9,144 m]), together with roomier pilot accommodation. It would have carried two 30mm Hispano-Suiza

This 'ant's-eye view' of the two-place SE 2415 Grognard II shows the unique compound curvature of the aircraft's fuselage, which optimised aerodynamic efficiency. The rear cockpit housed what would have been a radar operator had the aeroplane gone into production, a reflection on the growing complexity of airborne avionics in the 1950s. *Copyright Musée de l'Air et de l'Espace, Paris/Le Bourget*

12　SUD-EST SE 2410 GROGNARD I AND SE 2415 GROGNARD II (1950-1951)

Manufacturer's drawing showing some planned typical weapon loads for the proposed SE 2418 attack aircraft based on the Grognard prototypes. The aircraft would have two 30mm cannon in the lower forward fuselage plus the following stores combinations:

1. 32 x 60lb (27kg) rockets in fuselage bay.
2. 16 x 140lb (63.5kg) heavy rockets in fuselage bay.
3. 200 x 9lb (4.1kg) anti-personnel rockets in fuselage bay.
4. Four x 250kg (551lb) bombs in fuselage bay.
5. Three x 750lb (340kg) bombs in fuselage bay.
6. One x 1,000lb (454kg) bomb under each wing.
7. One x Matra air-to-air missile under each wing.
8. Four x 350kg (159kg) Napalm bombs in fuselage bay.

Type 603 cannon internally in the bottom of the fuselage and its attack armament included a battery of lower fuselage rocket projectiles or bombs and two underwing missiles. General characteristics were to have followed those of the earlier models – leading edge flaps, Lockheed Servodyne control boosters, adjustable tailplane, tail parachute, etc, and the pilot was to have been protected by almost half a ton of armour plate.

Note the exhaust aperture with a 'sugar scoop' lower fairing in this view of the Grognard II. The upper engine exhaust has curved baffles affixed to either side, much like that of the US Convair F-102A Delta Dagger. *Musée de l'Air et de l'Espace, Paris/Le Bourget*

91

13 FAF (F + W) N-20-2 Arbalète (1951)

FAF Arbalète

Span: 24ft 9.5in (7.56m)
Length: 24ft 8.5in (7.53m)
Gross wing area: 209sq ft (19.44sq m)
Gross weight: 3,968lb (1,800kg)
Powerplant: 4 x Turboméca Piméné I, 242lb (1.08kN)
Max speed/height: 354mph (570km/h) at 13,123ft (4,000m)
Ceiling: 26,247ft (8,000m) service ceiling (197ft/min [60 m/min] climb)

Switzerland has for a long time had a powerful Air Arm, and after the end of the Second World War it also made several attempts at developing and building a series of its own jet fighters. One of the most important programmes led to the N-20, which was built in prototype form but never actually flew. This was a product of the Eidgenössische Flugzeugwerke or Federal Aircraft Factory (FAF) at Emmen, Canton Lucerne, a company that ran an imaginative design team. The N-20 was intended to be a service aircraft, which means that it falls outside the parameters of this book. However, the fighter was preceded by a research and development programme, which had the objective of evaluating the aircraft's flight characteristics, and this took two forms, first a glider then a jet-powered aircraft.

Contract

A prototype contract for a single-seat, multi-role fighter called the N-20 Aiguillon ('Sting') was placed in May 1948. The fighter was especially tailored to meet Swiss conditions and requirements, and work on it had begun in 1945. The design work was completed in January 1947 and showed an aircraft that had a moderately swept flying wing (which some Swiss sources have described as a modified delta) and four Sulzer D-45 engines buried in the inner wings. Despite the fact that the wing was relatively thick, a large portion of the volume was to be filled by the engine airflow passing through in an arrangement that was referred to as the 'Durchströmte Flügel', which translates literally as 'through-flowing wing'. This effectively reduced the wing's thickness and drag, but four engines were still an unusual powerplant for a jet fighter. Regardless of the complexity of the power arrangement, the design of such an advanced aeroplane, which was to be capable of high subsonic and transonic speeds, was a big project for Switzerland to take on, so plans were made to build an approximately 3/5ths-scale model glider to assess the wing shape.

The first aerodynamic tests on the new wing were carried out at Emmen in a new large-scale wind tunnel. The glider, which was known as the N-20-1 and was built at Emmen, was constructed almost entirely of wood and had a retractable tricycle undercarriage and a relatively large all-over canopy. It was piloted by Major Laderach, the chief test pilot of the Kriegstechnische Abteilung (the Swiss Military Technical Branch), and he took the N-20-1 into the air for the first time on 17 April 1948. The tow was undertaken by a C-3604 piston-powered tug aircraft, another home-grown Swiss design. Altogether the glider completed a total of sixty-nine sorties before it was severely damaged by a crash landing on 1 July 1949.

The N-20-1 was subsequently replaced by a second test airframe called the N-20-2 Arbalète ('Crossbow'), which had the same span and

The F + W N-20-2 Arbalète scale model test aircraft. *F + W*

Below and bottom: Three-quarter port-side and full starboard-side views of the N-20-1 3/5th-scale model glider built as an aerodynamic research vehicle for the Aiguillon jet fighter programme. *F + W*

X-PLANES OF EUROPE

A view looking down on the glider while it was being towed to its release height. *F + W*

Above and right: These nose views of the N-20-2 Arbalète taken at Emmen show very well the aircraft's unusual engine arrangement and its wing shape. *F + W*

13 FAF (F + W) N-20-2 ARBALÈTE (1951)

length but introduced its own powerplant in the form of four small Turboméca Piméné I turbojets of 242lb (1.08kN) thrust. Although these were of very low thrust, their installation permitted the scale-model aircraft to examine the flight envelope rather more and progress the research further before the fighter was ready. The engines were housed in two pairs of pods mounted one above and one below the inner portion of each wing. As such the N-20-2 became the first jet aircraft to be designed, built and flown in Switzerland, and in its new form it completed a 16-minute maiden flight on 16 November 1951. Flight testing showed that the Arbalète possessed splendid manoeuvrability, and it reached a top speed on the level of 354mph (570km/h) at an altitude of 13,123 feet (4,000m), while the highest speed achieved in a dive was 447mph (720km/h). The stalling speed was 87mph (140km/h), and at an altitude of 1,640 feet (500m) the rate of climb was 336 feet per minute (102m/min).

Although the N-20 fighter programme was eventually abandoned, the Arbalète scale model was kept airworthy and busy for quite some time working on various items of research before it was finally retired in 1954, having completed ninety-one flights. The Arbalète was painted in a very bright yellow scheme and carried 52.8 gallons (240 litres) of internal fuel, which gave a range of about 155 miles (250km) and an endurance of 40 minutes.

The Arbalète is pictured here on a test sortie, flying over some of Switzerland's glorious scenery.
F + W

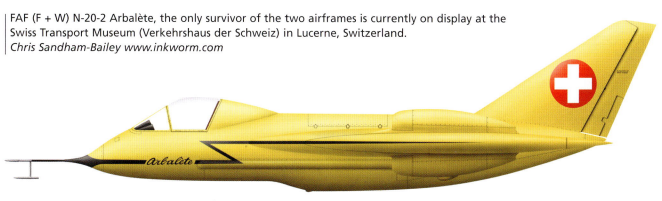

FAF (F + W) N-20-2 Arbalète, the only survivor of the two airframes is currently on display at the Swiss Transport Museum (Verkehrshaus der Schweiz) in Lucerne, Switzerland.
Chris Sandham-Bailey www.inkworm.com

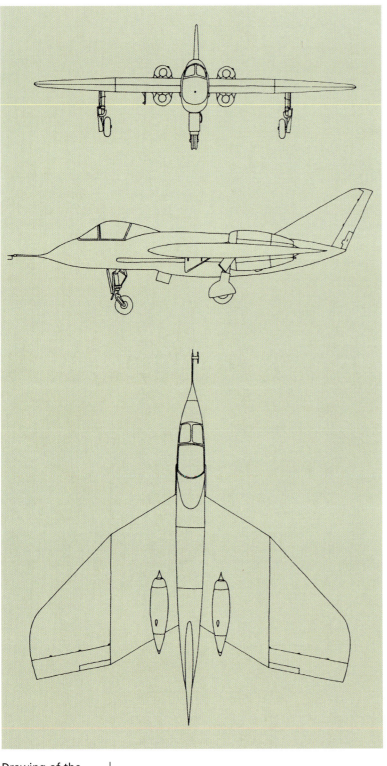

Drawing of the Arbalète.

The N-20 Aiguillon prototype was also built at Emmen and began its taxi trials and some short hops on 8 April 1952. By now the D-45 engine had been abandoned and in its place the fighter had four SM-1 engines installed (SM for Swiss-Mamba, a development of the British Armstrong Siddeley Mamba turboprop). This was as far as the fighter programme went because the funding from the National Defence Commission was brought to a stop and the Aiguillon was cancelled before a first flight could be achieved. In fact, although the type's taxi trials proved to be a success it was realised that the four engines were not supplying enough thrust, and at this stage it would have been too expensive to replace them with alternative power units. Despite the fact that the wing shape and the overall design showed promise, which had been proved by the glider and by the Arbalète, the N-20 failed because of its powerplant (although production plans had already been dropped before the cancellation). Today the unflown Aiguillon prototype is displayed in the Flieger Flab Museum at Dübendorf, and the Arbalète is at Lucerne.

13 FAF (F + W) N-20-2 ARBALÈTE (1951)

Above and below: The N-20 Aiguillon jet fighter prototype presented a very impressive appearance and is seen here around the time of its taxiing tests with parts of its skinning still in natural metal finish. Sadly, the aircraft never became airborne. *F + W*

14 Fairey Delta 1 (1951)

Fairey Delta 1

Span: 19ft 6.5in (5.96m)
Length: 26ft 3in (8.00m)
Gross wing area: 155.7sq ft (14.48sq m)
Gross weight: 6,769lb (3,070kg) at December 1951
Powerplant: VX350: 1 x RR Derwent 5, 3,500lb (15.6kN); VX357: 1 x RR Derwent 8, 3,600lb (16.0kN)
Max speed achieved: 397mph (639km/h)
Ceiling: Unknown

On 1 May 1949 Fairey Aviation achieved the first launch of a pilotless delta-wing rocket-powered model with a 9ft 3in (2.82m) span, called the HALA. This had been designed at Stockport, but in December 1946 Fairey at Stockport and Heston together had also prepared a full-size research aircraft brochure based on the delta-wing arrangement, and this was presented to the Ministry in February 1947 as the Type R. In due course the model programme became a back-up to this full-size aeroplane.

Type R

Although Type R was a private venture, the MoS eventually agreed that it was likely to provide some valuable information, and on 13 September 1947 Specification E.10/47 was allocated to the project. A Mock-up Conference was held on 28 January 1948, and on 19 April a contract was placed for three aeroplanes, serials VX350, VX357 and VX364; the type was eventually named Delta 1. At the time the Delta had no known vices, and briefly its virtues were:

- Large and compact internal volume for stowage of payload and fuel (time would show that this did not benefit the Delta 1 very much because of its small size).
- Very rigid structure due to a low aspect ratio and generous wing root depth.
- Tip stalling eliminated at high incidence without using drag producers such as tip slots.
- Excellent lateral control characteristics due to very low inertia and damping in roll.

From May 1950 studies were made to ramp-launch the R at all angles from horizontal to 80°, but in due course ramp-launching was abandoned altogether and the first Type R received a nosewheel undercarriage to enable it to perform normal take-offs. Had the ramp method been continued, 'swivelling' jetpipes, which were considered necessary for initial control in a vertical take-off, were to have been fitted to the second machine.

As a precaution, the decision was taken to fit a fixed tailplane for early flights at speeds below 300 knots (345mph/556km/h) to increase damping in pitch. Fixed wing slats would also be used for preliminary low-speed flights to reduce wing drop (both slats and tail were to be removed later, although the tail never was). The jetpipe was to have been split into four exit branches, terminating at a swivelling end, universally mounted and connected to the pilot's controls. This would have allowed the jet efflux to be deflected, thereby providing control about all axes during the vertical stage of a ramp launch (normal aerodynamic control would be ineffective because of the very low aircraft speed). However, once ramp-launching was out, a single jetpipe was fitted and later the holes built into the rear fuselage to house the split

DELTA WING RESEARCH AIRCRAFT
THE FAIREY AVIATION CO. LTD.

An artist's impression of a Type R (Delta 1) on the ramp ready for a vertical take-off. *RAF Museum*

An artist's impression of the original Type R (Delta 1) as originally proposed in February 1947. *RAF Museum*

pipes were faired off. Fairey's design used conventional light alloy construction with frames and stringers. It was a very small aeroplane with a short tubby fuselage, and the delta wing was quite thick at the root but clipped at the tip to permit streamlined fairings to be attached. Power-operated ailerons were placed along the trailing edge of each wing with a split air brake inboard, and a relatively large fin and rudder were employed with the small fixed horizontal slab surface on the top set at -5°.

Preparations for flight

The first E.10/47, VX350 (Ministry documents never called it Delta 1, but from here we will), was built at Heaton Chapel and, well behind schedule, began taxi trials at Manchester Ringway on 12 May 1950. Gordon Slade and Peter Twiss took turns in the cockpit and the aircraft behaved well with no tendency to swing in crosswinds. Taxi tests opened at Boscombe Down on 1 September, but progress was halted by hydraulic problems. Work on VX357 was also practically at a standstill; its fuselage was structurally complete with much of the fuel system in place, but the wings were still in their jigs. The part-complete VX364 was cancelled on 11 January 1950. Finally, in January 1951 VX350's taxi trials were resumed and the aircraft was taken up to 138mph (222km/h).

On 21 February Gp Capt Slade made a series of hops and achieved unstick at 155mph (250km/h), and on 12 March he completed a successful 17-minute maiden flight. During the flight a lateral oscillation at slow speed was experienced, which was so severe on take-off that it frightened the pilot, but it was much less pronounced on the approach to landing. Various modifications were agreed to, but they brought more delay. Intermittent flying did continue,

X-PLANES OF EUROPE

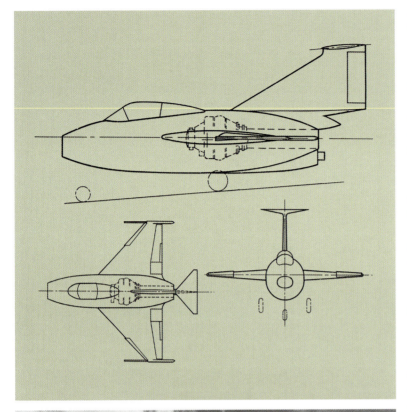

A manufacturer's three-view drawing of the Fairey Delta 1. *Author's collection*

however, and by 20 September a total of 3 hours 15 minutes had been compiled in ten flights. A landing accident forced another halt and it was during the repairs that the opportunity was taken to remove the swivelling nozzle fittings. Speed had been raised to the maximum allowable with the tail (345mph/556km/h), but the lateral oscillation appeared more marked at the higher speeds; partial extension of the air brakes at these speeds also produced a sharp longitudinal oscillation. VX350 was displayed at the 1951 SBAC Show where its fast rate of roll and high landing speed were impressive features, but it was transported to Farnborough by road, not by air.

On 23 November 1951 a meeting between MoS and Fairey officials, including Fairey's designer R. L. Lickley, discussed the difficulties in flight testing the Delta 1 caused by its unpleasant handling characteristics and short endurance. The lateral handling characteristics were described as like being balanced on a knife edge (the aircraft was very sensitive in roll), and with the engine throttled back the rate of sink was very high. This was due to the high aircraft density and also possibly to the large size of the fuselage relative to the wing. The knife-edge stability and high sink rate therefore made the approach on landing a tricky, if not dangerous, business. The longest flight had lasted just 25 minutes, and on another occasion only 4 gallons (18 litres) of fuel remained after landing, but the limited endurance was partly due to the fact that all flying so far had been done at low altitude. (In truth there was precious little space in the Delta 1 in which to put fuel – the tanks were located in the wing leading edges and held just 130 gallons [591 litres].) Lickley added that the rate of climb was lower than originally estimated because of the aircraft's high weight (the machine was actually 2,600lb [1,179kg] above the original estimate). Sink rate, high wing loadings and low endurance were all features of new jet aircraft designs, but on the Delta 1 they were badly compromised by its poor handling. In fact, VX350 was 'grounded as a dangerous aircraft'.

An example of Fairey's vertical take-off HALA series of pilotless models. *Author's collection*

This air-to-air view shows the Delta 1's large air intake and just how big the cockpit was in relation to the rest of the aircraft. The pilot, however, was still pretty cramped. *Author's collection*

Ground view of the sole Delta 1 to fly. Note the leading-edge slats. *Author's collection*

X-PLANES OF EUROPE

VX350 being prepared for public display at the 1951 Farnborough Show. *Phil Butler collection*

A manufacturer's picture of Delta 1 VX350 taken by Jack DeConinck in July 1953. The short stocky appearance of this aeroplane is most pronounced at this angle. *Author's collection*

Some fascinating results were obtained by calculation. For example, for 1° of aileron at 230mph (371km/h) the initial acceleration in roll on the Gloster Meteor fighter was 12°/sec/sec, while on the Delta 1 and the Boulton Paul P.111 delta research aeroplanes (qv) it was 40°/sec/sec. It was a big surprise that the Fairey and P.111's roll sensitivity were the same. Nevertheless, Company Chairman Sir Richard Fairey was very concerned about the Delta 1's flight characteristics and ruled that his firm would do no more work on the aircraft. By now Fairey's attention was firmly on the supersonic Delta 2 (qv), although both technical problems and financial difficulties had influenced the decision to end work on the Delta 1. The aircraft had been built to a fixed price and the Ministry would only be bearing one-third of the total cost. With so much technical uncertainty, Fairey was not prepared to do more until a satisfactory financial agreement had been made.

Continuation

In April 1953 Fairey completed a summary of VX350 flying so far, even though it hadn't flown for 19 months. After modifications to the aileron control, the initially severe lateral oscillation had been made much less so and

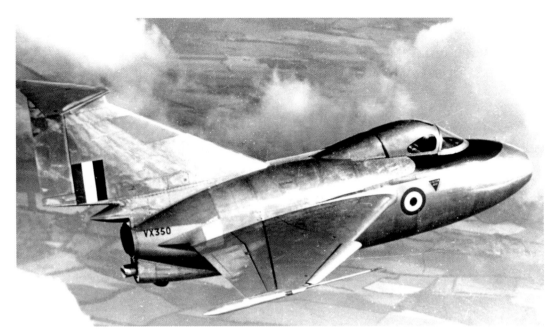

Another July 1953 view showing how the 'torpedo' fairings of the original swivelling pipe arrangement aft of the wing had been substituted by smaller and neater trailing-edge fillets. The wingtip fairings initially contained anti-spin parachutes, but these were later replaced by a housing placed beneath the jetpipe. *Author's collection*

latterly this had come to be regarded as more of a nuisance than a serious handling difficulty. With the wingtip slots and tail, the maximum speed was still limited to 345mph (556km/h), but the longitudinal stability was quite satisfactory up to this speed and very stable in all flight conditions. Including circuits and bumps, fourteen landings had been made. The basic aircraft was designed for a dive speed of 651mph (1,047km/h) EAS, or Mach 0.95, whichever was the lower. In the absence of a crosswind, the take-off characteristics were quite satisfactory and the aircraft would almost fly itself stick-free. The best landing technique was to approach at 184mph (296km/h) with air brakes extended, slow to 173mph (278km/h) on nearing the end of the runway, and hold off at 161mph (259km/h); touchdown was made at 155mph (250km/h).

Flight testing resumed on 5 June 1953 after the restrictions were lifted. Ten hours had been accumulated by 12 August, at which point VX350 was accepted off contract from Fairey to the Ministry. A&AEE Boscombe Down received the aircraft and removed the fixed leading edge slats, which at last made VX350 a useful research machine for general delta behaviour. An increasing understanding of low-speed handling allowed the rolling characteristics and the lateral and longitudinal stability to be examined with confidence, although a preference to fly the Delta 1 in fair weather remained. All test flying was made from either Boscombe or Farnborough, but at a low rate. In the meantime VX357 had been fitted with its Derwent engine at Stockport in January 1951, but it never flew.

VX350 ended its flying days after an accident at Boscombe on 6 February 1956. D. G. Taylor, a test pilot undergoing familiarisation in preparation to fly the Delta 2, found the undercarriage would not lower completely on the approach. The nose leg came down and one main leg dropped partially, but the other did not drop at all, and Taylor veered off the runway onto the grass. The aircraft was badly damaged and was clearly not worth repairing. On 9 October VX350, which during its career had sported an excellent high-polish metal finish, was taken away for use as a target at Shoeburyness.

15 Handley Page HP.88 (1951)

Handley Page HP.88

Span: 40ft 0in (12.19m)
Length: 39ft 10in (12.14m)
Gross wing area: 286.0sq ft (26.60sq m)
Gross weight: 13,197lb (5,986kg)
Powerplant: 1 x RR Nene 2 (R.N.2), 5,000lb (22.2kN)
Max speed: c Mach 0.85
Ceiling: Unknown

The scale-model Avro 707s, which were built to flight-test and assess the previously untried delta-wing planform of that company's Vulcan bomber, have already been discussed. Another V-bomber, the Handley Page Victor, also introduced a new, very advanced and complex wing shape, called the crescent wing. Accordingly, research aircraft were also ordered to perform the same function for this wing, but the only aircraft to fly, the HP.88, experienced a very short and tragic career.

Crescent wing theory and models

The theory for the crescent planform considered that the bomber's performance would benefit by having a wing of moderately high aspect ratio with a high degree of sweepback to provide a high critical Mach number. It was expected that if the wing had a constant angle of sweep it would experience tip-stalling and also unfavourable pitching behaviour when the aircraft stalled. The crescent was essentially a working compromise between high sweep with low aspect ratio and moderate sweep on a thin wing of reasonably high aspect ratio. The relationship between thickness/chord ratio and angle of sweep would vary progressively along the span to give, approximately, a constant critical Mach number over the entire surface. Sweep angle was at its maximum near the fuselage and at a minimum at the tips, and the centre section could be thick and strong enough to accommodate the engines and the undercarriage. This combination of sweepback and wing thickness was also expected to provide good stalling and stability characteristics.

The go-ahead for the HP.80 (which would become the Victor) was given in 1947. The original proposal brochure had also outlined the use of a quarter-scale towed glider to assess the new wing's behaviour. Although Handley Page started work on this HP.87 project, it was soon abandoned (no information or drawings have ever been traced for it). Instead, on 6 April 1948 a contract was issued for two model HP.88 jet-powered research aircraft at 2/5ths scale. However, since Handley Page was full with work the construction of the HP.88 was soon sub-contracted to General Aircraft at Feltham, a move that in due course would bring this new aircraft four designations in all, despite the fact that only one airframe was ever completed. General Aircraft allocated its GAL.63 designation to the HP.88; later, in 1948, General Aircraft was acquired by Blackburn, so when the programme was moved up to Brough GAL.63 was replaced by Y.B.2. But that was not the end. Unlike the Avro 707s, the HP.88 used a fuselage from another research type, an aeroplane called the Supermarine Type 510. Supermarine joined in and called the aircraft the Type 521. This was all entirely sensible for the companies concerned, and great material for historians.

HANDLEY PAGE HP.88 (1951)

There are not many photographs of the Handley Page HP.88, and very few were taken in the air, primarily because the aircraft had such a short life. This flying shot is one of the best and was taken on 26 July 1951. It shows very well the fairings on each inner wing covering the Fowler flap actuators, and the large mass balance arms above and below the wing trailing edge. *BAE Systems, Brough*

Handley Page did all of the aerodynamic research, but Blackburn and General Aircraft worked out the structure and detail design. Specification E.6/48 was raised in April 1948 to cover the HP.88, stating that the Supermarine fuselage would be mated with a 0.4 linear scale HP.80 wing and all-moving tailplane. However, the 510 fuselage required the HP.88's wing to be mounted in a low position while the HP.80 had a high-position wing, so there was already a mismatch between the two. The tailplane positions were also different, and there were other variations (as one would, of course, expect when using an existing fuselage); then, after the HP.88's wing had been built, the design of the bomber wing was altered to permit an increase in its critical Mach number.

Two HP.88s were ordered with serials VX330 and VX337, but in October 1949 VX337 was cancelled to save money. The objective was to demonstrate the stability and control of the crescent wing over the full speed range expected from the full-size bomber (up to 576mph [926km/h] at 50,000 feet [15,240 m]), and to examine its low-speed handling and drag characteristics. Supermarine's fuselage was built in traditional monocoque form, and stressed-skin construction was used throughout the airframe. Although based on the 510 body, that aircraft had been a swept-

Handley Page HP.88, first flew on 21st June 1951, broke up in flight during high speed trials. Powered by one Rolls-Royce Nene 102 turbojet.
Chris Sandham-Bailey www.inkworm.com

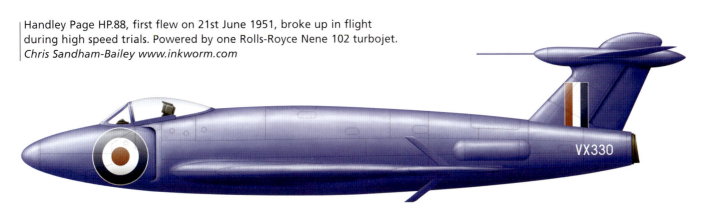

105

Top: This well-known detailed port-side view of VX330 was taken just after the aircraft had been painted but prior to its first flight – the ejection seat has not been fitted. *BAE Systems, Brough*

Midddle: This view from the starboard side shows the seat now installed. Unusually for a jet, the HP.88 employed a tail-wheel-type undercarriage, a legacy of the Supermarine Attacker jet fighter. *Phil Butler collection*

Bottom: This official Ministry of Supply 'walk-around' image of the HP.88 was taken in June 1951 at Carnaby. Note the side fuselage intakes. *Phil Butler collection*

Further Ministry photographs, all showing the flying surfaces and air brakes deployed. *Phil Butler collection*

wing version of Supermarine's straight-wing Attacker fighter, so the HP.88 essentially used an Attacker-type fuselage. A fuel bay (four tanks) came aft of the cockpit, with the Rolls-Royce Nene engine next, and a near-standard 510 undercarriage with tail wheel was fitted.

The principal changes to the fuselage were new attachments for the wings and tail together with strengthening of certain frames to carry these attachments and to absorb the different weight distribution. A forward main spar and auxiliary rear spar, built up with ribs, formed the wing structure, but only the main spar stretched to the tip, and it was bent at the outermost kink. The rear spar went part way along the wing and was then overlapped by a second rear spar, which had the aileron attached, and ended at the tip. The ailerons were interconnected to the flaps to keep trim changes to a minimum. HP.88 had both leading and trailing edge flaps and the flying surfaces were fitted with extensive pressure-plotting equipment. Very prominent on each wing was a large mass balance arm protruding forward 2ft 6in (76cm) above and beneath the wing trailing edge, and a pair of large fairings on the inner wing that covered the Fowler flap actuators. The fin used a two-spar structure and had a slab 'all-moving' tailplane or tailevator near the top with a long bullet fairing. There was no separate elevator hinged to the tailplane – the pitch was controlled by varying the tailplane incidence – and large air brakes were installed on either side of the rear fuselage. Unlike the Avro 707s, the HP.88 was fitted with a pressure cabin, but it continued the tradition of bright colours, and shortly before its first flight was painted in a splendid royal blue livery.

Hardware

VX330 was completed in January 1951 and made its first taxi runs at Brough between 20 and 25 February. On 14 June it went by road to Carnaby and on 21 June completed its maiden flight. The trip lasted just 5 minutes because the pilot, Flt Lt Gartrell 'Sailor' Parker, who was Blackburn's chief test pilot, found that the rate at which the rudder could be applied by the powered controls was too slow. Consequently, the power unit was bypassed to provide a direct coupling between rudder bar and rudder, and that permitted the control surface to be applied more quickly.

On 7 July VX330 flew for half an hour and Parker found that the rudder control had improved, although it was heavy. Above 265mph (426km/h), however, the aircraft became oversensitive to control in the pitching plane – any gust of wind would start the aircraft pitching. Attempts at correction made the feature worse, but releasing the controls or holding them firmly would allow the disturbance to dampen out. Subsequent testing showed that VX330 was extremely difficult to control above 295mph (475km/h), and Parker felt that the pitching oscillation 'could very easily get completely out of control' and that it was 'very similar to the feeling in a tail-less aircraft of being balanced on a knife edge'.

Angle pieces were added in stages to both the upper and lower surfaces of the tailplane trailing edges, and by the twelfth flight the pilot could report that he was able to stop the pitching, once it had started, until the speed went above 426mph (685km/h). Above that, however, there was an increase in frequency of pitch with increase in speed. By 5 August VX330's control had been made satisfactory up to Mach 0.82 (518mph [833km/h]), although it was still sensitive above that, so for the time being this figure was fixed as the limiting speed at altitudes below 20,000 feet (6,096m).

A second pilot to fly the HP.88 was Handley Page's Flt Lt Douglas Broomfield. On 23 August he flew the aircraft to Handley Page's facility at Stansted in readiness to practise a routine for the upcoming SBAC Show. However, on 26 August, during Flight 28, VX330 crashed, killing Broomfield. He had begun a low run over the airfield runway and after levelling out at around 300 feet (91m) the HP.88 began to pitch. After two or three oscillations it assumed a violent nose-up attitude, then broke up, spreading wreckage across the airfield. The accident report states that there was no evidence of a pre-crash defect or failure in any of the engine parts, and that the primary fuselage failure occurred in the region of frame 14 (to the rear of the wing trailing edge). Analysis of flight recording

One more official photograph of the HP.88, showing again the flap actuator fairings and the mass balance arms, as well as the substantial bullet fairing at the fin/tail junction. *Phil Butler collection*

HANDLEY PAGE HP.88 (1951)

Both of these air-to-air photographs were taken on 26 July 1951 during a manufacturer's test flight. *BAE Systems, Brough*

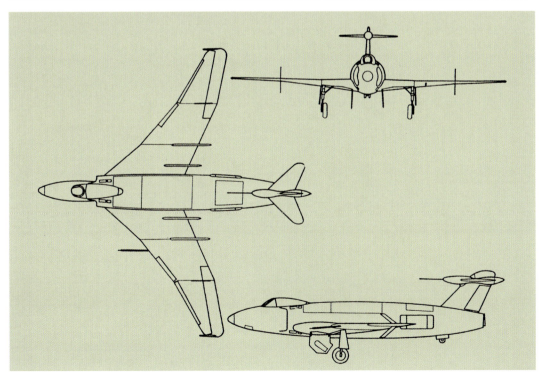

HP.88 drawing. *Dr David Baker, Aviation News*

X-PLANES OF EUROPE

Although of poor quality, this unique image shows the HP.88 breaking up over Stansted. The fuselage has failed in the region of the engine bay and the engine itself is almost certainly the object seen ahead of the forward fuselage. The wings are still attached, but they too broke away before the aircraft hit the ground. In this modern era of aviation we often forget the risks that courageous test pilots took almost every day in a much earlier and more dangerous era of flight test and development. The taking of this photograph was also a remarkable piece of work. *British National Archives (AVIA 54 – 121)*

equipment carried in the port wing root showed traces at +12g and -7g at 525mph (845km/h), and again at +7g and -5g at 475mph (764km/h). VX330 had completed just 13 hours 29 minutes of flight time and Broomfield had flown the aircraft five times.

No explanation could be given as to what the true effect of the progressive addition of angle pieces to the tailplane trailing edge was, but flight tests confirmed that these additions delayed the onset of extreme sensitivity to a higher speed. Wind tunnel work by RAE Farnborough suggested no definite cause for the accident, but the report suggested that it was 'associated with the violent oscillations in the pitching plane observed by witnesses and recorded by the vg recorder carried by the aircraft'. These oscillations at low altitude had produced accelerations that went beyond the Design Ultimate Factor (the maximum load that a structure was designed to withstand without breaking) and as a consequence the fuselage failed. The cause of the oscillations was not determined. (Today it is thought that inertia coupling between the tailplane and the powered controls may have been the reason for the massive load on the airframe, which caused this catastrophic failure.)

It is thought that the HP.88's final run was the fastest that VX330 ever achieved at low level. On 2 January 1952 the remains of the aircraft were Struck Off Charge. Since the scale-model aircraft was lost so soon after its first flight we will never really know just how beneficial it would have been to the full-size bomber. Little was learned in the time available, and the extensive system of pressure-plotting equipment installed in the HP.88 was never fully used. The loss brought no delay to the Victor programme.

16 SAAB 210 (1952)

SAAB 210
Span: 20ft 10in (6.35m)
Length: 28ft 10.5in (8.80m)
Gross wing area: 210A 260.2sq ft (24.2sq m); 210B 247.3 (23.00)
Gross weight: 2,590lb (1,175kg)
Powerplant: 1 x AS Adder, 1,050lb (4.7kN)
Max speed/height: 339mph (545km/h) at 2,000ft (610m)
Ceiling: Unknown

Sweden is a country with a relatively small population and a very limited defence budget, yet since the late 1940s it has been a major player in the design and development of jet fighter aircraft. This has happened primarily through the efforts of SAAB (Svenska Aeroplan Aktiebolaget), its most important aerospace company, which first established a reputation in the fighter field with the splendid J29 swept-wing aircraft that flew in September 1948. Only a year after that landmark event SAAB and the Svenska Flygvapnet (Swedish Air Force) began looking for a follow-up. They decided very quickly that any new fighter interceptor must be supersonic to ensure that it would be able to handle incoming enemy bombers flying at transonic speeds and high altitudes. In 1950, after prolonged studies, the design team led by Erik Bratt settled on a double-delta-wing configuration. This was dubbed the Gapande Flundran ('Gaping Flatfish') and the resulting fighter become known as Project 1250, and eventually the Type 35 Draken. In 1951 Bratt observed that bombers would soon be flying at close to supersonic speeds, which meant their interception would require an aircraft having a top speed of rather more than Mach 1. The delta planform would help to achieve such an objective, but the double-delta configuration required substantial testing to ensure it would perform satisfactorily.

Scale model
A large amount of wind tunnel time would be needed to assess the double-delta form and establish both its low- and high-speed qualities, because at this stage there was no delta-winged aircraft in service anywhere in the world. This

SAAB 210, known as the Little Dragon (Lilldraken), powered by one Armstrong Siddley Adder turbojet. Currently on display at the Swedish Airforce Museum (Flygvapenmusuem) in Linköping, Sweden.
Chris Sandham-Bailey www.inkworm.com

X-PLANES OF EUROPE

The SAAB 210 scale-model test aircraft is seen in March 1952. This aeroplane was built to carry out an assessment of the wing shape of the forthcoming SAAB Draken jet fighter. *Copyright SAAB AB*

configuration offered great possibilities, including a small frontal area coupled with a thin wing, and the largest possible internal volume for fuel, undercarriage and equipment. In order to test the wing in practice the Flygvapnet and SAAB decided to build a reduced (roughly 70%) scale experimental aircraft for tests at low speeds. At the start the scale aircraft was called Project 1251, but in due course it was redesignated SAAB 210. Work began in May 1950 and it was unofficially known as the Draken ('Kite' or 'Dragon'), but of course when the Type 35 fighter was officially named Draken the 210 automatically became the Lill-Draken ('Little or Mini Dragon').

As built, the 210 had a nose that protruded only just ahead of the air intakes. It had a single vertical fin and double-delta wings with the inner wing blended into the fuselage to the point that it looked rather like a large leading edge root extension. There was no horizontal tailplane, and a tricycle undercarriage, with relatively large wheels, was used. The pilot sat beneath a large canopy and the fuel capacity was 76 gallons (345 litres). To carry the required measuring equipment the 210 had to be designed for a very low wing loading and a low weight (two contradictory requirements), but this was necessary to keep the take-off distance within acceptable limits.

The only suitable jet engine available at the time to power this lightweight aircraft was the British Armstrong Siddeley Adder, which was essentially a development of that company's Mamba turboprop with the reduction gear and propeller drive taken away. The Flygvapnet bought two of these units, which in fact proved to be a bit too weak for the required purpose. With a thrust of just 1,050lb (4.7kN) they supplied only a small fraction of the thrust provided by the Rolls-Royce Avon that would power the first full-size Type 35 Drakens. On hot days some flights had to be abandoned because the extra heat reduced the power output even more (which consequently extended the 210's take-off run and affected its handling). On occasion some short test 'hops' were conducted at night to gain the benefit of the cooler air, but despite these problems the 210 would still have plenty to do.

Flight time

In December 1951 the SAAB 210 was ready for its first flight. Taxi trials had started, and on the 10th the aircraft was actually lifted off the ground for a short hop, but then a spate of bad weather prevented the maiden flight from taking place until 21 January 1952. On that day SAAB chief test pilot Bengt R. Olow took the aircraft on a 25-minute sortie from the company's Tannefors airfield in Linköping. It had become the first full-size double-delta aeroplane ever to fly. It was also the first Swedish aircraft with fully hydraulically powered flight controls,

and in less than a week it was exhibiting the exceptional promise of this configuration at low speeds. Just a few months later the Flygvapnet ordered the construction of J35 Draken fighter prototypes based on these principles.

Continued testing with the 210 confirmed that it would be a key aid for the Type 35 project. Questions about the centre of gravity position and stability at low speeds were answered during the 1,000 test flights conducted with the 210 over several years. In fact, the c.g. could be altered in flight by the transfer of liquid between a pair of tanks, one of which was placed toward the front of the aircraft with the other to the rear, and all of this work was complemented by high-speed data from a new supersonic wind tunnel built by SAAB to its own design. Although the 210 had a top speed just a little short of 300 knots (345mph/556km/h), a great deal was achieved, and the intensive flight programme brought in several other pilots, including three from the Försökscentralen, the Flygvapnet's Flight Test Research Centre. In due course the 210's engine intakes were cut back and its nose extended. These changes helped SAAB to establish the definitive layout for its fighter. In its final configuration, with an even longer nose, the 210 presented what would become the standard arrangement for the Draken itself.

Above and below: These beautiful photographs of the 210 in flight show it in its original form with nose-type air intakes. The 'U' painted on the fin signifies 'Utprovning' ('testing'), i.e. test aircraft. *Copyright SAAB AB, photographer Bo Dahlin*

Eventually the 210 was given an extended nose. In flight its tricycle undercarriage was retracted but still partially exposed to the airflow. SAAB

The changes to the nose had to be made because when the 210 was flying at high angles of attack the original arrangement created vortices at the nose intake lips, and these proved to be detrimental to the aircraft's longitudinal stability. Other trials flights looked at changes to the wing shape, and at one stage the wing was modified to a point where it was not unlike the Concorde SST's ogee planform. Vortex generators were tested and the 210 programme also looked at buffet, ground effect and pitch control. An additional horizontal tailplane was manufactured, but plans to fit this were dropped when the test pilots refused to fly the 210 with it in place (model tests had earlier shown that the double-delta plus a tail was not good aerodynamically – it was unstable and landings appeared particularly dangerous). The 210 with its original nose, with the intake separated in the middle by a pyramid-shaped cone, became known as the 210A. After a 'proper' nose had been introduced with the intakes pushed back to each side of the cockpit the aircraft was redesignated 210B.

During Stockholm's 700th anniversary celebrations held on 6 July 1953 the 210, piloted by the Försökscentralen's Olle Klinker, performed a spectacular display over the centre of the city. The SAAB 210 made its last flight on 25 October 1956 and today the aircraft resides in the Flygvapenmuseum (the Swedish Air Force Museum). The testing carried out on the combined double-delta layout revealed that it was a most effective solution for Sweden's new fighter. Results showed that the centre-section triangle offered the lowest drag at supersonic speeds, while the delta shape of the outer wings considerably improved airfield performance and the aircraft's flying qualities in the subsonic range. Test flights performed with the scale SAAB 210 research aircraft confirmed that this new wing shape provided greater stability at low air speeds and a better centre of pressure position than was possible with a single delta wing. The Draken made its maiden flight on 25 October 1955, went on to be a top-class fighter, and stayed in Flygvapnet service for nearly 39 years. It also gained major export orders for Sweden, and the last in-service Draken, flying with the Austrian Air Force, was finally retired in 2005. Despite being underpowered, the 210 more than proved its worth at the start of the fighter's development programme. It was a great success and the double-delta wing has left its mark on aviation history.

17 Short S.B.5 (1952)

Short S.B.5

Span: 50°: 35ft 2in (10.72m); 60°: 30ft 6in (9.30m); 69°: 26ft 0in (7.92m)

Length: High tail: 54ft 9in (16.69m); low tail: 52ft 9in (16.08m) with probes

Gross wing area: 50°: 273.1sq ft (25.40sq m) net; 60°: 276.9sq ft (25.75sq m) net; 69°: 281.7sq ft (26.20sq m) net; 60°: 351.0sq ft (32.64sq m) gross

Gross weight: 50°: 12,000lb (5,443kg); 13,000lb (5,897kg) maximum permissible

Powerplant: 1 x RR Derwent 8 (R.D.7), 3,500lb (15.6kN); 1960 1 x BS Orpheus (BE.26), 4,850lb (21.6kN)

Max speed: 50°: 311mph (500km/h); 403mph (648km/h) maximum achieved

Ceiling: 10,000ft (3.048m)

The only fighter fully developed in the UK that was capable of supersonic flight on the level was the English Electric Lightning, which entered service in 1960. This was preceded by two P.1 prototypes, the first of which flew in 1954. The P.1s were essentially technology demonstrators, and had they been designed from the start as research aircraft they would qualify for inclusion in this volume, but they were always covered by a 'fighter' specification (F.23/49) with armament (the Lightning itself incorporated various improvements including a redesigned nose fuselage to extend the Mach number range). Both P.1 and Lightning featured a very highly swept wing and, more controversially, introduced a highly swept horizontal tail placed low on the rear fuselage. Experts at RAE Farnborough disputed English Electric's findings that suggested that this swept wing and low tail would perform entirely satisfactorily even at low speeds. The debate was so strong that a low-speed research aircraft, a 7/8ths-scale model of the P.1, was built by Short Brothers & Harland Ltd (usually referred to as 'Shorts') at Sydenham, Belfast, to test the characteristics of this planform. It was called the S.B.5.

Dispute

Original documents show that there was indeed serious concern in regard to the P.1's layout. The RAE's scientists favoured a high-set tailplane on top of the fin since the low tail could suffer from the effects of the wake coming off the highly swept main wing. There might also be certain flight conditions where the low tail was masked, which would prevent it from being effective. Consequently, Shorts was asked to build the one-off S.B.5 to a contract issued in 1950, and serial WG768 was allotted on 27 July. English Electric's wind tunnel tests had shown that quite small changes in the P.1 design could have a profound influence on the stability characteristics. Furthermore, Shorts noted that the very fact that this low-speed model was required at all indicated that there was no margin of certainty that the P.1 would have acceptable or even safe characteristics at low speeds.

In March 1950 Shorts submitted a brochure stating that the primary objective was to supply an aircraft to explore and provide information on the low-speed handling, and especially the take-off and landing behaviour, of aircraft with wings swept back to 60°. It was desirable that the aircraft be as much like the English Electric P.1 as possible to ensure that the data obtained could apply directly to that programme. Thus the S.B.5 would have a similar ground angle, wing planform, wing

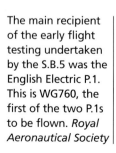

Dated September 1952, was taken before the S.B.5 research aircraft had been completed. The cockpit canopy, for example, is still to be fitted to the aircraft's forward fuselage. *Author's collection*

sections, vertical position of the tailplane, etc, and should be jet-propelled. A reliable engine was important and the Rolls-Royce Derwent was eventually chosen ahead of the de Havilland Goblin. From the safety aspect it was desirable to have the lightest possible wing loading but, if the handling characteristics of the P.1 were simulated at all accurately, it would be necessary for the wing loading to be comparable so that the dynamic response was not too different. It was therefore decided at this time to aim at a wing loading of 25lb/sq ft (122.05kg/sq m), but to provide for ballasting to bring the load up to 35lb/sq ft (170.87kg/sq m), which was approximately the same as the P.1 at its normal landing weight. This resulted in a 7/8ths linear scale to that of the P.1.

Shorts also arranged the wing geometry so that the angle of anhedral or sweep could be altered independently without affecting the wing incidence and, as far as possible, without having to manufacture complicated new root end fittings. In order to make the structural problems no harder than they needed to be, it was agreed with the MoS that the S.B.5 tailplane thickness/chord ratio should be increased to 8% from the P.1's 5%. At low speeds this change was unlikely to affect the aircraft's aerodynamics since the tailplane should never approach the stalled condition. The possibility of doing the same with the wing root was rejected on the grounds that here the stalling behaviour and stability might be seriously affected. Finally, the fuselage width had to be increased to accommodate the engine, and the nose shape was altered to match the smaller intake duct, which in the process gave the pilot a much better view. There

The main recipient of the early flight testing undertaken by the S.B.5 was the English Electric P.1. This is WG760, the first of the two P.1s to be flown. *Royal Aeronautical Society*

was, of course, only one jetpipe compared to the P.1's two, and the S.B.5 had alternative rear fuselages made for it, one with the high tail fitted and the other with the low tail.

The S.B.5 was covered by ER.100 (ER for Experimental Research), which was the first specification in a new 100-series introduced in 1950 to replace the old format that had ended in the year of issue (F.23/49 had been the twenty-third specification to be written in 1949). ER.100 was dated 28 October 1950 and declared that the aircraft was to be capable of being modified as follows:

1 50° wing sweep, high tail
2 60° wing sweep, high tail
3 60° wing sweep, low tail
4 70° wing sweep, high tail

The S.B.5 used a full-span tapered leading edge except on the 60° sweep/low-tail combination, when a part-span triangular leading edge was fitted. Also, for items 1 and 3 wing trailing-edge split flaps were employed, but on the others no flaps were used. Item 4 took the S.B.5 beyond the needs of the P.1 wing, thereby increasing the aircraft's value, and in the end the airframe actually flew with eight different configurations of sweep angle and leading edge arrangement.

The S.B.5 was quite a simple aircraft. In order to facilitate the three differing sweep angles the wings and the sets of wing root attachments were made very strong, and they carried the main fixed undercarriage whose adjustable rake was varied with the wing sweep angle. A total of 300 gallons (1,364 litres) of fuel was carried in a single tank and the aircraft was built with a conventional structure of light alloy. A mock-up was assembled during January and February 1951, and to illustrate the level of effort this project would consume, at least 12 Design Conferences were held by the Ministry during the development phase.

Moments of truth

After being moved by sea and road from its Belfast birthplace, on 2 December 1952 the S.B.5 made its maiden flight from A&AEE Boscombe Down with the favoured RAE high tail in place and the wing set at 50°. The pilot was Tom Brooke-Smith and the rather long take-off run revealed immediately that the Derwent did not provide enough power. A test programme to check the basic handling was completed over the next seven months, and WG768's first flight with the wing set at 60° was made on 29 July 1953, but still with RAE's preferred high tail. In August 1953 Roland Beamont, English Electric's chief test pilot, made his first trip in the S.B.5, and felt that the T-tail was far from satisfactory. In October WG768 returned to Belfast to have the low tail attached. After changes had been made to the inboard wing leading edges to give a greater droop and simulate the P.1's moveable flap, and the replacement low-position tailplane/elevator had been fitted, it flew for the first time in P.1 'configuration' (again from Boscombe) in January 1954. WG768 was then sent to RAE Bedford for performance trials, returning to Boscombe in February. The results confirmed that the English Electric wind tunnel research had been accurate and that the low horizontal tail did indeed provide the better flight characteristics at low speeds.

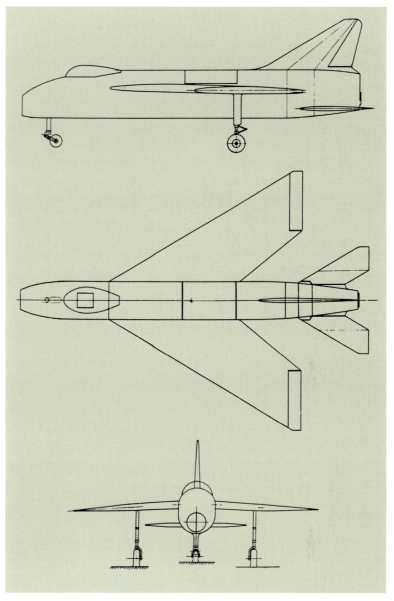

A drawing included in the March 1950 S.B.5 brochure produced by Shorts. It shows the wings swept 60°, a span of 30ft 6in (9.30m) and a length of 42ft 6in (12.95m), and there are no probes. *RAF Museum*

X-PLANES OF EUROPE

1953 WG768 in original form with a 50° swept wing, T-tail, and silver/black gloss colour scheme is seen in february 1953. Note the drooped leading edge, and that the nose probes are either not yet in place or have been temporarily removed. *Author's collection*

This moderate-quality image shows the S.B.5's underside detail and fixed undercarriage. *Author's collection*

SHORT S.B.5 (1952)

This nose view was taken as part of the publicity photography undertaken for the SBAC Farnborough Show in early September 1953. *Author's collection*

X-PLANES OF EUROPE

A side view from the publicity photography for SBAC Farnborough, September 1953. *Author's collection*

More photos of WG768 with its T-tailplane at the 1953 SBAC Show. *Author's collection*

Beamont's assessment of the S.B.5 in this form suggested that the aircraft was now fine for examining the slow-speed characteristics of this type of high-speed planform. The combination of a low power/weight ratio and high induced drag meant that he could vary the aircraft's speed to some degree just by altering slightly the angle of attack with the stick. Over a number of flights Beamont was able to collect plenty of experience in readiness to fly the P.1, but the S.B.5's poor rate of climb coupled with its low fuel capacity made it quite difficult to complete some parts of the programme. The Derwent running at full power needed 20 minutes to get WG768 to 7,000 feet (2,134m), which was considered the optimum for certain tests, yet the aircraft only had an endurance of around 40 minutes.

In spring 1954 Brooke-Smith identified a problem where sharp wing drop occurred when flying at 167mph (269km/h). This appeared after the outboard wing leading edge droop had been removed (it had not occurred with the full-span droop) and was caused by leading-edge vortices giving uneven airflow over the ailerons. RAE recommended that wing fences be fitted to the P.1 to prevent this problem happening on that aircraft, but in fact English Electric's solution was to introduce a small notch in the wing leading edge, which gave less drag than fences. On 24 June 1954 WG768 went to RAE Farnborough for handling trials, and on 1 September it was loaned to Shorts to attend that year's SBAC Show. It rejoined RAE Bedford on 20 September 1955 and in due course became employed on more general research, spending time at both Bedford and Boscombe. Trials made during this period included carrying asymmetric loads of 60, 100, 200 or 300lb (27, 45, 91 or 136kg) in underwing canisters at speeds between 104 and 230mph (167 and 370km/h). The fixed inboard leading-edge flap was eventually removed and replaced by full-span leading-edge droop of 10°, then, in due course, this was removed to leave a clean leading edge with no droop or flaps. In all, some 185 hours of flying was made with the wing set at 60°, most of it at heights of around 5,000 feet (1,524m).

These official Ministry views of WG768 with the low tailplane were taken in December 1953 after the aircraft had returned to Boscombe Down, but before it had flown in this condition. The nose view shows damage to the photographic negative behind WG768's port wing, which on close examination indicates that other aircraft in the original picture have been 'removed', probably for security considerations. *Ministry of Defence*

On 20 April 1958 WG768 was returned to Shorts to have its Derwent powerplant replaced by a more powerful Bristol BE.26 Orpheus. The sweep angle was now changed to its maximum (69° in fact, rather than 70°), a zero-zero Martin-Baker ejection seat was installed (which also required a new cockpit canopy), and the aircraft was repainted light blue gloss. WG768 now had a more pronounced continuous sweepback than any other aircraft in the world at this time. On 18 October 1960 the S.B.5 made its last 'first flight' from Bedford, this time with RAE Aero Flight's Denis Tayler in the cockpit. The increased sweep angle brought improvements to the performance, and on 6 December WG768 returned to Bedford to begin more research flying, with Tayler as a regular pilot. The S.B.5 later became involved in low-speed trials for the Concorde supersonic transport,

This shot was taken at Belfast by the Shorts photographer after the conversion to the low-tail position had been completed. A triangular moveable inner leading edge has also been fitted. *Short Brothers & Harland Ltd*

WG768 is seen on display at RAE Farnborough during the Establishment's Golden Jubilee celebration event held between 7 and 9 July 1955. The original cockpit canopy is well shown. *Author's collection*

Photographs of WG768 with its 69° sweep wing and pale blue colour scheme appear to be less common. However, this image shows the new canopy and the wool tufts that at one stage were fixed to the port wing. A miniature spotlight was placed on the fuselage spine to the rear of the canopy to permit a small cine camera placed on the fin to film the behaviour of these tufts in flight. *Author's collection*

An unusual rear-angle view of the S.B.5.
Author's collection

together with the Handley Page HP.115 (qv), which was also now at Bedford. At the conclusion of its test career, on 16 December 1965, the S.B.5 passed into the hands of the Empire Test Pilots' School, then based at Farnborough, to provide pilots with experience of swept wings flown at slow speeds. Here WG768 was given the code '28' and a much darker paint scheme, and was so used until Struck Off Charge in November 1967. On 22 January 1968 it was allotted to the Ministry of Defence (MoD) for 'exhibition purposes' with the ground airframe serial 8005M.

The S.B.5 could be described as a 'swing wing' aircraft, but of course it could not move its wings in flight – the angle of sweep had to be set prior to take-off and adjusting them was quite a task. The aircraft's primary objective was a success in that it proved that the slow-speed characteristics of the forthcoming P.1 and Lightning would be far superior with a low tail position than if a high tail were fitted. (In fact, other companies had also concluded that a low tail was the way forward – Supermarine's Type 553 proposal of April 1953 to the ER.134T requirement won by the Bristol 188 [qv] also featured a highly swept wing and tail, with the latter positioned low on the fuselage.) WG768 went on to complete a long career doing all kinds of research, which nullifies any criticism that might be made against the decision to build the aircraft in the first place. Overall the S.B.5 gave great value for the money and in the process never suffered a major setback or flight or engineering problem of any kind.

WG768 seen at Finningley on 12 September 1968, not long after its retirement from flying.
Roy Bonser-KEC

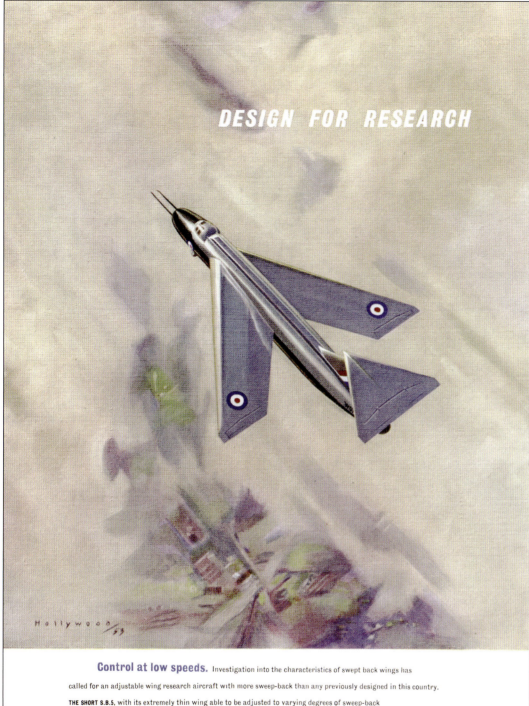

A 1953 painting by 'Hollywood' was used to compose this advertisement for the Shorts S.B.5.

18 Short S.B.1 and S.B.4 Sherpa (1953)

Short S.B.4 Sherpa
Span: 38ft 0in (11.58m)
Length: 31ft 11in (9.72m)
Gross wing area: 261.5sq ft (24.32sq m)
Gross weight: 3,300lb (1,497kg)
Powerplant: 2 x Blackburn Turboméca Palas, 353lb (1.6kN)
Max speed: 250mph (402km/h)
Ceiling: 5,000ft (1,524m)

Professor Geoffrey Terence Rowland Hill, photographed in 1947. *Royal Aeronautical Society*

Professor G. T. R. Hill is an unsung hero in British aircraft design. He is remembered for the pre-war series of Pterodactyl aeroplanes, but a large portion of his career was spent working on advanced wing design. Throughout the 1920s he became ever more concerned about the safety of flying and was profoundly concerned about the phenomenon of stalling. His thoughts on countering the problem came together in the swept flying wing Pterodactyl named after the prehistoric flying reptile and first flown as a glider in 1924, and as a powered machine in 1925. Further forms of Pterodactyl were built at Westland, in Hill's words the objective being 'to try to design an aeroplane, which would never, through an error on the part of the pilot, get out of control'.

During the war Hill worked with the Ministry of Aircraft Production (MAP) on special research. In 1942, as Scientific Liaison Officer between Britain and Canada, he was able to help the Canadians build an all-wing experimental glider. Later that year he made a trip to Northrop to view and discuss the tailless N1M flying wing aircraft. On leaving MAP, Hill was engaged as a consultant to Short Brothers, where he developed a gust alleviator called the 'Smooth Ride Flap', based on the principle that one did not need to eliminate the effects of gusts provided the effect was held below the threshold value. The threshold value was defined as 'that at which all normal passengers would retain their breakfasts'. His last important innovation in the field of wing design was the aero-isoclinic wing, which was developed with Short Brothers using the S.B.1 glider and S.B.4 jet aircraft.

Wingtip control

The term 'aero-isoclinic' describes a wing with an angle of incidence that remains constant regardless of flexure. The arrival of the jet engine brought the chance to reach previously impossible speeds, but there were difficulties. One was aeroelasticity, the upwards bending or flexing of the outer wing under air load with a consequent loss of incidence at the tips. This had always been present, but manoeuvring at higher speeds exaggerated the effect. The greater part of the outer wing would flex during steep turns or dives with the result that the action of the conventional aileron was severely reduced or even opposed, thus producing control reversal. Swept wings were much more liable to flexure or twisting under normal aileron loads than straight wings, so the wing designed for higher speeds consequently suffered the most serious flexing effects. The loss of tip incidence was most prevalent when pulling out of a dive, the reduced incidence acting like an upwards deflection of the elevator, which made the aircraft pull out more sharply than was intended. This effect was responsible on high-speed aeroplanes for a form of dynamic instability, which had sometimes proved to be fatal, and Hill's answer was the aero-isoclinic wing, which extended his work on the Pterodactyls. Here the wing was designed so that, as it bent, it was able to twist just sufficiently to preserve the correct incidence, a capability achieved by using all-moving wingtips.

In addition to the aeroelastic problem, conventional trailing-edge control surfaces were found to lose their effectiveness at transonic speeds, and the all-moving 'flying' tail had found increasing use as the solution. Hill extended this by replacing the trailing-edge ailerons with his moving wingtips, which, on a highly swept wing, functioned both as elevators and ailerons, thereby allowing the tail to be discarded altogether for a substantial saving in weight and drag. These moving tips brought a further advantage in that they could cancel out the effect of rolling moment induced by sideslip. The disadvantages were increased drag due to the discontinuity in the wing when the control surfaces were displaced (though tunnel testing on the S.B.4 test aircraft indicated that the drag rise was negligible) and the mechanical problems of fitting an all-moving tip, the surfaces having to be rotated around a long cantilever beam projecting from the wing. Finally, twisting the wing to keep the angle of incidence constant regardless of flexure was difficult to ensure, since if it twisted too easily the increased incidence and lift would be cumulative and twist the wing off the aircraft, a phenomenon called divergence.

Pterodactyl I first featured all-moving tips, the outer 7.5 feet (2.3m) serving as 'controllers' (what we today call elevons), which, when operated differentially, did the work of the ailerons, but in unison acted as the elevators. Experiments on the glider built in Canada to test the Pterodactyl VIII planform had revealed that removing the fins and rudders gave inadequate directional stability on the 'flying wing'. They also suggested that hinged elevons could not be made flutter-free and were liable to stall at the tips at slow speeds. But for high-speed aircraft Hill could see the merit in his earlier Pterodactyl configuration and, when faced with the problem of finding a design criterion for the wing stiffness in torsion, offered the idea that the torsion box should be placed well aft in the wing. This would give a rearwards location of the flexural axis, with the relation of stiffness in torsion and bending so adjusted that wing flexing would not produce any undesirable loss of incidence at the wingtips. In other words, the rear part of the wing was made torsionally stiffer than the front part.

Flight test

The design of the S.B.1 airframe, which received the British 'B' registration G-14-5, was placed in the hands of David Keith-Lucas, Shorts' chief designer. It had a wooden one-piece wing (of mainly spruce and plywood) and a stressed-skin fuselage, and became airborne for the first time with a winch launch on 14 July 1951. The pilot was Tom Brooke-Smith, and this was the first of Shorts' aircraft to be designed and built entirely at Belfast, following the company's move from Rochester (when it was officially re-titled Short Brothers & Harland Ltd). A second flight was made on the 17th, then on the 30th G-14-5 was taken from Aldergrove to 15,000 feet (4,572m) by a Short Sturgeon tug. Here Brooke-

The first flight of the Short S.B.1 glider to be made under tow used a Short Sturgeon tug, serial VR363, 30 July 1951. *Aeroplane*

The S.B.1 is seen again during its first aerotow. The Class 'B' serial G-14-5 is painted on the fin. *Short Brothers & Harland Ltd*

Tom Brooke-Smith sits in the cockpit of the S.B.1 glider. *Phil Butler*

Smith found the glider awkward and tiring to fly on the tow, but after release reported that in free flight it handled 'beautifully'. The next flight took place on 14 October. A longer towing cable had been introduced to counteract the turbulence from the Sturgeon's propellers, but this proved to be near disastrous because Brooke-Smith could not get the S.B.1 under control when it was off the ground. It was impossible to get the glider into the smoother air above the Sturgeon's wake and, after casting off, the pilot was unable to prevent G-14-5 from crashing. Brooke-Smith was injured and took some time to recover.

What was left of the S.B.1 was rebuilt as the S.B.4. A pair of Blackburn Turboméca Palas jets were mounted in the upper fuselage and fed by an intake placed behind the cockpit, and two small fuel tanks were housed in the fuselage. A new light-alloy fuselage was built to replace the wrecked S.B.1 body, but the wings and tail were repaired. The fuselage tail end and the fin and rudder were all built of wood, while the nose was made in fibreglass so that it could be split for access. To preserve the aero-isoclinic characteristic, the torsional stiffness of the wing leading edge had to be destroyed and this was done by providing a break in the skin on the under surface of the wing forward of the main spar. The wooden elevons were constructed around a built-up metal spar of octagonal section, and the undercarriage was fixed.

This work was undertaken as a private venture and the rebuild took the best part of two years. A new serial, G-14-1, was allotted to the aircraft and Brooke-Smith made another 'first flight' from Aldergrove on 4 October 1953. Test flying with Shorts continued for more than a year, and by the time Brooke-Smith demonstrated the S.B.4 at the 1954 Farnborough Show it had been named Sherpa. The data collected showed good handling at low speeds and gave indications as to how a full-size wing might behave at higher speeds, but the lack of power did limit the maximum speed. Keith-Lucas, however, would confirm that the S.B.4 had performed very satisfactorily and that it had succeeded in demonstrating the soundness of Hill's ideas.

Nose views of the S.B.4, which was not named Sherpa until later in its career. Note the dorsal air intake and the twin side fuselage jetpipes. *Phil Butler*

S.B.4 is seen on a test flight, with the wingtip controllers operating. The registration G-14-1 is painted on both the starboard wing upper surface and the fin. *Short Brothers & Harland Ltd*

This general perspective drawing from Shorts shows the Sherpa's wing structure. The section at the top shows the method of destroying the torsional stiffness of the leading edge. *Author's collection*

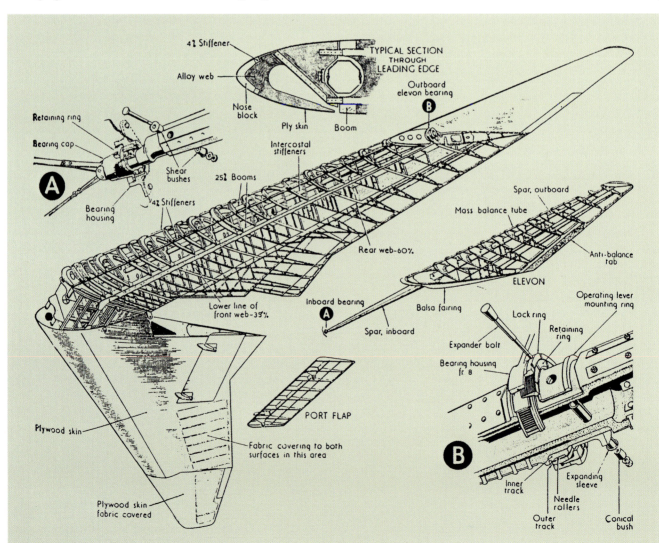

The S.B.4 reveals its underside detail as it banks away from the camera during a photo sortie. *Phil Butler*

When Shorts had completed its trials the S.B.4 was donated to the Cranfield College of Aeronautics. Flight trials, primarily for post-graduate research, began in April 1957 in the hands of Flt Lt A. J. MacDonald, the aircraft receiving another Class 'B' – G-36-1 – but in 1958 an engine failure brought things to a halt. Since the Palas was not a production engine, it was not until 1960 that the power units could be replaced, but a return to the air permitted research into the roll response of the wingtip controllers to continue. Overall, flying was carried out on a random basis, but a report made during the aircraft's early days at Cranfield showed that the College had found the Sherpa to be a very pleasant aircraft to fly in fine weather when, at low speeds just above the stall, ample control was available. However, in bumpy conditions the Sherpa tended to become a bit of a handful.

When the engines became time-expired in 1964 the Sherpa's fuselage and half of its wing were moved to the Bristol College of Advanced Technology for service as a laboratory specimen airframe. In May 1966 the Sherpa fuselage was retired (the wing had by then been destroyed) and went to the Skyfame Museum at Staverton to be reunited with the other half wing. Eventually Skyfame was closed, but today the fuselage belongs to the Ulster Aviation Society.

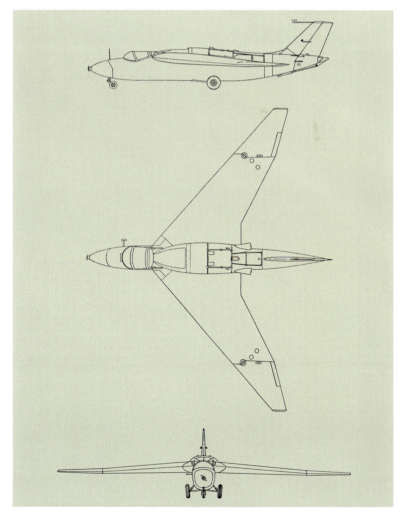

Short S.B.4 drawing. *David Baker, Aviation News*

X-PLANES OF EUROPE

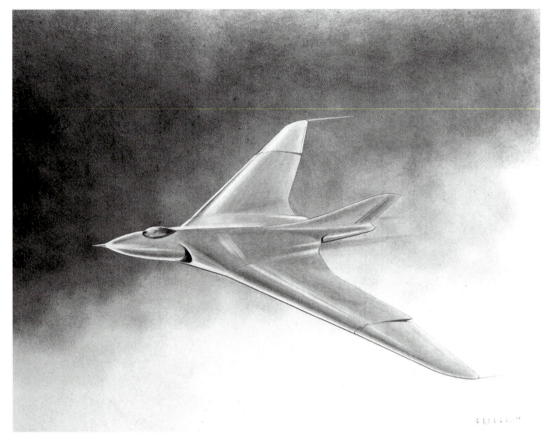

An artist's rendering of the high-altitude photo-reconnaissance P.D.8 of May 1952. Note how the tip controllers are slightly in opposition as they operate as ailerons for a banking manoeuvre. *Short Brothers & Harland Ltd*

High-speed project

The aero-isoclinic wing was applied to several other Shorts' projects, including the photo-reconnaissance P.D.8 proposal of May 1952. Investigations had shown that the wing was particularly suitable for high-altitude, long-range aircraft. There were also plans for a transonic research aeroplane to follow the S.B.4 called the P.D.10, which stimulated Ministry interest to the extent that Specification ER.145 was allocated to the aircraft (although the document was never written). A full P.D.10 brochure was submitted in July 1953, and Shorts reported that the design studies made with the aero-isoclinic wing had shown considerable gains in performance over conventional designs, especially at extreme altitudes where a large aspect ratio was an advantage. However, Shorts declared that little further useful work could be done until an aeroplane had been built and flown at high Mach numbers, so the new proposal took the fuselage from the Supermarine Swift fighter and fitted it with a new set of aero-isoclinic wings with all-moving tip controls. A proposed test programme was expected to verify a number of claims, namely:

- freedom from tip stalling
- freedom from adverse aileron yaw
- negligible loss of manoeuvre margin due to flexure of the swept wing
- negligible loss of control effectiveness due to proximity of control reversal speed

It was desired to design a wing as close to that of the P.D.8 as possible while still being suitable for the Swift – in other words, to show a family resemblance to the type of wing that might be

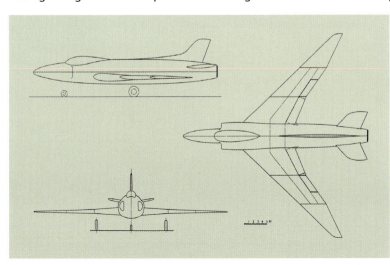

The general arrangement of the P.D.10 high-speed 'aero-isoclinic' wing research proposal of July 1953, which was to employ a version of the fuselage designed for the Supermarine Swift fighter. *RAF Museum*

An artist's concept rendering of the P.D.10. *Short Brothers & Harland Ltd*

used on an operational aeroplane. Although projects so far considered for the isoclinic wing did not have very high diving speeds, the aeroelastic problems that the wing hoped to solve occurred at these high speeds. It was thus proposed to design the P.D.10 to the Swift's diving speed (730mph [1,175km/h]), and it was assumed that the powerplant would be one afterburning Rolls-Royce Avon RA.7R jet. Maximum level speeds were calculated as 716mph (1,152km/h), Mach 0.97 at 10,000 feet (3,048m), and 677mph (1,089km/h), Mach 1.00, at 30,000 feet (9,144m). In the end the P.D.10 was not built, but it might have made for an interesting experiment.

Like the Pterodactyls that preceded them, Hill felt his aero-isoclinic wing ideas were never assessed on their true merits. He was very frustrated that, in spite of the Sherpa, the concept was never adopted for an operational aeroplane since the potential was there for an important improvement in air safety and air combat. Although official interest in the aero-isoclinic wing was considered strong at the end of 1953, no orders for further projects were forthcoming. The fact that the P.D.10 was not built leaves the assessment of the concept rather incomplete, the only 'high-speed' analysis having come from wind tunnel testing. Hill's design was, in essence, the world's first variable-camber wing. Today such airfoils are known as 'super-critical wings' and are designed and manufactured with digital technology; they are even built with composites for extra strength. Sadly, we may never know just how well the aero-isoclinic wing would have worked had it been used by a production aircraft.

19 Sud-Est SE 5000 Baroudeur (1953)

Sud-Est Baroudeur

Registration: SE 5000 01: F-ZWSB ('B' on fuselage), 02: F-ZWSJ 'J' SE 5003 01: F-ZWSS 'S', 02: F-ZWST 'T', 03: F-ZWTV 'V'

Span: 32ft 10in (10.00m)

Length: 44ft 10in (13.66m)

Wing area: 272.0sq ft (25.3sq m)

Max gross take-off weight (SE 5003 01): 15,763lb (7,150kg)

Powerplants: SE 5000 01: 1 x SNECMA Atar 101 B2, 5,290lb (23.5kN); SE 5000 02: 1 x SNECMA Atar 101 C, 6,175lb (27.5kN); SE 5003 01: 1 x SNECMA Atar 101 E4, 8,155lb (36.3kN); SE 5003 02: 1 x SNECMA Atar 101 D3, 6,285lb (27.9kN); SE 5003 03 for NATO trial: 1 x SNECMA Atar 101 E4, 8,155lb (36.3kN)

Max speed: Mach 0.97

Ceiling: Unknown

The SE 5000 Baroudeur tactical support fighter began life as a full private-venture project designed by Polish engineer Wsiewołod John Jakimiuk, who before the war had been with PZL in Poland and after the conflict had worked for de Havilland in Canada. However, the aircraft was really the conception of the company's President, Georges Hereil, who had been much impressed by the difficulties of operating jet fighters in Korea. The 3,000-yard (2,740m) runways then being laid down in France for NATO units flying the latest American aeroplanes confirmed Heriel's belief that something must be done to make more operationally flexible fighters. The result was the Baroudeur, whose name came from 'baroud', an Arabic word meaning 'battle' that had been adopted as a slang name by the French Foreign Legion to describe a tough, pugnacious and independent fighter. (Another variation was offered by Jacques Lecarme, chief engineer and test pilot at Sud-Est, who suggested 'Dog-fighter'.)

Designed by SNCASE at la Courneuve on the northern outskirts of Paris, the Baroudeur's overall configuration was fairly conventional for a swept-wing jet fighter, although the method by which the aircraft took off and landed was quite unusual. To save weight and reduce complexity the Baroudeur was designed to fly without conventional landing gear; instead it used a wheeled trolley for take-off and glider-like skids for landing. With this new arrangement the Baroudeur qualifies as a research aeroplane, although it was primarily intended for ground attack work.

The wheeled trolley could be used for take-off runs on either concrete or grass surfaces, while three retractable skids – two under the fuselage and one under the tail – were employed for landing on grass, and also for take-off from surfaces covered with snow or ice. After a relatively short 560-foot (171m) ground run the aircraft would leave its trolley at 140mph (225km/h); a drag parachute stopped the free-rolling trolley before it reached the end of the impromptu airfield. The aircraft could taxi on its skids, and if required could also take off with the trolley still attached. In fact, trials showed that it was possible to carry the trolley for 100 miles (161km) at a speed of 190 knots (352km/h). For his take-off the pilot was given a special air speed indicator (ASI) that operated a light on the dash when the flying speed was reached, at which point the pilot released the bomb-slip and

Airborne! A Sud-Est SE 5000 Baroudeur takes to the skies with its landing gear apparently already retracted. In actuality, there is no landing gear to retract, as the small lightweight jet fighter accelerated down the runway on, and took off from, a wheeled, rocket-powered trolley, seen at the lower left of this photograph. Once the jet was airborne, the take-off trolley was slowed and brought to a stop by a small drag chute. *Copyright Musée de l'Air et de l'Espace, Paris/Le Bourget*

Looking as though they are sitting on a typical alert during the early years of the Cold War, the three pre-production prototype Baroudeurs line up on a snow-covered ramp, with the canopy of the aircraft closest to the camera open and ready for its pilot. Note the small boarding ladder affixed to the side of the jet. *Copyright Musée de l'Air et de l'Espace, Paris/Le Bourget*

increased the incidence. The front support followed the nose and kept it steady until the aeroplane was airborne. As it flew off the trolley the brake connection was pulled free by a cable and the light would go out, and on release a touch of elevator would spring the aircraft into the air. Keeping the aircraft straight when using the trolley was a simple case of using the rudder, but taking off using the skids required more concentration to counteract the lateral rocking experienced as the Baroudeur rode over rough ground. The rear of the trolley could be fitted with up to six 1,654lb (7.35kN) STRIM 4AV JATO rockets, the number depending upon the requirements of the terrain.

For landing the pilot would bring the fighter down on its tail skid first, ride on it for 40 or 50 yards (36 or 46m), then drop gently on to the two magnesium alloy main skids positioned on the lower fuselage corners underneath the

This is the second prototype SE 5000, F-ZWSJ. There were several subtle structural differences between the first two airframes, namely larger wing fences and ventral fins on the second example. Note that the horizontal stabiliser is fixed to the upper vertical fin, and that the entire assembly pivots upwards or downwards for pitch trim control. Although it appears that the jet is sitting on low-slung tricycle landing gear, careful observation reveals the rocket-assisted ground trolley. *Tony Buttler collection*

leading edge of the wing. In late 1953 Jakimiuk reported that because of high friction the aeroplane was highly stable directionally, and in every landing made so far on the very stony soil at Istres the skid marks had been perfectly straight – even with a 12-knot (14mph/22km/h) crosswind component. Refitting the trolley after landing simply involved half-mounting the trolley using engine thrust before a final pull was made with a cable. On wet or slippery surfaces the pilot had controllable claws at the rear of the main skids to assist in slowing the aircraft, a feature that had been specially installed with a view to operations from ice. Company test pilot Pierre 'Tito' Maulandi, in charge of the Baroudeur project, showed during trials with taxiing on the skids that he could turn the aircraft through a radius of 70 feet (21m) to an accuracy of 3 feet (0.9m), which in other words meant that on landing he would not have to wait for a trolley before the aircraft could be moved away, but rather that he could taxi directly to the waiting trolley.

Previously, while the Baroudeur had still been under construction, Sud-Est had built a jury rig fitted with JATO rocket bottles to study

With a good top speed the Baroudeur would have seemed the natural choice to win the NATO competition for a new, small, lightweight fighter able to operate from soft or rough fields. However, the aircraft's take-off trolley concept proved to be too cumbersome for mass operation, and the Italian Fiat G.91 was chosen instead. On final approach for landing, this SE 5000 is controlling its descent with a drag chute. The aircraft's retractable landing skids can be seen clearly underneath the fuselage. *Musée de l'Air et de l'Espace, Paris/Le Bourget*

'If it looks right, it flies right' goes the age-old saying in aeronautical design, and the Baroudeur certainly looks right for a jet fighter of this era. Note the ample-size wing fences, root-mounted air intakes, and twin canted ventral fins below the aft fuselage. This is F-ZWSB, the very first SE 5000 built. *Tony Buttler collection*

Close up of the Baroudeur being loaded aboard its launch trolley.

the problems of taking off from unprepared surfaces. Indeed, trials with a mock-up had shown that even under these arduous conditions the skid shoe life was superior than the tyre life for a fast aircraft on grass.

Despite its unconventional take-off and landing, the Baroudeur was highly interesting in its own right. Every effort was made to make the structure simple, and it was designed from the start for production so that the jigs on which the two prototypes were made would also serve as prototypes for manufacture. Much of the structure was traditional, with the airframe built around the fuselage, and the first Baroudeur proved to be only 16kg (35lb) over the original weight estimate. Normal fuel was carried in the

The fighter makes a low level pass. *Wolfgang Muehlbauer*

The Baroudeur seen on public display with its launch trolley plus a selection of weaponry.

The skids are deployed as the Baroudeur prepares to land on a grass surface.

fuselage but the second prototype had provision for British Flight Refuelling Ltd probe-and-drogue equipment with a nose probe, as well as fittings for four 700-litre (154-gallon) wing drop tanks. Rockets or bombs could be carried on these same wingtip fittings.

Apart from its unique landing gear design, the aircraft featured a conventional shoulder-mounted 8% thick wing and cruciform tailplanes all with 38° of sweep at their leading edges. There were fully automatic slats and pressure-balanced and power-operated ailerons. At the start of the flight test programme the slats were locked open; then, after the first few flights, these were locked shut and fences were fitted at a flow-separation point. From spring 1954 the slats were released in stages (the wing fences were installed to control span-wise airflow and improve the aircraft's low-speed handling). The trailing edge was occupied entirely by the ailerons and flaps; the flaps were slotted but the inner portion was so hinged that there was no actual gap, which made, in effect, a simple split flap inboard. The wing root trailing edge fairing swivelled about a central axis and formed an ingenious balanced air brake. The wing structure was simple – a main spar, two auxiliary spars and closely spaced ribs with a relatively thin skin – and the aircraft was powered by a SNECMA Atar 101C turbojet with intakes faired into the aircraft's wing roots.

A drag chute helps to bring the aircraft to a halt.

Close up of the Baroudeur's landing skids, the aircraft having appeared to have touched down on sand. *Wolfgang Muehlbauer*

Pierre Maulandi took the first of two SE 5000 prototypes on its maiden flight from Marignane on 1 August 1953. The aircraft's flight envelope was explored initially to a speed of Mach 0.90 at 30,000 feet (9,144m), and after completing its early flight trials the prototype was taken on a tour of France, where it was allowed to demonstrate its off-field capability during visits to towns without proper airfields. Subsequent minor changes to the airframe included the introduction of ventral fins shod with steel to allow them to serve also as auxiliary skids.

The Baroudeur remained a private-venture programme until a decidedly doubtful Ministry finally awarded a contract in March 1954 to reimburse the cost of the two prototypes and also to cover three pre-production aircraft, to be designated SE 5003; a small follow-on series of aircraft was also planned but never built. To convince the Ministry, the Baroudeur had been flown from several sorts of terrain as might be met in any part of the world. The trials were conducted from December 1953 onwards off the stony ground at Istres, firm grass at Toulouse-Blagnac, heavy clay at Melun-Villaroche, on wet sand at La Baule, and in swampy ground at Tours. At the last-named venue the Baroudeur performed successfully, but the Dodge van sent to mount it on the trolley became bogged down!

The second prototype, 02, first flew on 12 May 1954, and some weeks later, on 17 July, the Baroudeur went supersonic for the first time when 02, piloted by Maulandi, achieved Mach 1 in a dive (the aircraft did not have the aerodynamic shape or sufficient engine power to go supersonic on the level). By mid-July 1954 Maulandi was testing 02 at Istres while 01 was in the hands of SNCASE chief test pilot Pierre Nadot at Toulouse-Blagnac, having been flown there on 5 July to continue the flight trials programme. The second machine had introduced longer wing fences, 3° of anhedral on the wings and bigger ventral fins, which were

This photograph and those on the next two pages show the Baroudeur after alighting on various grass surfaces and also sand.

now detachable (the anhedral and ventral fins helped to damp out yaw-and-roll oscillations), and the aircraft's handling characteristics were found to be very good – better than the Dassault Mystère IVA, which was due to enter service within a year. However, problems began to surface in late 1954 when cracks were discovered in the wing spars of both prototypes, so the first two Baroudeurs had to be grounded for several months for repairs to be carried out.

Both prototypes were shown to the public at the 1955 Paris Show. The take-off and landing of skid-equipped fighters had not previously been demonstrated in public, so attracted particular attention during the Show's flying display. To begin with an experimental Sud-Est SE 530 Mistral Mk 53 (a licence-built version of the de Havilland Vampire powered by an Hispano-built Nene 102 engine), fitted with an oversize nosewheel and flat non-retractable metal skids and shock absorbers in place of the main wheels, took off from the grass surface, then landed with a pull-up of not more than 400 yards (365m). The two Baroudeurs demonstrated their skid landing techniques and the special launching trolley. On the first demonstration one aircraft took off from the grass with rocket assistance while the other used the trolley. The first aircraft used a tail-breaking parachute on the final approach and skidded to a stop on the grass. It was then fitted with a launching trolley (the operation took about 2 minutes), then taxied out for another take-off; this time the take-off and landing was made with the trolley still attached.

The third aircraft, the first SE 5003, completed in July 1955, received an ATAR 101 E4 that permitted it to reach a speed of Mach 0.96 in a climb and Mach 1.1 in a dive. This aircraft was subsequently fitted with additional conformal fuel tanks on the sides of the rear fuselage, in part to give extra range (the original fuel capacity had been considered inadequate) but also to allow the aircraft to conform better to the newly discovered area rule, thereby improving the transonic performance. Indeed, the Baroudeur's impressive performance included a time-to-climb from ground level to 40,000 feet (12,192m) of only 7 minutes. Ground landing runs could stretch to 2,790 feet (850m) without using skid hooks or a drag chute, but many experienced pilots could stop the aircraft in as little as 1,150 feet (350m) after landing. Aircraft No 4 (the second pre-production machine) was used for armament trials, while the last Baroudeur to be built, which first flew on 3 March 1956, took part in 1957 in the NATO Light Weight Strike Fighter competition, which was eventually won by the Italian Fiat G.91. Despite the relatively problem-free development and testing of both the prototype and pre-production aircraft, not to mention its impressive performance envelope, in this competition the Baroudeur was deemed as being too radical for operation on a mass deployment basis, and as a result was never ordered into production.

In 1957 a British test pilot from the Aeroplane & Armament Experimental Establishment at Boscombe Down had the opportunity to evaluate the Baroudeur (in all, twenty-two pilots flew the type, including half a dozen from America). He

found that the controls were effective throughout the speed range, but a lack of harmony was present for small displacements at speeds above about 350 knots (649km/h). This was due to the increased sensitivity of the elevator and the rudder; in fact, at the highest speeds the elevator was so sensitive that it was easy to induce porpoising by over-controlling. The rate of roll was never very high and, although adequate for manoeuvring at medium airspeeds, it was becoming unacceptably low at the highest speeds. Also, the aircraft did not behave well as an aiming platform. Induced longitudinal short-period oscillations were slow to damp out and snaking occurred randomly under all flight conditions, being worse in turns.

The pilot found that the Baroudeur operated satisfactorily on grass strips, although taxiing on the skids was imprecise and caused grave doubts as to the capacity for precise ground handling on saturated surfaces, snow or sand. While the take-off trolleys would still be available to manoeuvre the aircraft on the ground, it was clear that difficulties would arise when several aircraft were operating at the same time.

By the time of the A&AEE trial Sud-Est had accumulated an impressive record of operation from a selection of different surfaces, including sand, snow and very rough ground, which indicated that the skid-equipped Baroudeur might be able to operate from terrain that would be impracticable for aircraft with conventional undercarriages, an advantage that could well outweigh its deficiencies in design and control. The A&AEE's tests showed that the Baroudeur's take-off distance without JATO or a bomb load when operating from grass was about 2,600 feet (795m) in zero wind, and 3,500 feet (1,070m) to reach an altitude of 50 feet (15m). Two 250kg (551lb) bombs, however, added around 125 yards (114m) to each of these figures. Using two JATO bottles, the aircraft needed 2,000 feet (600m) of runway to take off on dry ground and climb clear of a 50-foot (15m) obstacle. Choosing the skids for landing had minimal effect on the speed during the circuit because they had been so well streamlined.

The Baroudeur shown on display at the Air & Space Museum at Le Bourget is not an original aircraft. This static display example was cleverly salvaged from the military weapons practice range at Cazaux in 1979. Appearing very convincingly as a real aircraft, however, the display airframe is, in actuality, a blend of parts from all five of the Baroudeurs that were built. The forward and aft fuselage and right wing all come from the first aircraft, the left wing from another, and the centre fuselage and tail section are from the third aircraft. In mid-1954 test pilot Pierre Maulandi made an observation that is worth quoting since it reveals one of the big plus points of this aeroplane. Quoted in *Flight* magazine, Maulandi said that, for him, the Baroudeur 'had taken the worry out of jet flying. No longer did he have to start calculating where he could put down in the even of an engine failure as soon as he had taken off; now he knew he could land in any reasonably large field.' Had it become a production and service aeroplane it would have been interesting to see if the Baroudeur would have been a difficult aircraft to operate or not.

Sud-Est SE 5000 Baroudeur, powered by one SNECMA Atar 101D turbojet. Currently in storage and undergoing conservation at Dugny, France. *Chris Sandham-Bailey www.inkworm.com*

20 Sud-Ouest SO 9000 Trident I and SO 9050 Trident II (1953-1955)

Sud-Ouest SO 9000 Trident I

Registration: 01: F-ZWRY ('Y' on fuselage); 02: F-ZWSG 'G', lost during first flight
Span: 24ft 10in (7.57m)
Length: 47ft 2in (14.37m)
Wing area: 156sq ft (14.5sq m)
Max gross take-off weight: 12,125lb (5,500kg)
Powerplant: 2 x Turboméca Marboré, 882lb (3.92kN); later 2 x Dassault MD30 Viper, 1,642lb (7.3kN)
1 x SEPR Rocket 481, 9,920lb (44.1kN)
Max speed: Marboré: Mach 1.5; Viper: 1,060mph (1,707km/h), Mach 1.6
Ceiling: Marboré: 39,370ft (12,000m); Viper: 49,215ft (15,000m)

Sud-Ouest SO 9050-01 Trident II

Registration: 01: F-ZWTT ('T' on fuselage); 02: F-ZWTY 'Y'; 03: F-ZWTZ 'Z'; 04: F-ZWUK 'K'; 05: F-ZWUL 'L'; 06: F-ZWUM 'M'; 07: F-ZWUN 'N'
Span: 22ft 11in (6.98m)
Length: 41ft 8in (12.70m)
Wing area: 156sq ft (14.5sq m)
Max gross take-off weight: 13,007lb (5,900kg)
Powerplant: 2 x Dassault MD30 Viper, 1,642lb (7.3kN) (SO 9050 SE: 2 x Turboméca Gabizo, 2,425lb [10.8kN])
1 x SEPR 631 two-chambered Rocket, 6,615lb (29.4kN)
Max speed: 1,300mph (2,092km/h), Mach 1.92
Ceiling: 78,740ft (24,000m)

Lucien Servanty and his team of designers created the Trident series of aircraft in response to a requirement from the French Air Force for a lightweight single-seat high-performance supersonic interceptor capable of speeds of more than Mach 1 and able to reach approaching enemy bombers at altitudes of up to 49,200 feet (15,000m). NATO air forces also looked at the design for potential orders. These requirements came from the hard lessons of jet-powered aerial combat learned during airborne encounters in the Korean War, which had ended only two years earlier. Radical in layout, the Trident featured clean aerodynamic lines and was a relatively simple, lightweight aircraft employing turbojets for auxiliary power and a rocket motor for its primary thrust. Unusual elements were the mixed powerplant with wingtip-mounted turbojets and rockets in the tail, straight wings, and the location of all the flying controls in the tail. The aircraft was intended to be operable from rough and unprepared airstrips both for take-off and landing.

The aircraft had a pressurised cockpit that would detach as a unit in the case of an emergency, then parachute to earth. The finely pointed fuselage was very slender and had a circular cross-section; the main barrel section housed both types of fuel for the turbojet and rocket engines (including the jettisonable oxidant). All three members of the narrow-

With the top barrel of its SEPR 481 rocket engine firing for added thrust, the first SO 9000 Trident I rolls down the runway for take-off. *Copyright Musée de l'Air et de l'Espace, Paris/Le Bourget*

track tricycle undercarriage retracted into the fuselage. In the upper part of the rear fuselage section were the two air brakes, and the rocket engine was placed in the lower section. At the extreme end were the tail surfaces, which comprised three 'slab' controls turning about central hinge axes. The Trident thus had not only an 'all flying' tailplane, or 'ailavators' (not a true slab tailplane because of the anhedral angle and differential 'aileron' motion), but also an 'all flying' rudder, or 'slab fin'. Jacottet-Léduc irreversible servo controls and an autostabiliser developed by Ouest Aviation were used, and finally, also in the truncated tail cone, were the combustion chambers of the rocket motor and the brake parachute.

The straight and slightly tapered wings were set in the high mid-wing position and initially featured full-span high-lift flaps, but the flaps were later deleted after asymmetric deployment problems occurred during early flight testing. The aircraft's three tailplanes were each hydraulically boosted and articulated in their movement to provide yaw control with the vertical stabiliser, and a combination of pitch and roll control with the horizontal stabilators. In order to obtain a light but strong structure, new manufacturing techniques were adopted on the Trident, including the use of metal-honeycomb 'fillings'. As a result a breakdown of the weight showed that the fuel and oxidant weighed almost as much as the equipped airframe.

Two prototypes of the Trident were ordered on 8 April 1951, and the first of these flew for the first time on 2 March 1953; the pilot was Jacques Guignard. That flight was made solely on the power of two small wingtip-mounted Turbomeca Marboré II turbojets, each rated at 882lb (3.9kN) of thrust. After a successful inaugural flight the aircraft returned to its

The first Trident I taxies past the cameraman, in the process providing detail of the aircraft's spindly undercarriage and the anhedral given to the tailplane. *Wolfgang Muehlbauer*

home base at Melun-Villaroche airfield near Paris and was able to land on the grass strip with the aid of its low-pressure 'soft-field' tyres. The aircraft was first seen by the public at the Le Bourget Air Show in June 1953 after arriving on a short flight from Melun-Villaroche, but again on that occasion it was powered only by the auxiliary jet engines mounted at the wingtips, which ensured that the display was somewhat sedate.

The second prototype was written off on its first flight on 1 September 1953 when it was again piloted by Jacques Guignard. The aircraft failed to gain sufficient height on its climb-out from the runway in the very hot conditions at Melun-Villaroche, and after a long run it collided with a utility pole at the end of the airfield. Although he was seriously injured, Guignard recovered and later returned to flight testing the Trident. In the meantime, development continued with the first prototype, newly recruited test pilot Charles Goujon taking over piloting duties on the next flight, made on 16 January 1954. Goujon also made the first flight using the Trident's primary powerplant on 4 September 1954, the triple-barrel SEPR 481 liquid rocket motor providing 9,920lb (44.1kN) of thrust. The motor was developed by SEPR in cooperation with SNCASO and the barrels could be fired individually or in any combination. The aircraft now accelerated at a much higher rate, but on 26 October, on what was planned to be its sixth 'full power' flight, the rocket failed on take-off just after the aircraft had left the runway and with the undercarriage already retracted. Now flying on the thrust of only the wingtip-mounted Marboré

Pictures of the SO 9000 Trident I on the ground. *Wolfgang Muehlbauer*

X-PLANES OF EUROPE

Close-up of the SO 9000's rocket motor. *Wolfgang Muehlbauer*

A side view representation of the Sud-Ouest SO 9000 Trident I. *Chris Sandham-Bailey www.inkworm.com*

turbojets at maximum gross take-off weight, the Trident barely made it back to the runway. It was subsequently grounded.

More jet power was certainly required, and as a consequence Armstrong Siddeley Viper ASV 5 turbojet engines with 1,642lb (6.7kN) thrust, built under license by Dassault as the MD 30, were fitted to the Trident's wingtips. Now equipped with engines that offered nearly twice the power of the Turbomécas, the Trident I flew again on 17 March 1955. On 30 April the SO 9000 exceeded Mach 1 not only in level flight but also in the last stage of a climb, and without using the full power available from the rocket engine; indeed, it also exceeded Mach 1 in a shallow dive without using any rocket power. For its flying display at the Paris Salon a month later the aircraft taxied out for take-off using only the Vipers, only one of the three rocket chambers was used for take-off, and when the rocket fuel had been exhausted the aircraft flew past

Two flying shots of the first SO 9000 Trident I reveal the completely straight wing and the slim wingtip engine nacelles. *Wolfgang Muehlbauer*

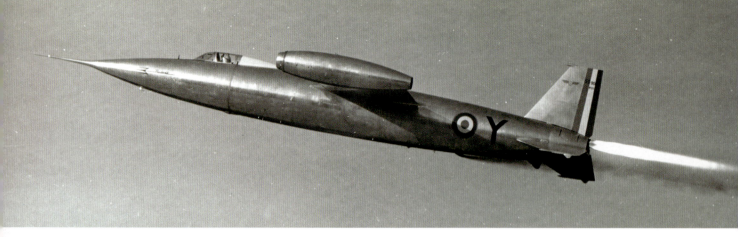

Another view of the SO 9000 in the air, this time firing its rocket motor. *Wolfgang Muehlbauer*

the crowds on the Vipers alone. An altitude of 52,000 feet (15,850m) was achieved in July.

The SO 9000 Trident I test programme ended on 10 December 1956, with the prototype having attained a top speed of Mach 1.63 – the highest speed flown by any piloted aircraft in Europe at that time. But nothing more could be achieved with this particular aircraft – something better was on the way. The SO 9000 had met its initial design objectives but was superseded by a more advanced development called the SO 9050 Trident II. The SO 9000 test programme had been conducted during 100 flights, with twenty-five of them made under rocket power. With rocket-thrust augmentation, speeds above Mach 1 were successfully achieved, but only in short bursts measured in seconds (i.e. less than a minute) rather than any sustained supersonic flight.

The logical next step

With the experience it had acquired from developing the unarmed and experimental SO 9000, the company now moved on to the SO 9050, two prototypes of which were ordered in 1954 as a fully armed missile-carrying light interceptor derivative. The objective was to produce an aircraft that could be used for interception at great heights at a short distance from its base, or for long patrol flights followed by a supersonic attack, and it was expected that the Trident II's high rate of climb would mean that it could reach a height of 50,000 feet (15,240m) in about 2.5 minutes after releasing the wheel brakes at take-off. This later version introduced many refinements, but one major change was the deletion of the ailerons and achieving lateral control by means of differential movement of the elevator halves. The Trident II also featured a smaller wing with reduced thickness and aspect ratio, the pilot's cockpit was enlarged, and a three-petal speed-brake configuration was relocated from the aircraft's wing to the rear fuselage. Additionally, taller struts were provided for the main and nose landing gear, providing more ground clearance on take-off and landing to permit a large air-to-air missile to be eventually carried under the fuselage on a centre-line pylon and ejector rack. A two-barrel SEPR 631 rocket motor with 6,600lb (29.3kN) thrust was fitted in the rear fuselage in place of the Trident I's three-barrel SEPR 481 – use of the rocket allowed for 4 minutes only at supersonic speed.

The first prototype SO 9050 was flown on 19 July 1955 by test pilot Charles Goujon, with its first flight under rocket power taking place on 21 December of that year. The second prototype flew on 4 January 1956, but was destroyed three days later during its second flight after experiencing an engine flame-out on each Viper; pilot Jacques Guignard was

Colour view of the first SO 9000 Trident I seen on public display, probably at the 1953 Paris Le Bourget Air Show. Note that the fairing behind the cockpit is painted white. *David Hedge*

Above left and above: The first SO 9050 fires up its rocket motor for a ground run, and then during flight. *Wolfgang Muehlbauer*

fortunately only slightly injured. A third prototype had meanwhile been ordered as a private venture and first flew on 30 March 1956. Ten weeks later a contract was placed for six pre-production aeroplanes, and a supplementary contract for four more aircraft followed, although the latter was cancelled on 24 October 1957 due to government funding cutbacks. Nevertheless, test flying now progressed relatively smoothly and safely well into 1957. On 8 January 1957 Charles Goujon established a new French speed record of Mach 1.96 at 15,700 feet (4,785m), but he tragically perished in SO 9050-01 several months later on 21 May when it was lost during a practice flight for the 1957 Paris Air Show. No cause for the explosion in flight that destroyed the aircraft was ever found.

The pre-production series SO 9050 Trident II SE differed from the prototypes principally in having 2,425lb (10.8kN) Turbomeca Gabizo turbojets in place of the Vipers, and provision for a radome nose-mounted AI radar system as well as a single weapon hardpoint on the fuselage centre line for a single Matra R 511 air-to-air missile. A different cockpit window arrangement providing better pilot visibility and an improved drag chute braking system were also installed in the first pre-production series Trident (the fourth SO 9050), which was first flown on 3 May 1957 by Jacques Guignard.

The first SO 9050 Trident II seen in flight carrying a Matra T10 air-to-air missile. *Wolfgang Muehlbauer*

The pre-production SO 9050 Trident II SE ('K') was the first to have Turbomeca Gabizo jets in the tip nacelles.

A Trident II climbs to the launch altitude in readiness for a test of the French Matra T-10 air-to-air missile, seen on the centre-line fuselage pylon. *Tony Buttler collection*

Responding to the ever-present threat of government budgetary cutbacks and to keep the aircraft in the public eye, Sud-Ouest engaged in a series of record flights for the Trident. Addressing the primary contractual requirement to climb rapidly to an established altitude, Sud-Ouest decided to go after the speed and altitude records held by the Nord Gerfaut (qv). On the first attempt test pilot Jacques Guignard took the Trident II to 49,000 feet (15,000m) in 2 minutes and 50 seconds. Four days later a new official record was established for an altitude run to the same height in only 2 minutes and 37 seconds, beating the Gerfaut's mark by 1 minute. On 19 April Guignard reached an altitude of 59,000 feet (18,000m) in just 3 minutes and 16 seconds, although, like the other records, this flight was considered technically unofficial since the aircraft had used its rocket power at take-off. Later the pilot rolled the Trident at Mach 1.8 with the controls fully deflected.

On 17 January 1958, during its brief career, the third Trident II pre-production prototype set a new world record when test pilot Roger Carpentier flew it to 74,803 feet (22,800m) and a maximum Mach number of 1.95, unofficially

This front three-quarter view of the Trident II displays the aircraft's clean lines and purposeful design. The relatively small diameter of the wingtip-mounted Dassault MD 30 Viper turbojet engines is evident in this photo. *Tony Buttler collection*

This rear view of the Trident II shows the three-chamber SEPR 631 rocket engines to best advantage. Note the use of anhedral on the aircraft's stabilators for maximum stability at high-Mach-number speed. *Musée de l'Air et de l'Espace, Paris/Le Bourget*

beating the record of 70,310 feet (21,430m) held by an English Electric Canberra B Mk 2, which had been boosted by a Scorpion rocket engine. Then Carpentier went on to reach the officially recognised record altitude of 79,452 feet (24,217m) in the aircraft on 2 May 1958 using a ballistic trajectory with the rocket motors being fired at an altitude of 35,430 feet (10,800m). His record lasted only five days, however, because US Air Force Major H. C. Johnson then took a specially modified, rocket-boosted Lockheed F-104 Starfighter, the NF-104A, to a record altitude of 110,000 feet (27,811m) over Edwards Air Force Base in California.

The SO 9050 Trident II undergoes a ground test firing of its SEPR 631 three-chamber rocket engine, which produced 6,630lb (29.5kN) of thrust. The rocket allowed for 4 minutes of sustained supersonic flight. *Musée de l'Air et de l'Espace, Paris/Le Bourget*

X-PLANES OF EUROPE

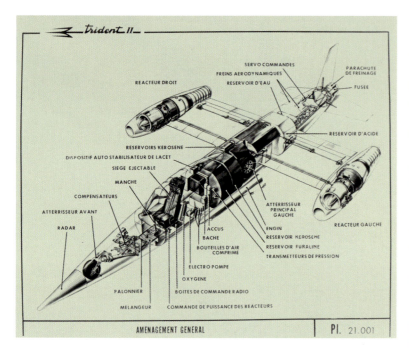

This cutaway rendering of the Trident II clearly shows the tightly packed components of this hybrid supersonic interceptor. *Copyright Musée de l'Air et de l'Espace, Paris/Le Bourget*

Despite these impressive aeronautical feats, the Trident programme was cancelled on 26 April 1958. At the time development work was under way on a version of the aeroplane called the Trident III with a thinner-section wing and higher-thrust afterburning Gabizo engines to give an even better performance. This variant was to be fitted with radar and was designed to reach speeds of Mach 2.3, but it was abandoned. Meanwhile, the incomplete SO 9050s were scrapped. In a press conference in May 1958 to announce that all further development of the Trident II was to be stopped, Georges Hereil, chief of Sud-Aviation, said that the aircraft's possibilities were 'far from exhausted but … it will no longer be possible to demonstrate them … because of restrictions in the national aeronautical budget'.

Instead of this hybrid jet/rocket aircraft the French government selected the Dassault Mirage as its choice for a new interceptor, reacting to the potential complexities of operating and maintaining a multi-engine aeroplane with rocket and jet engines. The two remaining flyable Trident aircraft were, however, sent to the Centre d'Essais en Vol (French Experimental Flight Centre) to perform research work, and on 8 July 1958 test pilot Jean-Pierre Rozier flew Trident II 06 to a new time-to-climb record, reaching 49,210 feet (15,000m) in only 2 minutes and 15 seconds. This figure could not be made public, however, due to serious concerns about the inevitable and unwelcome comparisons with the yet-to-arrive Mirage. The two Tridents were also used to give more pilots experience in flying high-performance aeroplanes at their maximum speeds at very high altitudes.

It should be noted that during this period of intense worldwide aeronautical testing and development, many American military test pilots flew a number of high-performance European aircraft during exchange programmes with the Empire Test Pilots' School at Farnborough in England and at the French military test facility at Istres near Marseilles. In this regard the Trident was flown and evaluated by US Air Force Capt Iven C. Kincheloe to gain experience before he was to fly the rocket-powered hypersonic North

A good assessment of the landing gear height can be seen here in this front view of the SO 9000 Trident II. The taller gear was employed to give greater ground clearance when the aircraft was carrying air-to-air missiles on its centre-line pylon. *Musée de l'Air et de l'Espace, Paris/Le Bourget*

The fourth of six SO 9050 Trident IIs rolls out on landing with drag chute deployed. Note the extended speed brake on the upper aft fuselage. *Musée de l'Air et de l'Espace, Paris/Le Bourget*

American X-15 as chief Air Force project pilot for that new research aircraft. Although Kincheloe did not particularly care for the Trident's marginal low-speed handling characteristics, he did enjoy the hybrid aircraft's high-speed manoeuvrability and spectacular rate of climb. In September 1956 he had become the first pilot ever to fly above 100,000 feet (26,000m), reaching 126,000 feet (38,405m) in the Bell X-2 rocket plane at Edwards Air Force Base.

In a grand finale of world records attained during the final days of the Trident's flight test programme, on 23 July 1958 a maximum-speed run of Mach 1.9 was achieved at 64,000 feet (19,500m), then on 6 October Rozier reach 85,300 feet (26,000m) during a flight that, with the Gabizos operating, was the highest altitude to be flown at that stage by a turbojet. It is understood that this was also the last flight made by a Trident. Finally, a maximum airspeed reading of Mach 1.97 was recorded on 23 July 1958 using highly calibrated and sensitive data-recording equipment on the ground, and with CEV test pilot Dominique Ferringo in the cockpit.

A most significant test and record-setting aircraft, the historic Trident I is now permanently displayed in the Hall of Prototypes at the Le Bourget air museum in Paris as a reminder of how remarkable this series of aeroplanes really was.

The first Trident II carrying what appears to be a dummy missile. Note how the mainwheel undercarriage doors leave a huge hole in the side of the fuselage. *Wolfgang Muehlbauer*

21 Rolls-Royce 'Flying Bedstead' (1953)

The Rolls-Royce Thrust Measuring Rig (TMR), better known as the 'Flying Bedstead', was, as far as is known, the first jet-lift aircraft to fly anywhere in the world. Its construction was first suggested by Dr A. A. Griffith of Rolls-Royce as a means of demonstrating the practicability of controlling a jet-lift vertical-take-off aircraft in hovering and low-speed flight, and to undertake research into the control powers and the degree of artificial stabilisation that such an aircraft would need. The aircraft, which was first known as the 'Jet-Borne Test Rig', was on the Secret List, and the TMR title was almost certainly used as a cover to disguise the real purpose of the research programme. It relied on jet lift (engine thrust directed downwards) rather than the use of aerofoil surfaces like wings or rotor blades, and, having no wings, would never travel very far horizontally.

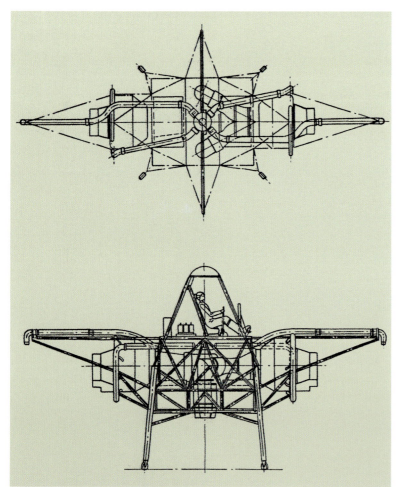

A drawing of the Rolls-Royce Thrust Measuring Rig. *British National Archives*

A novel idea

The Ministry of Supply research programme that resulted in two TMRs being built was opened in 1952. Both aircraft were assembled by the Rolls-Royce facility at Hucknall, although the first example's autostabiliser was designed and built at Farnborough. Their construction consisted essentially of a tubular framework inside which two Rolls-Royce Nene turbojets were mounted horizontally. Fuel tanks were fitted below the engines, a platform above carried the pilot and the autostabiliser, and there was a crash pylon, which was intended to protect the pilot in the event of the aircraft overturning. The TMR was 28 feet (8.53m) long and 14 feet (4.27m) wide.

In order to eliminate gyroscopic torque, the engines were mounted back to back and the jetpipes had right-angle bends with cascades to reduce the thrust losses in turning. The jetpipe from the forward Nene was bifurcated and terminated in two nozzles on either side of the larger single nozzle from the rear engine; these exhausts were deflected downwards directly underneath the TMR to supply vertical thrust. The thrust line from each Nene thus passed through the TMR's centre of gravity so that an engine failure would not result in any moment being applied. A four-leg long-stroke undercarriage

ROLLS-ROYCE 'FLYING BEDSTEAD' (1953)

The first Rolls-Royce Thrust Measuring Rig, or 'Flying Bedstead', is seen on display at RAE Farnborough's Golden Jubilee event held between 7 and 9 July 1955. *Phil Butler collection*

This nose view of XJ314 shows the side control nozzles or puffer pipes. It is assumed that the van parked next to the TMR was used to monitor the aircraft during its test flights. *Courtesy Jet Age Museum*

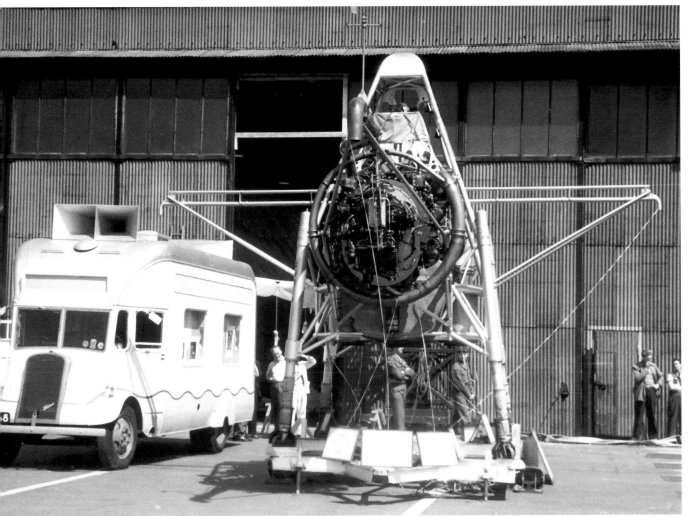

A three-quarter-angle view of XJ314 shows how the control nozzles were placed out at the aircraft's extremities. *Courtesy Jet Age Museum*

with small castoring wheels was used, and at take-off the TMR's maximum all-up weight was 7,650lb (3,470kg). The maximum thrust available from the engines (including jet control thrust) was about 8,100lb (36.0kN), which gave a nominal maximum thrust-to-weight ratio of 1.06:1 (in practice at take-off this was reduced by the recirculation of hot gas into the engine intakes).

The development of the control system was the main justification for building and operating the TMR. Normal aerodynamic forces and moments were absent, so had to be provided artificially. The TMR was controlled by air jets placed at its extremities, and these provided the moments located fore and aft for pitch and yaw control and on outriggers for roll control. A total of 9% of the mass flow of each engine was bled from the compressor and ducted through non-return valves to a collector box in the centre of the aircraft. It was then ducted through further pipes containing butterfly valves to control nozzles (puffer pipes) at the extremities. With the controls neutral, the pitch control nozzles produced equal thrusts of 290lb (1.29kN) each and the roll control nozzles produced 38lb (0.17kN) each. A control movement in pitch or roll then moved the corresponding pair of butterfly valves, increasing the thrust from one nozzle and decreasing that from the other, so that a control moment was produced without appreciably altering the total lift. The pitch control nozzles were pivoted about fore and aft axes, and movement of the rudder bar rotated them differentially, through a maximum of 30° each, to produce a yawing moment.

Translational moments of the aircraft were made by pitching or rolling it to produce a horizontal thrust component and therefore a horizontal acceleration. Height control was purely by means of the engine throttles, which were arranged so as to resemble the collective pitch lever of a helicopter. For the autostabiliser, while the yaw and height controls were purely mechanical, the pitch and roll controls were electrically signalled throughout with no provision for mechanical reversion. Hucknall also built a 'gantry' for use in the initial trials, in a form designed to offer no restraint to the Bedstead's movement within a restricted space while preventing it from going outside that space. The gantry also prevented the Rig from ever exceeding 10 feet per second (3.05m/sec) rate of descent, so a pilot in difficulty could close the throttles without fear of destroying the aircraft in a crash landing.

Flying on the spot

It was some time, November 1954 in fact, before the first TMR was recognised as a military 'aircraft' by the allocation of serial XJ314. Fuel capacity was 190 gallons (864 litres), which gave a flight endurance of about 11 minutes. With 50 gallons (227 litres) remaining, fuel warning lights came on, telling the pilot that about 3 minutes flying time was left, at which point the flight would be terminated.

The value of the gantry was demonstrated on 6 July 1953 during the first attempt to fly the TMR. In fact, it keeled over because the four undercarriage legs did not perform evenly – when the power was reduced, two of them retracted as required but the other pair remained fully extended, which put the rig off balance. After modifications had been made to the legs, the TMR first flew on 9 July with Wg Cdr J. H. Heyworth of Rolls-Royce aboard. The first series of flight tests was concluded on 19 November and the next set began on 31 January 1954. Gradually the degree of control was improved to the point where Capt R. T. Shepherd was able to make a first free flight outside the gantry on 3 August 1954. When Rolls-Royce's test programme came to an end in December 1954, XJ314 had made 224 tethered flights that totalled roughly 9 hours of flight time. Fifteen free flights were subsequently made (totalling 1 hour and 45 minutes flight time) up to 50 feet (15.2m). It had hovered in winds up to 20 knots (23mph/37km/h) and achieved a forward speed of 10 knots (11.5mph/18.5km/h).

By this stage experimental evidence was accumulating from the TMR and from model work at RAE that jet lift and control was likely to be satisfactory for the vertical flight phase. It was now thought desirable to investigate the transition from vertical to horizontal flight and vice versa, and the proposal to do so was the start point for the Short S.C.1 (qv).

In January 1955 XJ314 was transferred by road to RAE Farnborough, and in March, after receiving some modifications, it began a new series of trials. The practicability of controlling the aircraft had been demonstrated at Hucknall, but the Farnborough tests would investigate in depth the stability and control problems of a hovering jet-lift aircraft. On 21 June 1956 XJ314 was transferred to RAE Bedford where testing continued until 16 September 1957. On that day it was severely damaged in an accident. XJ314 was being hovered by Sqn Ldr S. J. Hubbard when part of the control system failed and the aircraft finished on its side. After basic repairs had

The 'gantry' that was used to restrain the TMR during the early part of its trials programme. *British National Archives*

It is uncertain if this image shows the first TMR XJ314, or the second XK426. However, it does show the original crash pylon over the cockpit and was taken at Rolls-Royce Hucknall. The jetpipes are just visible on the bottom of the main body. *Phil Butler Collection*

X-PLANES OF EUROPE

The presence of the tow tractor and the steps up to the cockpit confirm that XJ314 was indeed quite a large aircraft. *Author's collection*

been made it was sold to the Science Museum in London, England, in 1961.

The passing of XJ314 to RAE meant that Rolls-Royce was unable to continue its own jet-lift research, so in 1954 the decision was made to build a second identical 'Bedstead', known as TMR.2, and another gantry. It was serialled XK426 and received two Nene 103 engines (XJ314 had Nene 4s) and a new autostabiliser from Louis Newmark Ltd, which had been built using the original RAE drawings. A first tethered flight was made on 17 October 1955 and a first free flight on 12 November 1956. After XJ314's crash, and with Rolls-Royce's programme almost complete, XH426 passed to RAE Bedford's hands. However, soon after midday on 28 November 1957 Wg Cdr H. G. F. Larsen started the engines in readiness to make a test flight, but on opening the throttles XK426 climbed high up the gantry, then bounced back hard on the starboard rear leg. The throttles were opened again and the aircraft was handled very erratically before coming down at an angle hard on the starboard legs, which made XK426 crash into the gantry and fall on its side. Larsen appeared to have lost control and in the crash he hit his head on the gantry structure and was killed. It was a tragic end to the Flying Bedstead's career. Parts of the wreck were used to repair XJ314.

Results

The RAE's tests with the TMRs were made with varying amounts of artificial stabilisation (including a few without stabilisation) and showed that some artificial stabilisation was necessary in pitch and roll for operation in other than very favourable weather conditions. Yaw stabilisation was not essential for hovering flight. For safety reasons the TMR was not normally flown at the RAE unless the wind speed was 10 knots (11.5mph/18.5km/h) or less. A reduction in lift was experienced if the aircraft was tilted to counteract the effects of the wind. Very little flying was done in 'manual' because the pilots who tried it found that, while manual control was possible in good conditions, it required a great deal of concentration, particularly in roll.

The biggest problem in flying the TMR with artificial stabilisation was the height control, due to the slow response of the engines to throttle movements. The elderly Nenes were modified production units and their response to the throttle was slow when compared to newer specialised lifting engines (or with the response of a helicopter rotor to movements of the collective pitch lever). Once in the air, power had to be reduced to stop climbing, then, as the TMR descended, power would

Opposite: Detail shots of XJ314 taken at Farnborough in July 1955. The later version of crash pylon has now been fitted. Note the serial number painted down the right-hand undercarriage leg. *Courtesy Jet Age Museum*

The first TMR, XJ314, is pictured in flight with the undercarriage legs now pressurised to their maximum length. *Phil Butler collection*

have to be increased again. The art in hovering at a certain height was to pick the moment when to reapply or reduce the power. Once a pilot had mastered this difficult skill he had no real problems in flying the aircraft.

The RAE's main conclusion from its TMR trials was that any practical jet-lift aircraft must have some artificial stabilisation while hovering if it is to operate in other than very favourable weather conditions, and artificial stabilisation appeared to be essential in both pitch and roll. At this time (1961), the RAE and others felt that autostabilisation was essential for Vertical Take-Off and Landing (VTOL) aeroplanes (as it was for the Short S.C.1 – qv), but Hawker Aircraft had found a different way to provide the lift with its P.1127 design (qv) – vectored thrust. Hawker chose not to use high levels of autostabilisation (given their potential failure modes) but instead to rely on pilots compensating for the handling difficulties that resulted. It is understood that for a while this difference in opinion proved to be quite controversial between the parties concerned.

Flight in the TMR or Flying Bedstead was not necessarily pleasant or unpleasant, but it was described as difficult, and piloting required full concentration at all times. The main problem was height control, and the Nene didn't provide a rapid enough response, even at high power. The type of research undertaken by the Bedstead was eventually matched by similar efforts in France and Germany (featured elsewhere in this book) and in the Soviet Union with a test rig called the Rafaelyants Turbolyot. Later in America came the Lunar Landing Research Vehicle, or LLRV, which was developed as part of the Apollo space programme, and was also known as the Flying Bedstead. The TMR remains one of the most unusual aircraft ever built in the UK. It achieved much but demanded respect from its pilots.

22 Nord 1402 Gerfaut I and 1405 Gerfaut II (1954-1955)

Nord Gerfaut I (N 1402-01)

Registration: F-ZWSH ('H' on fuselage)
Span: 21ft 11in (6.68m), later 24ft 7in (7.50m)
Length: 32ft 6in (9.90m)
Wing area: 204.3sq ft (19sq m), later 279.6sq ft (26sq m)
Max gross take-off weight: 10,412lb (4,723kg)
Powerplant: 1 x SNECMA Atar 101 D 2, 6,173lb (27.4kN)
Max speed/height: Mach 1 at 32,810ft (10,000m)
Ceiling: 50,525ft (15,400m), maximum reached

Nord Gerfaut II (N 1405-01)

Registration: F-ZWUE ('E' on fuselage)
Span: 24ft 7in (7.50m)
Length: 37ft 4.5in (11.39m)
Wing area: 279.6sq ft (26sq m)
Max gross take-off weight: 11,860lb (5,380kg)
Powerplant: 1 x SNECMA Atar 101 F, 8,377lb (37.23kN); later 1 x Atar 101 G, 9,900lb (44.0kN) with afterburner
Max speed/height: Mach 1.13 at 35,435ft (10,800m)
Ceiling: 50,525ft (15,400m), maximum reached

The Gerfaut ('Gerfalcon') was developed to further the studies in delta-wing aerodynamics and design characteristics that the company had begun with various models and a glider test aircraft called the Arsenal Ars.1301. Designed by Jean Galtier, the Gerfaut was built as a single-seat research aircraft and was the first French delta-wing aircraft fitted with high-power engines.

Jean Galtier started his career in aviation with the Bernard company, then in the 1930s went to the Fouga company. In 1937 he moved to the Arsenal de l'Aéronautique (the one-time equivalent to the British Royal Aircraft Factory) at Chatillon-sous-Bagneux, where he designed the VG 30 series of piston fighters. After the war came the VG 70 research aircraft (qv) and the large VG 90 naval jet fighter. Unfortunately for Arsenal, the company lacked an experienced jet pilot, so little flying was done with the swept-wing VG 70, while both flying prototypes of the VG 90 were lost, one due to control-booster failure and the other from the undercarriage uplock releasing during a fast high-g manoeuvre.

For the next step Galtier was asked to devise a short-range interceptor that would combine high speed with a rapid rate of climb. His response had a delta layout because he felt this offered the best solution for obtaining sufficient wing area for climb and manoeuvrability, while at the same time having the necessary low thickness/chord ratio to delay the compressibility-drag-rise; it would also give enough structural depth to provide stiffness. As well as the usual wind tunnel work required for any new aircraft, the Gerfaut programme was as noted based upon full-scale glider testing using a wooden craft called the Ars.1301. This had been built originally with a swept wing to provide research

X-PLANES OF EUROPE

The Arsenal 1301 glider was originally fitted with a swept wing to test the configuration for a planned rocket fighter.

Right and below: It was then fitted with a 60° delta wing specifically to test the surface for the Nord Gerfaut and Griffon prototypes that followed.

The 1301 glider is photographed just after release from its tug aircraft, in this case a Sud-Est Languedoc.

for a now abandoned supersonic rocket fighter project called the Ars.2301, but for its Gerfaut work the 1301's swept wing was replaced by a delta, which was flown both with and without a canard trim plane. The glider employed wings of very low thickness/chord ratio and used a variety of tail configurations; for its flight tests it was air-launched by an aerotow using a Douglas DC-3 or a Sud-Est Languedoc transport. At this time information in the public domain on the Gerfaut was sparse, but it was an open secret that this glider model work was intended to assist the design of a small transonic fighter (although the Gerfaut was purely experimental).

The Gerfaut was virtually designed around an uninterrupted circular straight-through duct, which supplied air to an Atar turbojet. This simplified the air feed arrangement and was a key factor in the aircraft's excellent performance, but it gave an odd humped-back appearance to the aircraft itself. What the straight-through duct did was to allow the Atar 101 D to develop its maximum thrust of 6,200lb (27.6kN) with minimal duct losses, while the stubby fuselage with the cockpit placed on the top provided an excellent view for the pilot.

The wing had two main spars (swept back respectively at 28° and 6°), between which the main undercarriage legs retracted into the fuselage, a spar very close to and following the line of the leading edge, and a control-surface spar lying parallel with the trailing edge; these were supplemented with for-and-aft ribs and stiffeners. The use of elevators and ailerons on the wing trailing edge in addition to a trimming tailplane was an unusual combination, and in addition unconventional constructional methods were employed on this wing with a good amount of high-tensile steel within the structure. Each trailing edge carried a flap and a conventional powered aileron, both of minute dimensions owing to the small span. No leading-edge flaps or slats were fitted and the leading edge was very sharp; the wing held no fuel or equipment. Above the engine and duct was the superstructure housing the cockpit and the fuel, while the nosewheel of the Messier undercarriage retracted rearwards. There was a large fin, and the tiny delta tailplane was a one-piece all-moving surface. Air brakes were fitted on each side of the jetpipe and their leading edges were curved to fit snugly against the rear fuselage when they were open.

Colour view of the Nord 1402 Gerfaut I F-ZWSH ('H').

X-PLANES OF EUROPE

This front view of the Nord 1405 Gerfaut II shows the gaping maw of its nose air intake and the relatively thin delta-wing structure. Note the wide stance of the single-wheel, inwards-retracting main landing gear, which gave the Gerfaut excellent ground handling characteristics. *Copyright Musée de l'Air et de l'Espace, Paris/Le Bourget*

The Gerfaut's moderate gross weight also resulted in a low wing loading; in fact, the pace of construction moved ahead so rapidly that a 'high-speed' wing (with a span of 21ft 5in [6.5m] and area of 204sq ft [19sq m]) was completed ahead of a 'low-speed' version (of 24ft 7in [7.5m] span and 282sq ft [26.2sq m] area). Both wings had a sweep angle of 57.5° and a thickness of 5.5%, which made their wave-drag characteristics quite similar; the intention had been to let chief pilot André Turcat gather experience with the larger surface, then to fit the small one for subsequent high-speed trials. However, fortified by several hours of flying practice at Boscombe Down in England with the delta-wing Avro 707C (qv), he was able to perform all of the initial trials using the small wing. At the Paris Air Show of 1953 British test pilots from Avro were quizzed about the results of their findings flying the delta-wing Avro 707 family. On that aircraft span-wise flow anomalies were discovered that led to standard fixes such as the addition of longitudinal wing fences for improved performance and stability. The team from Avro invited the French design team to visit their factory, and that was when test pilot André Turcat was invited to fly the Avro 707C. He duly completed a brief course on deltas at Boscombe Down in the autumn of 1953.

Meanwhile, the design of the Gerfaut was started in September 1952 and the prototype was completed on 26 September 1953. The first taxi trials were made on 20 October and the first flight (by André Turcat from Istres) was performed on 15 January 1954. This was the first delta aircraft to be built in France and the maiden flight lasted 7.5 minutes, during which the undercarriage was not retracted. After the initial flight tests Turcat noted that only limited control was offered by the wing control surfaces, but he had begun to explore the aeroplane's inherent instability through experiments with pilot-induced oscillations.

First to Mach 1

On 3 August 1954, during its thirty-fourth and final flight in its original form, the Gerfaut became the first French aircraft to reach the speed of Mach 1 in level flight without any additional thrust augmentation (afterburning), eight days before the English Electric P.1 (predecessor of the Lightning fighter) achieved

this feat – indeed, the Gerfaut was the first aircraft in Europe to do this. On this sortie Turcat broke through the sound barrier while flying at about 34,000 feet (10,360m) over Istres, and of course he did not have the benefit either of additional rocket engines like the Trident I (qv), nor did he employ the stepped altitude technique used by the Dassault Mystère VIB fighter.

After this the Gerfaut I was fitted with the larger 282sq ft (26sq m) wing, in which form it became known as the 1402B or Gerfaut IB, the earlier arrangement now being known as the 1402A or IA. As such Turcat flew it for the first time in its new form on 17 December 1954. When first completed, the only major change was the wing itself, the root leading edge of which was joined to the fuselage at a more forward position (just ahead of the cockpit) than on the old wing. However, further modifications were added pretty quickly – additional fins under the rear fuselage to improve stability, two rows of vortex generators around the rear fuselage, and a large bulge around the fin root (which also housed the drag chute). The aircraft was also now equipped with an Atar 101 D turbojet engine offering 6,600lb (29.3kN) of thrust, and with its larger wing the Gerfaut IB went on the achieve a maximum speed of Mach 1.2 at 50,000 feet (15,240m) on two occasions in early 1955. On 26 October the aircraft was flown by André Turcat to a maximum speed of Mach 1.3 in a 65° to 70° dive starting from 50,000 feet (15,240m). Although the initial instrument readings indicated a speed of Mach 1.27 at 32,000 feet (9,910m), Turcat's skills as a test pilot came into play when a small peak was discovered on the instrumentation print-out to get the official centre to recognise an official true airspeed of Mach 1.3 for the record flight.

The Gerfaut IB went on to be evaluated by the CEV test pilot squadron in Bretigny (in the autumn of 1955), and in May 1956 it was used to flight test the new Nord 5103 air-to-air guided missile, which in service became the AA.20 (these were aerodynamic sorties only – the missile was not released). The aircraft was also employed towards the end of its career as the safety and photo chase plane during the flight test programme of the more advanced Nord 1500 Griffon I (qv). The Gerfaut I airframe made its last flight on 2 July 1959. One feature of this aeroplane in flight was a mysterious whistling sound heard only at certain speeds – it was some months before the cause was traced to the joint between the engine and the fuselage.

The second airframe

The final iteration of the Gerfaut series was the Nord 1405 Gerfaut II, which was at first equipped with an improved and more powerful Atar 101 F turbojet that produced 8,400lb (37.3kN) of thrust with afterburner. This second aircraft represented a considerable redesign over the original 1402, although in appearance it looked pretty similar to the first. However, it was longer, which brought improvements from the transonic aerodynamics point of view while also providing more room for fuel. The wing area was again increased, although the wingtips were now clipped. The Gerfaut II made its maiden flight from Istres in the hands of Michel Chalard on 17 April 1956, and the aircraft was found to be comfortably supersonic on the level while also possessing an excellent rate of climb.

As a result the Gerfaut II went on to claim a series of world time-to-height records from a standing start by reaching altitudes of 6,000 metres (19,685 feet) in 1 minute 17 seconds, 9,000 metres (29,528 feet) in 1 minute 33.7 seconds, 12,000 metres (39,370 feet) in 2 minutes 17.4 seconds, and 15,000 metres (49,213 feet) in 3 minutes 46 seconds, all accomplished in three flights made by André Turcat on 16 February 1957. (Turcat would later achieve more fame flying the Nord Griffon and Concorde supersonic transport.) Then on 28 February Michel Chalard set a time-to-height record for 3,000 metres (9,842 feet) of just 51.0 seconds. (Later in 1957 Chalard was tragically

This interesting view of the Gerfaut II shows the aircraft's 'double bubble' fuselage structure, with the turtle deck aft fairing of the pilot canopy seemingly mated to the more circular cross-section of the fuselage and engine casing below. *Musée de l'Air et de l'Espace, Paris/Le Bourget*

This in-flight view of the Gerfaut II reveals a four-piece 'flower petal' engine exhaust port. Note the rather pronounced clipped and squared tips on both the delta wing and horizontal stabiliser. *Musée de l'Air et de l'Espace, Paris/Le Bourget*

The Nord 1405 Gerfaut II takes to the skies. High-mounted cruciform tailplanes solved the problem of wetted area turbulence behind a low-mounted wing, blanking out an equally low-mounted horizontal stabiliser. Take-off speed was 195mph (312km/h) at maximum gross take-off weight. *Copyright Musée de l'Air et de l'Espace, Paris/Le Bourget*

An unusual modification to the Nord 1405 Gerfaut II was the addition of a small streamlined upper nose radome for testing the Aida airborne radar system. Note the two Dassault Mystère fighters in the background and the Esso fuel tanker truck. *Musée de l'Air et de l'Espace, Paris/Le Bourget*

killed in a crash of a Nord 2501 Noratlas transport.) The previous records held before these flights were made on 31 August 1951 by English test pilot Flt Lt Richard B. 'Tom' Prickett in a twin-engine Gloster Meteor fighter fitted with powerful Armstrong Siddeley Sapphire engines, and the Gerfaut's figures stood until they were beaten by a substantial margin by US Marine Corps Major Edward N. LeFaivre flying a delta-wing Douglas F4D-1 Skyray on 22 and 23 May 1958. In early June 1957 the record-breaking Gerfaut II was shown to the public at the Le Bourget (Paris) Air Show, Turcat performing two air displays during the event.

Subsequently the Gerfaut II was used in mid-1957 for advanced flight testing of the experimental AA.20 air-to-air missile, with releases being made over the Levant Isle firing range and launches at supersonic speeds of up to Mach 1.35. Supersonic launches were first made on 22 and 24 July, and at the same time the aircraft was fitted with the Atar 101 G turbojet capable of producing 7,000lb (31.1kN) of dry thrust or 9,700lb (43.1kN) in afterburner. Later the aircraft was used to test some of the equipment destined to go into the Nord Griffon, then, after the abandonment of the light interceptor programme and the concept of guiding those aircraft to their targets from the ground, it was employed testing nose-mounted radars. The Aladin intercept radar system was the first to be fitted (in May 1958), followed by an example of the Aida radar, in each case the equipment being housed in a fairing above the nose intake. The trials were undertaken by the CEV, which also made the Gerfaut II available to other pilots to give them experience in high-speed flight.

Despite its promising performance, the Gerfaut was never turned into a service aircraft for the French Air Force. The last flight of the Gerfaut II was made on 7 August 1959, and in 1961 both Gerfaut airframes joined their other pioneering French stable mates, the Grognard I and II (qv), to be obliterated as fixed ground targets on the National Military Test Range at Cazaux – quite an undignified end for France's first true supersonic aircraft. In some respects the Gerfaut series replicated the delta-wing research undertaken by the Fairey Delta 2 (qv), although the British aircraft was sleeker and had more in common with the Dassault Mirage series. The Gerfauts have been described as delicate aeroplanes and their aerodynamics did give some problems, but they were remarkable machines that certainly (in English-language publications at least) have never been given the attention and credit they deserve.

The Nord 1405 Gerfaut II F-ZWUE ('E') proceeds down the runway past a Sud-Ouest SO 4050 fighter-bomber. *David Hedge*

23 ONERA Deltaviex (1954)

ONERA Deltaviex

Registration: F-WBHA
Span: 11ft 2in (3.40m)
Length: 23ft 3.5in (7.10m)
Wing area: 53.76sq ft (5sq m)
Max gross take-off weight: 2,028lb (920kg)
Powerplant: 1 x Turboméca Marboré II, 880lb (3.91kN)
Max speed: 249mph (400km/h)

The very unusual one-off Deltaviex prototype was designed as a test-bed aeroplane by a team from ONERA, the Office Nationale d'Étude et de Recherches Aéronautiques (the French National Research Establishment), led by an engineer called Aliette; the aircraft's objective was to examine a variety of new ideas and devices for flight control. There was also the objective of evaluating the low-speed performance of a very highly swept 'arrow-shaped' wing, which of course was well suited for aircraft required to fly at high supersonic speeds. Despite its name this was not really a delta-winged aircraft, but instead featured a wing of 6% thickness that was swept at an angle of 70° at the leading edge. It is understood that the name 'Deltaviex' was just a pronunciation of 'Delta VX', this theory for the aircraft's official designation having been offered many years ago by *RAF Flying Review* magazine.

The all-metal Deltaviex was built in 1953 by SNCASO to the ONERA design. A Turboméca Marboré II turbojet was installed in the rear fuselage and the horizontal variable-incidence tailplane was also sharply swept and could be adjusted from +1° to -4°. To provide boundary layer control for the inner portions of the wings,

The very small ONERA Deltaviex research aircraft had a swept delta tailplane and very highly swept wings. Note the air intakes above the wings.

collector manifolds took bleed air from the engine compressor (2% in total) and vented it out through holes of 0.028 inch (0.7mm) diameter placed at the trailing edge of the flap. This was the first application of the jet flap principle to an aircraft (as opposed to the blown flap concept), and the amount of air blown could be varied between each flap, thereby permitting lateral control to be obtained by the use of differential pressure. (Jet flap was also examined by the Hunting H.126 – qv.) Both the elevators and the orthodox ailerons (the latter fitted for low-speed flight) were horn-balanced. This tiny experimental machine measured little more than 11 feet (3.35m) in span, weighed just about 2,000lb (907kg), and at different stages was fitted with three different cockpit canopies.

Prior to its first flight from Bretigny in 1954 the Deltaviex was mounted in the large wind tunnel at Modane to permit data to be collected to make a comparison against the results accumulated from subsequent flight testing (some reports suggest that this tunnel work may have occurred after its flying career had ended).

Left and Below: Two photographs showing the ONERA Deltaviex with what is believed to be the original cockpit canopy. The relative size of the pilot inside confirms just what a tiny aeroplane this was. *Michel Benichou via Wolfgang Muehlbauer*

X-PLANES OF EUROPE

The little research aircraft, which apparently was always painted in this pale grey colour scheme, comes into land to complete another test flight. *Michel Benichou via Wolfgang Muehlbauer*

The Deltaviex seen at rest after a new raised canopy had been fitted.
Michel Benichou via Wolfgang Muehlbauer

Robert Fourquet was the pilot who took the aircraft on its maiden flight, and the first sortie to be made with the air bleed system functioning fully also took place from Bretigny, on 21 September 1955. A report in *Flight* magazine in November 1956 stated that 'because of the sharp wing sweep the machine is sensitive on the controls and laterally unstable'. (The secret existence of the Deltaviex was first unveiled to the French press on 8 November 1956, by which time it had acquired a small dorsal fin.) Accounts suggest that at one stage the roll control appears to have been dangerously unstable, but flights with an automatic control proved successful in damping the roll. A good number of test flights were performed with the Deltaviex and the magazine's note added that 'having flown for a number of hours piloted by Fourquet, the Deltaviex is shortly to be scrapped'. However, in 1984 the airframe was discovered in a garage and today it still exists at Toulouse. It will hopefully be rebuilt as a full museum exhibit.

24 Payen PA 49 Delta (1954)

Payen PA 49 'Katy'

Registration: F-WGVA
Span: 16ft 11in (5.16m)
Length: 16ft 9in (5.10m)
Max gross take-off weight: 1,426lb (647kg)
Powerplant: 1 x Palas Turbojet, 331lb (1.47kN)
Max speed: 311mph (500km/h)

The Payen Model PA 49 Flechair, or 'Katy' (also known as the 'Delta Jet'), was the first French jet aircraft to be built with a delta wing. It was developed from the works of the noted French aeronautical engineer Roland Payen, who since 1931 had built up quite a track record producing various arrowhead-shaped aircraft designs, including the Payen 22 tandem-wing piston aircraft flown in October 1942. The miniature PA 49 research aircraft was essentially a scaled-down version of the proposed PA 48 Mars, and its cockpit was integrated into the airframe at the base of the vertical fin where it intersected the fuselage. The Mars, proposed to a French Air Ministry interceptor requirement in 1948, was to be a jet-powered flying wing aircraft with swept delta surfaces that would have a top speed in the region of 1,000mph (1,610km/h). Independent of government subsidy or sponsorship, Payen elected to move ahead with his own funding for the PA 49 project in the hope of producing and flying the first jet-powered delta-wing aircraft in France.

Registered as F-WGVA, the PA 49 was equipped with a very small Turbomeca Palas engine that provided only 331lb (1.47kN) of thrust. It was built entirely in wood and had a wing sweep angle on the leading edge of 55° and on the trailing edge of 27°. In fact, the swept trailing edge meant that the Katy was not really a true delta, but it also had no horizontal tailplane and that did make it a true tailless aeroplane. The wing, which featured full-span control surfaces with ailerons outboard and elevators on the inner portion of the wing, was blended into the fuselage and the air intakes for the Palas were placed in the wing root leading edge. The fin, which was situated directly behind the cockpit, was swept at 78° on the leading edge. Prior to its first flight, the Katy sported a low bicycle undercarriage with skids at the wingtips, but by the time it entered flight test it had been refitted with a fixed tricycle undercarriage.

When it came to being the first, however, luck was simply not on the side of Monsieur Payen. He was prevented from flight testing his aircraft until a regulation crash helmet could be obtained for his test pilot, Tony Oshenbein. Thanks to this critical delay, the PA 49 Katy finally flew for the first time on 17 January 1954, just two days after the Nord 1402 Gerfaut I (see above), but in doing so it had missed the distinction of becoming France's first jet-powered aircraft to fly with a delta wing. (Some sources give the PA 49's first flight as 16 December 1953, but in fact on that date the aircraft made a short hop only, something already practised several times by the Gerfaut by that time.) The PA 49 possessed only a fairly mediocre flight performance, especially at low speeds, but had further aerodynamic refinements been made to the aircraft, or had more powerful engines been available, such a limited performance might very well have been much improved.

X-PLANES OF EUROPE

The diminutive Payen Delta is shown off to the public. The name 'Katy' is painted on the red portion of the extreme nose. *David Hedge*

By late April 1954 the little aeroplane had been handed over to the CEV at Bretigny for trials, and it attended the Le Bourget Paris Air Show in late May 1957, by which time it had a spatted undercarriage. The modestly run flight test programme eventually accumulated an impressive total of nearly 300 flights, which confirmed the performance and flight characteristics of the small delta-wing aircraft, and also verified the effectiveness of the 'crocodile jaw' split-rudder configuration used for both yaw and airspeed control. This unique feature was also studied thoroughly for use on the Concorde supersonic airliner. Although the split-rudder design was not subsequently used on that aircraft, it was later successfully employed by the Rockwell International Corporation for the vertical stabiliser configuration on its fleet of delta-wing Space Shuttle Orbiters. Could Roland Payen have ever imagined the ultimate contributions to both French and international aviation made by his little experiment? Today, the Payen PA 49 is proudly displayed at the Musée de l'Air et de l'Espace at Le Bourget.

Author's note: I was privileged to meet Monsieur Payen, although rather unexpectedly. During a whirlwind tour of Europe to catch a chartered Concorde in January 1998, a stop at Orly Airport for lunch was in order. From that restaurant I could see a collection of classic aircraft across the runway representing a fair portion of French aviation history. There was a Sud Caravelle twinjet airliner, a Dassault Mirage supersonic fighter, a very rare Dassault Mercure transport, the magnificent Concorde, and a Payen aeroplane – all part of the Delta Museum collection. A short drive led me to the site, and upon arrival I began to take pictures of the various aircraft. Shouting down from the top of the Concorde's boarding stairs, the elderly curator of the museum vigorously insisted upon collecting the entrance fee before any photos could be taken. Later, during a tour inside the Concorde, the same 'curator' explained with great verve and enthusiasm exactly how he had designed the first French delta-wing aircraft. That gentleman was none other than Monsieur Roland Payen himself!

25 Fairey Delta 2 (1954)

Fairey Delta 2

Span: 26ft 10in (8.17m)
Length: 51ft 7.5in (15.73m) with probe
Gross wing area: 360.0sq ft (33.48sq m)
Gross weight: 14,532lb (6,592kg), maximum tested
Powerplant: 1 x RR Avon RA14R, 9,500lb (42.2kN) dry, 14,500lb (64.4kN) afterburner; both aircraft also flew with RA28
Max speed/height: Mach 1.82 at c37,000ft (11,278m)
Ceiling: At least 55,000ft (16,764m)

On 10 March 1956 the Fairey Delta 2 research aircraft smashed the World Speed Record over the South of England. This remains one of the finest achievements in British aviation history, but the Delta 2 proved to be an exceptional aircraft in pretty well everything it was asked to do. One aeroplane also became the high-speed test bed for the Concorde supersonic airliner.

Supersonic project

In August 1948 Fairey Aviation was officially requested to design an aircraft with a sufficient ratio of excess thrust to weight to enable it to fly at supersonic speeds. Fairey's proposals were completed in September 1948 and concluded that the requirements were best met by an aircraft employing very high sweepback on the wing and tail and powered by two reheated Rolls-Royce Avon engines. Fairey was subsequently asked to investigate the possibilities of a single-engined machine, and the research moved on to low-aspect-ratio delta wings. Advantages over the highly swept wing with tail were a low structure weight, the possible use of conventional control surfaces, more space for fuel and the undercarriage, and the elimination of early longitudinal instability. The studies eventually led to a 60° swept delta-wing layout called the Type V. This allowed a comparatively low wing loading, which was important to Fairey since the team had decided from the outset to try to design an aeroplane that would not only fly fast but would also handle well at low speeds and make no abnormal demands for take-off and

WG774 lined up, ready for take-off. *Author's collection*

X-PLANES OF EUROPE

A lovely view of WG774 banking away from the camera to reveal the famous delta wingplan. Author's collection

landing. The go-ahead was given on 16 May 1950. Two aeroplanes (WG774 and WG777) together with a static test specimen were ordered on 27 July, and Specification ER.103 of 29 September was written around the aircraft.

The Type V (later re-titled Delta 2) was expected to investigate the problems of flight at transonic and supersonic speeds up to Mach 1.5 and at least 45,000 feet (13,716m). Both prototypes were single-seaters with no armament, and the design resulted from a logical line of development encompassing the Delta 1 (qv), unmanned flying models, and numerous supersonic studies. Two impressive features were the wing's thickness/chord ratio, the lowest known anywhere when it was designed in 1949, and the hydraulically drooped nose, which could be angled down 10° to improve the pilot's view on the approach (a feature later revived on Concorde). The aircraft also had integral fuel tanks where the wings were sealed to act as fuel cells, the wings themselves being built in light alloy with stressed skin over three main and two supplementary spars. The powered flight surfaces stretched along the full length of the wing trailing edge, the inner surfaces serving as the elevators and the outer as ailerons. To minimise frontal area the fuselage was kept as slim as possible, just enough to enclose a Rolls-Royce Avon RA14R. Special aluminium forgings were used to provide strength around the engine, while the fin had a three-spar structure and a power-operated rudder.

The Mock-up Conference was held on 27 June 1950, but Fairey became so heavily involved in the urgent Gannet anti-submarine aircraft programme (another Fairey design) that construction did not commence until late 1952. The first flight was pushed back by a full year, and it was not until the middle of 1954 that WG774 was complete. It was then taken by road from Hayes to A&AEE Boscombe Down where, on 6 October, Peter Twiss took it on a

The first Fairey Delta 2 lands after its display at the Farnborough Show on 6 September 1955. Author's collection

WG774 is seen relatively early in its career before it had broken the speed record. *Author's collection*

25-minute maiden flight. There was little in the way of publicity, principally due to the need for security, but Twiss was pleased with the handling characteristics. A smooth test programme saw the speed increased slowly until Mach 0.9 was reached in November. Then on 17 November the engine stopped with WG774 at 30,000 feet (9,144m). Fortunately Twiss was able to glide back to Boscombe and, on breaking cloud at 2,500 feet (762m), found that he was lined up with the runway. He made a successful 'dead-stick' wheels-up landing, without the droop nose, which brought him the Queen's Commendation for Valuable Service in the Air. WG774 was damaged and, on return to Hayes, had to have the starboard wing replaced by the static-test specimen wing. Flying resumed in August 1955.

The first transonic run was recorded on 28 October in a shallow dive from 35,000 feet (10,668m) and was notable by its smoothness. After a gentle nose-down trim change at about Mach 0.95 there was no indication that WG774 had passed from high subsonic into supersonic flight except on the instruments. All early supersonic flying was made without afterburner, but even dry power was enough to take WG774 to Mach 1.1. When reheat was introduced, Twiss found that the acceleration after lighting was 'an embarrassment to accurate flight test results, which … gave the pilot a feeling of loss of control'. Virtually an 'on-off' selector, this had the effect of nearly doubling the available power at 36,000 feet (10,973m), and a more selective reheat control was clearly needed. It was also found necessary to light reheat during the subsonic climb, which resulted in the pilot experiencing what felt like 'a meteoric climb to altitude'. Overall, the early flight development went very smoothly, and four sorties per day were frequently achieved.

Fairey Delta 2, powered by one Rolls-Royce Avon 200. WG777 currently on display at RAF Museum, Cosford, UK. *Chris Sandham-Bailey www.inkworm.com*

When it first appeared, the new high-speed 'shape' of the Delta 2 must have impressed most people in the aviation world, despite so many other advanced aircraft designs having flown already during the 1950s. *Author's collection*

A wonderful record

During October 1955 it became increasingly clear that the Delta 2 was fully capable of beating the World Speed Record of Col Horace A. Hanes, who on 20 August 1955 had taken a North American F-100C Super Sabre to 822mph (1,323km/h). It was the ease with which the Delta 2 passed into the supersonic regime without the violent behaviour experienced by other aircraft in the transonic region that strengthened Fairey's determination to set a new record. In November, when the aircraft reached Mach 1.56, Fairey decided there was a sufficient speed margin available to push the record into four figures. Due to concerns that the Americans might go for 'the first over 1,000mph', once the attempt was under way the whole operation was kept 'in the dark' as much as possible. A cover story was actively promoted that proved to be so successful that many engineers working on WG774 knew nothing about these plans until two days before the first record attempt.

RAE Farnborough designed, produced and operated the timing camera and apparatus at either end of the course (which used the wing trailing edge as its reference point). Twiss had to fly exactly over the sight line of the cameras at a

Record-breaker! Test pilot Peter Twiss took WG774 to 1,132mph (1,822km/h) on 10 March 1956. *Bill Harrison collection*

specific altitude. The height rule tolerances meant an allowable difference of only 328 feet (100m) between the two 'entry gates', a problem solved by using a specially calibrated de Havilland Venom to measure the height as the Delta 2 passed by. This 'flying technique' for position error tests was a difficult air-to-air interception problem because the Venom had to take off at least 7 minutes before WG774. RAF radar vectored the two machines into suitable positions, but the process of getting the Delta 2 at the right position and height at the right moment called for meticulous timing and superb piloting skills. In addition, a natural contrail (condensation trail) was absolutely essential for the timing cameras to track the Delta and measure its speed, so prior to each attempt a Gloster Meteor made a meteorological flight to confirm the current condensation height (above which contrails would form). All record attempts were made at about 38,000 feet (11,582m).

After take-off from Boscombe, an economical climb and acceleration to the maximum dry thrust speed was made in a climbing turn. Reheat was then lit when the aircraft had been lined up with the 9.67-mile (15.56 km) course, which stretched between Chichester and RNAS Ford. For a successful attempt, two runs had to be made in opposite directions within 30 minutes of each other. Good weather was also needed, and on 7 March 1956 it cleared beautifully and held for several days. Seven pairs of test runs saw four-figure speeds recorded on each occasion, but technical problems with the ground equipment prevented useable results from being obtained. Finally, during an attempt on 10 March everything worked perfectly. The west-to-east run recorded 1,117.6mph (1,798.2km/h), the east-to-west 1,146.9mph (1,845.4km/h), giving an average 1,132.2mph (1,821.7km/h) and a mean Mach number of 1.731. Peter Twiss had advanced the World Speed Record by a remarkable 37%. The time spent in excess of Mach 1.6 was 2.8 minutes and the aircraft was still accelerating at the end of each run.

When the record was announced the popular press went crazy and worldwide the achievement was received with great enthusiasm. The Air Ministry's Stuart Scott-Hall was, at the time, in the United States and found that the Americans 'were quite astonished'. Capturing the record gave the British aircraft industry a huge lift. Twiss eventually conceded the record to a McDonnell F-101A Voodoo, which set a figure of 1,208mph (1,944km/h) on 12 December 1957.

On 24 June 1956 Wg Cdr H. Bird-Wilson of the RAF Staff flew WG774. On his second flight he lit reheat at Mach 0.88 and found that he accelerated to Mach 1.57 in just 2 minutes 20 seconds. The acceleration was 'extremely smooth', and once the transonic trim change had been trimmed out, he was impressed by the performance and by the responsive controls throughout the speed range. In June WG774 was used for interceptor trials, the first time a vehicle had been available to give ground controllers experience of supersonic aircraft. The SBAC Farnborough Show of 1956 was graced by the presence of both Delta 2s, which were flown together by Twiss and Gordon Slade.

WG777 began its flying career, again with Peter Twiss in the cockpit, on 15 February 1956. Apart from slight differences in equipment and instrumentation, and the removal of the underwing flap system, the second aircraft was identical to WG774. On 18 April it passed into the hands of RAE Bedford for use in high-speed measurement, stability and handling research. When these trials began, WG777 was powered by an Avon RA28 of 9,300lb (41.3kN) thrust dry and 13,100lb (58.2kN) with reheat.

Below left and below: These close-up detail shots show the Delta 2 on display at a Farnborough Show. Note the 'eyelid' style of jetpipe. *Author's collection*

X-PLANES OF EUROPE

WG774 is seen in landing configuration with undercarriage down and nose dropped. Note the long nosewheel leg. *Author's collection*

To France

There was now a necessity to perform supersonic testing at heights below what was allowed in the UK, so another venue was found at Cazaux near Bordeaux in south-west France. Agreement was reached with the French Air Ministry to use an Air Force station. On 11 October 1956 WG774 flew to Cazaux and in 4½ weeks completed fifty-one flights before returning on 16 November. A considerable extension of the flight envelope was achieved and valuable practical information on the intensity of sonic bangs on the ground was also obtained. All except five flights were made by Peter Twiss, the rest being flown by Gordon Slade, who brought the aircraft back to Bedford. One discovery made in France was difficulty with the Delta 2's transonic trim change, which previously was thought to be mild. Twiss reported that the change, which occurred at Mach 0.95, became more marked as the IAS was increased. This trim change had become a most unpleasant feature.

In the very smooth weather conditions over France, the opportunity was also taken to make some high-speed manoeuvres, which included turns of up to 4g at Mach 0.9 at 2,000 to 3,000 feet (610 to 914m). The maximum g that could be applied at supersonic speeds dropped from approximately 3g at 20,000 feet (6,096m) and Mach 1.3 to 0.75g at 3,500 feet (1,069m) and Mach 1.05. There was never any buffeting or instability during these supersonic manoeuvres. Rolling performance remained good up to the highest EAS/Mach number combination attempted, and a rate of 250° per second was attained on some high subsonic rolls.

After the Cazaux trials some extensive modifications were made to WG774. Then, between 19 August 1957 and 4 March 1958 a series of fifty-nine UK-based flights was made, which included preliminary work on a convergent/divergent reheat nozzle and 'zoom climbs' to higher ceilings. A number of climbs to more than 50,000 feet (15,240m) were made using a technique where the aircraft was accelerated up to the tropopause at a relatively high Mach number, pulled up 2 to 3g in a 20° to 30° climb, and held at that angle until the desired altitude was reached. A maximum 55,000 feet (16,764m) at Mach 1.25 was achieved after reheat was cancelled at 52,000 feet (15,850m). The aircraft continued to zoom for several thousand feet.

Another splendid image of WG774, taken prior to the aircraft's record in March 1956. *Author's collection*

To Norway

In 1957/58 plans were made for an Avon development programme, which required supersonic flights at a range of heights up to 40,000 feet (12,192m). The 30,000 feet (9,144m) limit for UK supersonic flight would again prevent a large portion of this programme from being completed at home, and this time French air space was not available. However, a Royal Norwegian Air Force offer to use air space over Hardangervidda, a vast wild and sparsely populated area north-east of Stavanger, was accepted. On 5 June 1958 WG774 flew to Sola to begin the research, which covered compressor blade strain gauging, the investigation of centre bearing loads, and intake pressure distribution plotting. Low-altitude supersonic trials took place between 5 June and 2 July, and twenty flights were made covering the envelope between Mach 1.25 at 7,000 feet (2,134m) and Mach 1.6 at 40,000 feet (12,192m). WG774 returned to Bedford on 2 July.

Other work planned for WG774 in 1958 included testing various nozzles (an ejector nozzle, a ventilated nozzle, and a simple convergent-divergent nozzle), wing leading edge pressure-plotting to correlate with RAE's work on WG777 below thrust boundaries and energy climbs, and transonic flutter tests. In 1959 it was used for more trials before, in 1960, going to Bristol to be rebuilt as the BAC.221 (qv). During 1957 WG777 was used for aerodynamic tests at supersonic speeds, but the work also covered lateral stability, performance, pressure-plotting and kinetic heat trials. WG777's 1958 programme included the measurement of thrust and drag throughout the aircraft's Mach range, wing pressure-plotting, the examination of dynamic stability, the study of buffet at subsonic and transonic speeds, measurement of wing and fin loads with strain gauges, and research into kinetic heating on the wing. When WG777 was released from service on 27 June 1966 it had completed 429 flights.

Another September 1956 display image. It appears that all of the Delta 2's public performances were undertaken by WG774 because few, if any, such pictures show the second aeroplane. *Author's collection*

In the mid-to-late-1950s Fairey proposed several fighter projects based on its Delta 2. None were ordered and the firm never flew a jet fighter, but the two Delta 2s experienced long and immensely successful careers. The maximum speed ever reached by the type was Mach 1.82 (Peter Twiss to the author, 1998) at about 37,000 feet (11,278m), but the lack of fuel was a limiting factor. Higher speeds, however, would have brought other problems such as high skin temperatures. The author was also told that 0 to 40,000 feet (12,192m) in 4 minutes was possible with reheat. The Delta 2 was the last fixed-wing type to be designed and built by Fairey and proved to be a superb research aircraft. It was not built to set records, but was used over a long period to collect a tremendous amount of supersonic knowledge; however, the Delta will always be remembered for pushing up the World Air Speed Record by such a huge margin.

WG774 prepares to take off for another display at Farnborough. The aircraft's all-metal finish shows through in many photos. *Author's collection*

X-PLANES OF EUROPE

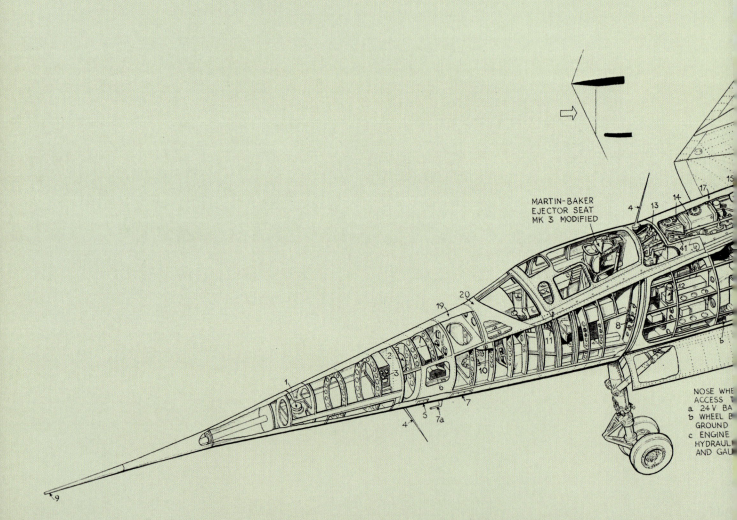

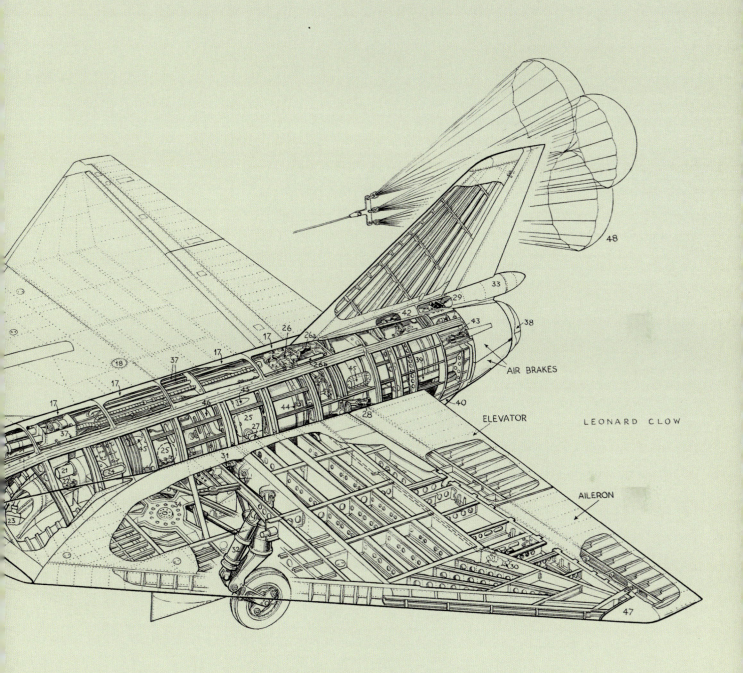

X-PLANES OF EUROPE

A beautiful publicity photograph that was probably taken prior to the 1956 Farnborough. This angle shows detail of the wing root air intake arrangement. *MoD*

Below and opposite top: WG774 was repainted in 1957 as the 'Holder of the World Absolute Speed Record'. Easily seen is detail of the droop nose and how the nose undercarriage doors had to be opened to permit the nose to drop. In black and white this scheme looks very attractive, but in fact it was a mauve/pink colour, which some thought was a ghastly choice for any aeroplane. *Ministry of Defence*

One of the relatively few photographs known to exist showing WG777 during its service life. Such rarity is probably due to the machine having spent most of its time in Ministry hands, and consequently it did not attend many air shows. By 1956 WG777 had been painted in an attractive blue colour scheme. This shot was taken at Thurleigh (Bedford) between 1957 and 1959. *Author's collection*

A three-view drawing of the Fairey Delta 2. *Author's collection*

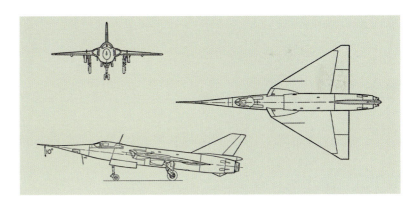

Photograph of the first Delta 2 WG774 taken sometime during the late 1950s when the aeroplane was flying with RAE. *Clive Rustin*

183

26 Nord 1500 Griffon I (1955) and Griffon II (1957)

Nord Griffon I (N 1500-01)

Registration: F-ZWUX ('X' on fuselage)
Span: 26ft 7in (8.10m)
Length: 47ft 8.5in (14.54m)
Wing area: 344.1sq ft (32sq m)
Max gross take-off weight: 13,992lb (6,347kg)
Powerplant: 1 x SNECMA Atar E 101 F2, 6,500lb (28.9kN) dry, 8,377lb (37.2kN) with two-door 'eye-lid' afterburner
Max speed/height: Mach 1.30 at 28,000ft (8,535m)
Ceiling: Unknown

Nord Griffon II (N 1500-02)

Registration: F-ZWUI ('I' on fuselage)
Span: 26ft 7in (8.10m)
Length: 47ft 8.5in (14.54m)
Wing area: 344.1sq ft (32sq m)
Max gross take-off weight: 14,870lb (6,745kg)
Powerplant: 1 x SNECMA Atar E 101 E3, 7,715lb (34.3kN)
1 x Annular Ramjet, 15,250lb (67.8kN)
Max speed: 1,448mph (2,330km/h), Mach 2.19
Ceiling (achieved): 59,055ft (18,000m)

Nord Aviation produced the Griffon series of experimental research prototypes (Nord 1500-01 and -02) as the next-generation aircraft after its supersonic Gerfaut 1400 series. The Mach 2 Griffon was the company's ultimate response to a 1953 directive from the French Air Ministry requesting the development of a high-performance manned interceptor aircraft capable of eliminating high-speed enemy aerial threats during the Cold War. Two prototypes were ordered in August 1953.

From the beginning of the programme this research aircraft was considered to be ahead of its time. The overall configuration featured a virtually straight flow-through barrel-section fuselage that was fitted initially with just an Atar turbojet. But later this conventional powerplant was augmented with a ramjet engine that fired in conjunction with the turbojet. The well-proven 60° sweepback delta-wing design flown on the Gerfaut series served as the main wing, and small, fixed delta-shaped canards (foreplanes) were fitted to the aircraft's nose section just below the cockpit to augment stability in the pitch axis. The great advantage of these surfaces was that, as the centre of pressure moved aft when the speed of sound was reached, the nose plane could be used to lift the nose instead of depressing the tail, thereby adding lift at a critical time. The foreplane was in fact a simple fixed surface that provided a nose-up moment to counteract the nose-down trim change produced by the delta wing as it approached sonic speeds.

Roll and pitch control were derived from elevons on the wing (the aircraft had no separate horizontal stabilator), and low-pressure tyres, flaps and a braking parachute would enable the Griffon to operate from many types of airfield. Despite the fact that these were unarmed experimental research aeroplanes, the Griffon was designed to meet the French Air Force performance and operating requirements for being able to take off from a 3,000-foot (914m) grass runway, respond immediately to

These left and right profile views of the Nord 1500 Griffon I show the unique lines of this revolutionary aircraft. *Tony Buttler collection*

launch, and intercept and kill any aerial threat. Consequently, there was space in the nose for a radar, and a pressurised cockpit and the fuel storage area were located in a hump above and forward of the air intake.

The Griffon's design resulted from tests and studies begun in 1953 by the Aviation Arsenal Establishment (which was subsequently integrated with the Nord Aviation Company). From the beginning the engineers at Arsenal, while adopting the same general form of delta as their English colleagues at Avro, Boulton Paul, Fairey and Gloster, used it quite differently. Much of the English work centred on 45° delta wings with a chord of 8 to 10% (some of the aircraft concerned feature elsewhere in this book), but Nord had already started working on the Gerfaut I (qv) with a wing of 60° and a chord of 5%. A delta wing of this angle (and of 4.5% thickness/chord ratio) was adopted in 1953 for what became the Griffon, and at the time was probably unique among modern wing designs in that it was first tested out on a glider. Actually, the word 'glider' only indicated the absence of an engine; its flying qualities as a glider were not good even in the strongest of thermals, and the aircraft resembled an electric iron more than it did a flying machine. The flights performed by the Arsenal 1301 glider fitted with a delta wing, released at 21,000 feet (6,400m) after a tow by a four-engine SNCASE SE 161 Languedoc transport aircraft, were short and the landing required a considerable amount of skill on the part of the pilot, but the information acquired from these flights proved to be extremely useful to the Griffon (and the preceding Gerfaut). This glider has of course already been referred to earlier in this book. The designer of the Gerfaut, Jean Galtier, was also the man most responsible for the design of the Griffon.

A turbojet giving high thrust at low speed paired with a ramjet matched to high Mach numbers was not ideal, and Nord improved upon this by employing a common air intake for both engines. With a variable-area ramjet nozzle, the compressor did not impose its law on the common air intake and could make full use of the high intake efficiency provided for the ramjet. In a programme split into two stages, the aircraft was to fly first with an afterburning SNECMA Atar F and no ramjet, after which a ramjet was to be disposed about a SNECMA Atar E3 with 7,700lb (34.2kN) of thrust. It was decided to test a small turbo-ramjet built around a Turboméca Palas, but a scale model was first tried based on a combustion chamber from a Sud-Ouest SO 1100 Ariel helicopter. Both units were tested extensively at Gatines and Modane, the Palas unit reaching Mach 0.8 in free stream in the huge tunnel at Modane-Avrieux in 1954. A decision to equip the second Griffon airframe directly with the turbo-ramjet was taken at an early stage. During this time of rapid technological advancement, with scores of radical new aircraft concepts being proposed worldwide almost monthly, the only other advanced interceptor aircraft in development that featured such an innovative hybrid turbojet/ramjet powerplant was the all-titanium delta-wing Republic XF-103 Thunderwarrior built in the United States. That extraordinary aircraft, however, never moved past the mock-up stage and was cancelled in 1957.

The Griffon I (Nord 1500-01)

At the start of the project the aircraft was actually named Guépard ('Cheetah'), but by mid-November 1955 (after its maiden flight, in fact) it had been renamed Griffon (due, it is understood, to the merger of SFECMAS with SNCAN to form Nord Aviation). The Griffon I was actually equipped initially with a single Atar 101 G21 turbojet with afterburner, but later flew with the uprated Atar E turbojet, which was capable of producing 8,398lb (37.3kN) of thrust. The main purpose of the Griffon I arrangement was to experiment with the high-speed mode of the engine. It was first flown on 20 September 1955 (as the Guépard) piloted by French test pilot André Turcat, and although the aircraft was somewhat underpowered compared to the later Griffon II it still managed to reach supersonic speed, achieving Mach 1.15 on its first supersonic flight on 11 January 1956. The maximum speed achieved during the test programme was Mach 1.30 at 28,000 feet (8,560m). Although the initial flight tests encountered difficulties with engine performance above 30,000 feet (9,144m), the aircraft's overall handling characteristics were generally judged to be excellent.

While testing the soft-field operating characteristics (and just prior to the aircraft's delivery to CEV for evaluation), on 19 June 1956, André Turcat suffered an accident when the nose gear collapsed as he took the aircraft across a grass field (in a test required by the covering specification). This brought a six-week delay to the flying programme and the Griffon I did not get airborne again until 26 July. Plans for adding a ramjet to the Griffon I in its original configuration were never carried out, but for a few flights it did have its rear fuselage temporarily modified in a more bulky form to permit an assessment to be made of the aerodynamic behaviour of the forthcoming Griffon II. The heavily worked first prototype's flying career came to an end with Flight 156 on 16 April 1957.

A classic chase plane view of the Nord 1500 Griffon I prototype in flight high over the French countryside. *Tony Buttler collection*

This front view of the delta-wing Nord 1500 Griffon I shows the original air intake diameter for the aircraft's single Atar E 101 F turbojet, which in full reheat produced 8,398lb (37.3 kN) of thrust. *Copyright Musée de l'Air et de l'Espace, Paris/Le Bourget*

Below and top next page: Views of the original Griffon I with the small air intake. *Wolfgang Muehlbauer*

The Griffon I seen after landing with the drag chute deployed. *Wolfgang Muehlbauer*

Opposite side rear views of the Griffon I. *Wolfgang Muehlbauer*

This in-flight view of the improved Nord 1500-02 Griffon II gives a good comparison of the deeper aft fuselage dimensions and larger air intake diameter of the later aeroplane. *Tony Buttler collection*

Griffon II (Nord 1500-02)

Nord built this airframe directly as the Griffon II (Nord 1500-02) by installing an Atar 101 F engine of 7,735lb (34.3kN) thrust into the 59-inch (150cm) barrel section fitted within the ducting for the ramjet. The exhaust of the Atar turbojet exited into the Nord-designed ramjet exhaust rings. This aircraft also differed from the original design in having a larger-diameter air intake and a rear fuselage that was longer and deeper; the former characteristic anhedral tail surfaces were deleted, and the siting of the braking chute was altered (from the dorsal back of the rear fuselage to a position just below the small-area rudder). There was also the addition of an integral onboard electronic computer designed to regulate the fuel flow rate of 8,800 gallons (334 litres) per hour required by the ramjet when running at full power; this device automatically regulated the throttle settings relative to altitude and speed. Finally, the peculiar geometry of the fore part of the Griffon's fuselage necessitated the use of straight boundary layer fences, which on the Griffon I appeared above the intake and were joined to the bottom of the cockpit nacelle; on the Griffon II these fences were now curved due to the increased intake diameter.

This three-quarter front view gives a good indication of the Griffon II's vast aft fuselage area, which housed the turbojet/ramjet powerplant combination. Unique 'Griffon II' nose art is also visible on the forward fuselage. *Tony Buttler collection*

The record-setting Griffon II poses on the ramp with the prototype of a new series of aeroplanes that would emerge as France's most successful fighter design, and one of the world's most revered fighter aircraft, the Dassault Mirage III. *Musée de l'Air et de l'Espace, Paris/Le Bourget*

Being such a different type of power unit, the ramjet presented a difficult case for a test programme. Its functioning demanded a high-velocity airflow, so in the first instance its test bench had to be a wind tunnel. In addition, the scale of dimensions was a major unknown variable in the problems of combustion, so a scale model could not be used in the tunnel – it had to be a full-size engine. Further, the supply of air was a problem as important as that of combustion, so it was the aircraft itself that had to be tested in the tunnel (bearing in mind that the velocity of the air blown into the engine must be that for the aircraft). At the time of the Griffon's development few tunnels of that size existed and they were only capable of providing piecemeal results. Consequently, as far as its burning conditions were concerned, the ramjet, as the main propulsive power of the aircraft, was still an unknown factor the day the Griffon II first took off to light up the ramjet. The need to design a practical aircraft that would take off and return under its own power led Nord, like ramjet pioneer René Leduc previously (qv, Leduc 0.10, 0.16, 0.21 and 0.22), to place a turbojet in the belly of both the ramjet and of the aircraft, thus creating the combined turbojet/ramjet.

The first flight of the Griffon II was made on 23 January 1957 at the Istres test base in the hands of test pilot Michael Chalard. A standard routine was that the Griffon II would take off and climb out using turbojet thrust and the ramjet would be switched on when flying on the level or in a slight dive. Although ramjet power could only ever by used for just a few minutes, such was the available thrust that high supersonic Mach numbers were achieved very rapidly indeed. The man in charge of the whole flight test operation was engineer Bernard Curis.

The ramjet was first lit in April, Mach 1.0 was exceeded in May, and by December of that year the aircraft had reached Mach 1.85. That figure was attained at 42,000 feet (12,802m), surplus thrust still sufficing for a climb of 28,000 feet per minute (8,534m/min) at that point. Further Mach increases were slow because the limits of the turbojet were being approached, but the Mach 2 area had become a fact by October 1958, the turbojet being throttled back at Mach 1.8; Mach 2 itself was exceeded on 24 October, just three days after the turbojet-powered Dassault Mirage III had achieved that feat. By March 1959 kinetic heating effects on the Griffon II's airframe structure (built mostly in Dural TO 4 G-1 aluminium alloy) had limited an extension beyond the figure of Mach 2.1 at 61,000 feet (18,593m) – and still accelerating – reached so far. However, on 13 October 1959 the aircraft achieved Mach 2.19 (equivalent to 1,448mph/2,330km/h) at an altitude of 50,000 feet (15,240m).

Opposite: This is the Nord 1500-02 Griffon II's larger-diameter air intake for its Atar E 101 E3 turbojet, which produced 7,735lb (34.4 kN) of thrust. Although smaller than the Griffon I's turbojet, total thrust on the Griffon II was augmented by the use of an annular ramjet engine producing 15,290lb (68.0 kN) of thrust. This potent powerplant combination pushed the Griffon II to several world records. *Musée de l'Air et de l'Espace, Paris/Le Bourget*

Photographs showing the Nord Griffon II in flight.
Wolfgang Muehlbauer

The Griffon II's ultimate claim to fame, however, was perhaps the shattering of a world record held until that time by the Douglas XF4D-1 Skyray fighter. That aeroplane, piloted by US Navy Lt Cdr James Verdin, had flown a 100km closed circuit at an average speed of 753.4mph (1,211km/h). By comparison, the Griffon II flown by André Turcat achieved a blistering 1,020mph (1,643km/h), and in recognition of this feat he was subsequently awarded one of the highest American honours, the Harmon Trophy. This was the highest speed ever recorded at that time in Europe, and to achieve the 100km record the Griffon II carried an underfuselage drop tank to increase its range, the tank being jettisoned prior to lighting the ramjet. Several forms of tank were flight tested and the extra fuel proved vital in achieving the highest speeds. The US Air Force was also very interested in the study of supersonic flight by this dual-mode propulsion system and funded some of the Griffon II testing up until 1960. As part of this effort US Air Force Capt Iven C. Kincheloe made four flights in the Griffon in late April 1958, only a few months before his untimely and tragic death in the crash of a Lockheed F-104 Starfighter in the United States.

After pushing the top speed to higher and higher figures, the test team moved on to a wider study of the aircraft's flight characteristics. In particular the effort looked into acquiring more control of the ramjet, although later the tests also embraced the effects of kinetic heat on the structure. Nord engineers encountered the greatest difficulty in trying to reduce the flux of exhaust gasses in the ramjet operating mode. The engine only produced either full thrust or nothing at all, with shutting down the ramjet as the only option while still accelerating beyond Mach 2. The ramjet offered 80% of the total 9,260lb (41.2kN) of thrust at 45,000 feet (13,716m), and 5,510lb (24.5kN) thrust at 52,000 feet (15,850m). Frequent damage was sustained by the jetpipe, which required regular dismantling for repairs, although as control of the ramjet grew this problem began to disappear. Plans for a Mach 3-plus Super Griffon would have brought an all-welded steel structure to remedy that problem.

By 1960 the rate of test flying had dropped off considerably thanks to reduced levels of finance being made available to the project; in fact, there were no flights at all between February and July of that year. The Griffon II did attend the June 1959 Paris Air Show and the record-breaking aircraft's flying display included a vertical climb with the ramjet lit. Some of its final flights were made at the 1961 Show, and the test programme came to an end on 5 June 1961 after 337 test flights had been completed.

Nord 1500 Griffon II, power plant one ATAR 101E-3 turbojet and one Nord Stato-Réacteur ramjet. Currently on display at the French Air and Space Museum, Le Bourget, France. *Chris Sandham-Bailey www.inkworm.com*

A hypothetical view of how the Griffon might have looked in a typical scheme of the French Air Force during the 1960s. *Chris Sandham-Bailey www.inkworm.com*

Here the second Griffon is seen at one of the two Paris Air Shows which it attended. *Wolfgang Muehlbauer*

A rival to the Griffon was the pure turbojet-powered Dassault Mirage III, seen here standing alongside the Nord aircraft. The Mirage III went on to achieve spectacular sales both in its home country and abroad. *Wolfgang Muehlbauer*

Neither the Griffon I nor Griffon II was ever fitted with operational tactical military equipment. Nord pursued studies for a Mach 3 'Super Griffon', but that advanced design was never ordered and the engine that would have powered it, the Super Atar, with its 19,850lb (88.2kN) thrust, was also abandoned. The prototype Griffon II now resides at the Musée de l'Air et de l'Espace at Le Bourget Airport near Paris, while famed French test pilot André Turcat had to wait 15 years to break his own speed record when he flew the Concorde at Mach 2.02. In that aircraft Turcat also beat his personal-best altitude record with a flight to 73,000 feet (22,250m). Several French and foreign pilots flew the Griffon II and remarked on its smoothness and the insensitivity of its intake system to high incidences. Acceleration could be maintained in turns and it was that capability that largely accounted for the 100km closed-circuit record performance. Deliberate extinction of the ramjet did not disturb flight, ramjet fuel/air mixture could be varied in flight, the ramjet could be lit over a wide speed range, and (very fortunately) there was no unfavourable interaction between the two engines. In fact, the flying qualities came as a pleasant surprise and showed themselves to be exceptionally right from very low speeds for this type of aircraft (110 knots, 204km/h) up to the maximum attained.

Rare colour view of the Griffon II taken during its flight test programme. *David Hedge*

In 1959 André Turcat wrote of his experiences of flying the Griffon (in *Shell Aviation News* magazine). He reported that the only difference between the Griffon I and its successor fitted with the ramjet was the size of the air intakes and outlets, the air consumption having to be tripled as a result of adding the ramjet. In fact, the narrowness of these orifices on the Griffon I caused some real difficulties. For example, the Griffon I displayed rolling characteristics that were very different with the afterburner lit from those without it – good in one case, frankly horrid in the other. These characteristics led Nord to install ventral fins on the smaller outlet as a temporary measure, but the results were inconclusive.

During early flying up to 32,500 feet (9,905m) and Mach 0.65 trials were made with all forms of 'lighting up' and 'putting out', and sometimes the pilots saw a flame completely detached from the ram and several yards/metres behind it, joined only by a fine thread of light to the so-called combustion chamber. Flight tests with the ramjet also had to be carried out in a rather special way, which resulted from the fact that thrust increases as the square of the speed, a well-known characteristic of the ramjet. Thus, until such time as speed, thrust and drag had reached their optimum adjustment, the power output continued to grow with speed, in such a way that the increase of thrust was even greater than the square of the speed, although increase in drag was only proportional to speed. Consequently, the aircraft would continue to accelerate throughout any given test, in contrast to the performance of other types of aircraft, which reached their maximum speed at a rate that became slower and slower as the maximum was approached. The pilots, therefore, had to take care to ensure that the ramjet did not take the Griffon outside the safety limits fixed for the specific test they were performing.

With the ramjet the Griffon could 'barrel roll' or make tight turns at supersonic speed without any reduction of speed. In fighter combat, loss of altitude in a manoeuvre was equivalent to disengagement – what was termed the margin of manoeuvre. This was reached when the supplementary aerodynamic drag – induced drag – absorbed the surplus thrust available at the Mach number in question. Here the ramjet had the great advantage, like the rocket, of conserving this surplus intact, if not improved. The margin of manoeuvre also remained intact, the Griffon continuing to accelerate in tight turns at high Mach numbers.

In spite of the unknown factors that had existed at the moment of the first lighting up, test results gave the Nord test team the impression that the combined turbo/ramjet was unequalled as tomorrow's propulsion unit for European interceptors, but of course that did not prove to be the case. In fact, the Griffon programme was eventually discontinued in favour of aircraft powered by a more conventional means of propulsion – turbojets. The visual and audible images of the aircraft in flight remained, however. One eye-witness stated that the Griffon II climbed 'like a bat out of hell', and the roar of the ramjet 'engulfed the 'drome leaving one deafened and speechless!' Without doubt, for its time the Griffon II was one of the most spectacular and impressive aircraft in the world.

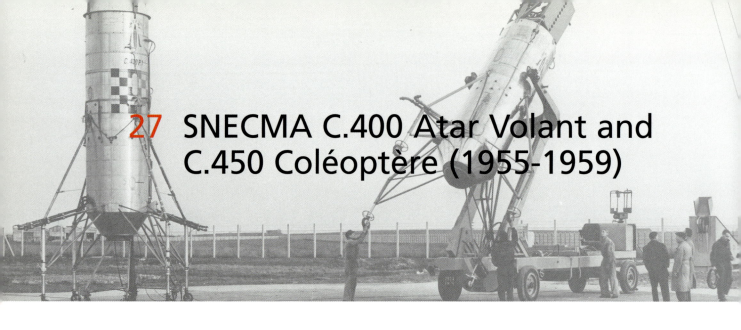

27 SNECMA C.400 Atar Volant and C.450 Coléoptère (1955-1959)

SNECMA C.400 P-2 Atar Volant

Registration: F-ZWUZ
Total height (with landing gear installation): 27ft 4.5in (8.34m)
Fuselage height: 19ft 8in (6m)
Fuselage diameter: 4ft 11in (1.50m)
Max gross take-off weight: 5,732lb (2,600kg)
Powerplant: 1 x Atar 101 DV, 6,395lb (28.4kN)

SNECMA Coléoptère C.450-01

Span (circular wing diameter): 10ft 6in (3.20m)
Length: 26ft 4in (8.02m)
Max gross take-off weight: 6,614lb (3,000kg)
Powerplant: 1 x SNECMA Atar 101 E5V, 8,160lb (36.3kN)
Max speed (intended): 497mph (800km/h)
Ceiling (intended): 9,850ft (3,000m)

SNECMA (Société Nationale d'Étude et de Construction de Moteurs d'Aviation), the National Company for the Design and Construction of Aviation Engines, worked on an entirely new application of turbojet power to solve the problem of VTOL performance. The company simply mounted a pilot on top of a vertically situated jet engine and created an aircraft that resembled a stovepipe, but which lifted vertically off the ground. The craft used an Atar engine, the name of which came from Atelier Aéronautiques de Reichenbach, an aeronautical workshop in the city of Reichenbach, Germany, where in the months following the end of the war German turbojet technicians and engineers had gathered together to form a team in the former Dornier factories within the French occupied zone. Their new engine was initially derived from the wartime BMW 003 design but was larger and more powerful and was to be built by SNECMA. The Atar was a single-shaft turbojet and the first Atar 101 was ground tested on 26 March 1948; it was to be built subsequently in many versions over many years.

The idea of a vertical-take-off aeroplane with an annular (ring-shaped) wing came from another German engineer, Helmut von Zborowski. During the war Zborowski had been in charge of rocket development at BMW and was responsible for the existence of the nitric acid/aniline motor used widely for guided missiles. With the conflict over he went to France and worked for the Société d'Études de la Propulsion par Réaction (SEPR) before establishing his own company, the Bureau Technique Zborowski, or BTZ, which subsequently led to his involvement with the Coléoptère. BTZ was created in 1952 but was formally incorporated as 'Société Anonyme BTZ' in 1957. The name Coléoptère means 'Beetle', but this particular aircraft had more in common with a 1950s science-fiction novel.

The following ground views of the same scene show the tether rig attached to the top of the C.400 P-1 and the C.400 P-2 being erected into launch position. Note for scale the size of the ground personnel. The P-2's pilot cockpit stood more than 25 feet (7.6m) off the ground.
Musée de l'Air et de l'Espace, Paris/Le Bourget

The basic idea was to utilise the lift of an annular wing that housed and guided the propulsive jet and was characterised by an internal flow duct, a thin aerofoil section and a low aspect ratio. In addition to aerodynamic lift, the propulsive jet would produce a lifting component when at incidence (incidence in this case referring to the direction of gravity, with lift regarded as a force opposed to gravity).

Engine manufacturer turned aeroplane maker

The early stages of SNECMA's interest in VTOL aircraft followed the usual path of model testing, using a SNECMA Ecrevisse pulse-jet with 100lb [0.44kN] thrust, wind tunnel work, the development of a gyro-stabilisation system, then the use of a test bed craft. The latter was built to assess the problems of propulsion, control and stabilisation and their application to VTOL, and embraced remote-controlled tests in a safety gantry, tethered tests with a pilot, then piloted free flight tests. The model tests started in March 1954 with the Ecrevisse placed at the centre of an annular framework, and were performed inside a hangar with the models on remote control. In 1955 a special vertical test rig was built to trial an Atar's oil system for duration-running in the vertical position; gimbal-rig tests were also made on the effectiveness of Atar jet deflection devices, and there were mobile bench investigations into ground effect. After all of this preparation into the basic problems of single-engine vertical flight control, an Atar was installed into a 'flying' engine/fuselage housing named the Atar Volant, or 'Flying Atar'.

In fact, four different test bed machines were eventually constructed, the first three of which were designated C.400 P-1, P-2, and P-3, while the final iteration was the C.450-01, a more refined, fully enclosed cockpit-equipped aeroplane-style design. The construction of the first full-scale Atar Volant test bed was begun in 1955, and the four 'aircraft' to be built can be described in more detail as follows:

C.400 P-1:

This was a pilotless remotely controlled research vehicle formed around a single gimbal-mounted Atar 101 DV turbojet producing 6,400lb (28.4kN) of thrust. It was fitted with a jet-deflection nozzle for directional control, mounted vertically inside a nacelle, and the entire structure sat on a tubular four-wheel undercarriage. An annular fuel tank was placed around the centre of the nacelle, with radio control equipment above it, and the vehicle was equipped with gyroscopic stabilisation control. The C.400 P-1 was first tested on a special gyroscopic ground rig in 1955, then flight tested while safely tethered in a specially built gantry in 1956 to investigate stabilisation and the influence of the wind. In all a total of more than 250 flights were made (under the remote control of pilots Lucien Servanty and Auguste Morel) to study the craft's basic stabilisation and handling near the ground in hovering flight. The early stages of this work culminated in the C.400 P-1 successfully completing its official French Air Ministry acceptance test in September 1956.

C.400 P-2:

This was another test rig similar to the C.400 P-1 but with a platform positioned above the engine intake at the top of the fuselage to accommodate an open cockpit for a pilot. This included an ejection seat, an instrument panel and basic 'flight' controls, although the craft could only hover in ground effect. Directional control was obtained by using jets of engine bleed air, which were strong enough to turn the craft laterally on its castering wheeled landing gear. Annular tanks containing 1,102lb (500kg) of jet fuel surrounded the cylindrical engine compressor casing, which gave the test machine an endurance of slightly more than 4 minutes at sea level. Weight at take-off was 5,730lb (2,600kg), 90% of the thrust of the Atar at peak rpm, and on 8 April 1957 this machine successfully completed its official acceptance tests flown tethered under a special safety gantry by company test pilot Auguste Morel.

The C.400 P-2's first free (untethered) flight took place at Mélun on 14 May 1957, again with Morel aboard, and this was undertaken without the aid of special launching or landing devices. The 'aircraft' then stole the 1957 Paris Air Show at Le Bourget in June when Morel sat down in the cockpit, fired up the turbojet, and rose in a thick cloud of dust and noise. The now-hovering test rig skulked across the main runway in a hover, was tilted forward and aft by approximately 20°, and spun around quite rapidly on its vertical axis. The grand finale for this performance was a climb to an altitude of 500 feet (152m), then a controlled descent, which left the aviation-savvy crowd literally gasping for breath. To the casual observer the tubular aircraft with its lone pilot sitting exposed to the elements seemed distinctly unsafe, but the very fact that he could manoeuvre the aircraft in this manner was an undeniable achievement. By June 1957 a height of more than 1,500 feet (460m) had been reached, and by the spring of 1958 the P-2 had made a total of 123 tethered and free flights. In addition, on 13 September 1957 the C.400 P-2 was flown by a civilian pilot, Pierre Voisin who was also a reporter for the French newspaper *Le Figaro*.

C.400 P-3:

This was the final development of the C.400 P-2 and was built around an Atar 101 E turbojet with 7,700lb (34.2kN) thrust. Fitted with a tilting ejection seat mounted inside an enclosed cockpit, this machine more closely resembled an aeroplane – at least the forward fuselage of an aeroplane – but it did not have lifting surfaces. However, to test the effects of airflow on the craft's jet exhaust during simulated rapid vertical descents, this version was also mounted horizontally on a high-speed railcar with its tailpipe facing forward. It was then towed down the track at speeds between 25 and 50mph (40 and 80km/h). The C.400 P-3 was essentially built as a full-scale but non-flying Coléoptère and in fact it only ever 'flew' in the wind tunnel and on the train.

The Atar Volant was one of several turbojet-powered VTOL aircraft from around the world that were built specifically to supply the answers to the problems of stabilisation and directional control, although unlike the Rolls-Royce 'Flying Bedstead' (qv) the Volant had just the one power unit (mounted vertically, unlike the Bedstead's horizontal Nene units). Consequently it was susceptible to the gyroscopic toppling moments incurred when the engine's axis or rotation was moved through an angle.

The Coléoptère: a revolutionary experimental aircraft

Flight testing of the P-3 was followed by the addition of an annular wing to the 'flying' fuselage. This was a Zborowski design and based on SNECMA's acquisition in May 1956 of the European rights to the patents of the Bureau Technique Zborowski 'Coléoptère'. The aerodynamicist on the aircraft was Dr W. Seibold, who was well known for his work in both German and French research establishments. The effort undertaken by BTZ had actually begun back in 1950 and embraced a lot of tunnel and model research.

In 1958 the West German government disappointed the British and French aircraft industries by ordering an American aircraft instead of British or French interceptors for the re-established German Luftwaffe. Instead of a suitable European design, the German Air Force ordered the supersonic Lockheed F-104 Starfighter. Even though this aircraft was regarded as an interim interceptor, it was believed that at some point an advanced high-performance VTOL fighter would be developed. A vertical take-off and landing capability would eliminate the need for miles of long concrete runways at fixed (and vulnerable) air bases, and would turn any section of road or open field into a potential launching pad. A fast time-to-climb for this VTOL aircraft was also a mandatory requirement because West Germany would experience only the shortest of warnings should an aerial attack ever originate from points east, such as the Soviet Union.

With the Coléoptère, a major step towards the development of this new VTOL interceptor appeared to have been taken. At one stage the French Ministry of Defence reported in Bonn that it had awarded 'a secret development contract to a French firm for a new type of vertical-take-off fighter'. Development work on this project had been going on in France for more than six years, with SNECMA working closely with Nord Aviation, since both companies were integral parts of the newly structured national French aircraft industry. Like its pioneering test bed predecessors, the Coléoptère was essentially a jet engine adapted to run while situated in a vertical attitude relative to the ground. It would sit on its tail while on the ground, and had a small, enclosed fighter-like cockpit mounted as the craft's forward fuselage above the cylindrical aft engine and circular wing. In the United States work had been under way for years on similar types of VTOL interceptors, such as the Lockheed XFV-1 Salmon and Convair XFY-1 Pogo. Both of these aircraft were developed for the US Navy and were powered by geared turboprop engines driving contra-rotating three-blade propellers. (Only the Convair Pogo ever successfully transitioned from vertical to horizontal flight, and back again.) The first US pure-jet VTOL fighter concept was the delta-wing Ryan X-13, which for ground transportation was mounted on a truck bed; this was then raised to permit the aircraft to fly away vertically and to land vertically. The Coléoptère was also mounted on a raised truck bed-type of ground vehicle – in other words it had its own special trailer to allow it to be moved horizontally across the ground. However, it differed from the X-13 by taking off from and landing on the ground, and it derived its lift strictly from an annular wing surrounding the engine casing.

This photo shows the Coléoptère being erected into the vertical position in preparation for a hovering flight test. The yellow ground transporter and handling apparatus closely resemble the truck bed used to transport and erect the US-built Ryan X-13 Vertijet. Unlike the French VTOL test aircraft, the X-13 completed successful transitions from vertical to horizontal flight and back again for landing on its vertically positioned truck bed. *Pierre Boue via J. C. Carbonel*

Another major difficulty was in having a precise and reliable method for balancing the aircraft on its hot column of exhaust gasses emanating from the engine during take-off and landing. Even more important was the need to control precisely the transition from vertical to horizontal flight and back again. Aerodynamically, the aircraft had no appreciable forward momentum during these transitions, and had the engine ever flamed out the pilot would have had no choice but to eject immediately or plummet to the ground in the rapidly descending aircraft. SNECMA already had some experience with directional control of high-speed airflow by mechanical means by utilising metal fins mounted directly in the jet exhaust. The problem with this technique was that it took several long seconds before control authority would take effect on the aircraft's attitude. This was completely unacceptable near the ground, when the aircraft's stability depended on rapid response to control commands by the pilot. SNECMA engineers therefore developed a unique directional control nozzle that consisted of a number of auxiliary jets using engine bleed air and completely surrounding the outlet of the main engine. These nozzles essentially deflected and diverted the main jet exhaust blast to achieve rapid directional control for the aircraft.

An additional engineering challenge was overcoming the torque created from the spinning turbine compressor blades inside the vertically situated engine. To augment directional control, four swivelling cruciform rudder fins were mounted at the bottom of the annular ring, just above the four struts of the aircraft's castering landing gear. The complete engine assembly weighed 5,600lb (2,540kg), yet the jet engine could produce 7,700lb (34.2kN) of static thrust. With its thrust-to-weight ratio now defined as being greater than 1:1, a complete vertical lift-off by the aircraft from a standing position on the ground became feasible.

An experienced test pilot with a sensitive touch could control the Coléoptère's basic hovering flight with careful operation of the stick and throttle. It would take superhuman effort, however, to control both pitching and rolling

X-PLANES OF EUROPE

Half-aeroplane, half annular-wing-and-engine, the C.450 was an odd-looking but purposeful design. Note the pilot's ejection seat tilted forward 20° for better visibility and ground reference when the aircraft was in vertical flight during take-off and landing.
Pierre Boue via J. C. Carbonel

Opposite:
This photograph of the Coléoptère in hovering flight shows good detail of the pilot's 'down view' window below the cockpit, used for aligning the aircraft when it was near the ground. Note the four tapered and swept-back stabilising fins to be used when the aircraft was in high-speed horizontal flight.
Pierre Boue via J. C. Carbonel

One can only imagine the noise levels that would have been experienced by anyone this close to the aircraft, which had to be running at near full power. *Pierre Boue via J. C. Carbonel*

forces at the same time. An automatic stabilisation system was therefore required for safe, controlled flight. This consisted of a complex system of gyroscopes and gyro meters, which detected the aircraft's movements on all three axes and operated the jet steering system. Directional nozzles counteracted tilting, while auxiliary air jets compensated for any tendency of the aircraft to rotate about its own axis while situated in a vertical attitude. Overall, the Coléoptère required a very intricate and very complicated flight control system just to maintain stable flight, and the seat tilted and rotated in the cabin to permit the pilot to be seated horizontally

Ground view of the Coléoptère loaded aboard its transporter. *Pierre Boue via J. C. Carbonel*

C.450 Coléoptère powered by one SNECMA Atar 101E.V turbo. *Chris Sandham-Bailey www.inkworm.com*

throughout all of a flight. Nevertheless, judging heights and distances was a formidable challenge for the pilot. After his experience with the C-400 P-2 Morel did not have too much trouble dealing with height (in metres) during a landing, but altitude (in dozens of metres) was just another matter! Helicopters were used to provide him with altitude indicators.

The C.450 Coléoptère made its first vertical take-off on 17 April 1959. The initial tests on the ground were followed by tethered flights, then free flights began on 5 May. The third free flight was made on 20 June and soon afterwards final preparations were underway for an attempt at a transition into horizontal flight. Indeed, before the Coléoptère could be considered a truly successful VTOL fighter concept it had to demonstrate that the annular wing could make the difficult transition from vertical to horizontal flight, and also support the aircraft successfully in horizontal flight. The aircraft also had to demonstrate convincingly that it could accomplish the much more difficult task of transitioning from horizontal flight back into a hover, then perform a stable tail-first landing. On 25 July 1959, while attempting to transition from vertical to horizontal flight at an altitude of 300 feet (91m) above the Melun-Villaroche Air Base near Paris, the Coléoptère departed from controlled flight, crashed and was burned out. Test pilot Auguste Morel ejected successfully from the tumbling aircraft but was injured. The loss of the sole Coléoptère put an abrupt end to the flight test career of this unique and revolutionary flying machine, as well as the French quest for VTOL flight using a single vertical turbojet powerplant. Plans for further aircraft developments with annular wings were also brought to an end.

SNECMA's experiences with the Coléoptère firmly demonstrated that vertical flight with an aircraft powered strictly by its engine in a vertical attitude (and without a standard wing to provide lift in flight) represented both formidable and insurmountable control problems. With the loss of the Coléoptère, the American Ryan X-13 was left to hold the title at that time as the world's only successful jet-powered VTOL fighter prototype to take off vertically, transition from vertical to horizontal flight and back again, and land vertically on a predetermined spot powered only by its main engine.

28 Saunders-Roe SR.53 (1957)

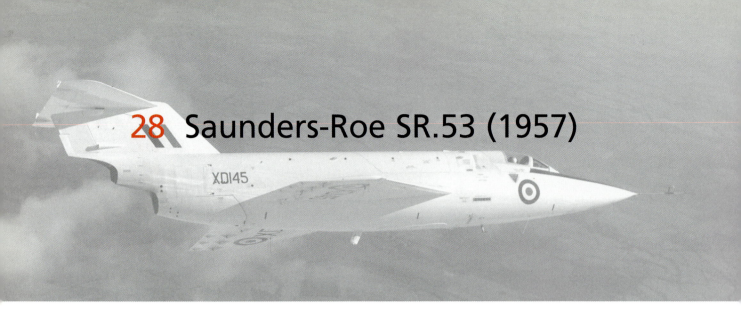

Saunders-Roe SR.53

Span: 28ft 1in (8.6m) with wingtip AAM

Length: 46ft 4.5in (14.14m)

Gross wing area: 271.3sq ft (25.23sq m)

Gross weight: 20,238lb (9,180kg) overload

Powerplant: 1 x de Havilland D.Spe.1A Spectre, 7,000lb (31.1kN); 1 x AS Viper 101, 1,640lb (7.3kN)

Max speed/height: estimated Mach 2.1 at 60,000ft (18,288m); maximum achieved Mach 1.46

Ceiling: maximum achieved 56,900ft (17,343m)

During the Second World War the German Messerschmitt Me 163 Komet rocket fighter left a huge impression on Allied Air Forces through its phenomenal speed and rate of climb. By the late 1940s new fighters powered by the first generations of jet engines were still offering a performance that was inferior to the Komet because a jet engine did not provide enough power at altitude. Aircraft drag is reduced with increasing altitude, but at the same time a turbojet loses its efficiency; however, at height a rocket motor becomes more effective. In fact, it was calculated that a rocket-powered fighter or interceptor might cut time to height by as much as 80%, be capable of faster acceleration, and have a ceiling of at least 80,000 feet (24,384m). For the late 1940s and early 1950s these were extraordinary possibilities, and plans were drawn up for a rocket interceptor to meet the threat of enemy aircraft penetrating UK defences at very high altitudes, at heights beyond the reach of other interceptors.

The outcome was the SR.53 from the Saunders-Roe Company (Saro) based at Cowes on the Isle of Wight. This aircraft was designed from the start as a service type, but its inclusion in this book is explained by two factors:

- It used a power source (a rocket motor) that had only previously been tested on existing types like the Hawker P.1072 trials aircraft adapted from a P.1040 prototype. The SR.53 was the first all-new British design to be built with a rocket motor powerplant (although as explained later a turbojet was also fitted).
- In due course the SR.53 became a research and trials airframe for the later and larger Saro SR.177.

Rocket power

British research into rocket motors was opened in 1946 on two types, the Armstrong Siddeley Snarler and de Havilland Sprite. However, these units were not flight tested until 1950 and 1951, by which time both firms were developing more powerful motors with 8,000lb (35.6kN) of thrust called, respectively, the Screamer and Spectre. In January 1952 the Air Staff issued a requirement for a rocket-propelled interceptor under Specification F.124T. This was perceived as a last-ditch defence to high-flying enemy aircraft with an outstanding rate of climb (sea level to 60,000 feet [18,288 m] in 2½ minutes). Armament was to be a battery of 2-inch (5.1cm) air-to-air rockets and de Havilland Blue Jay (Firestreak) air-to-air missiles. Avro, Blackburn, Bristol, Fairey, Saunders-Roe and Westland submitted designs.

Several of the competing teams highlighted problems in having a rocket-only powerplant. For example, landing an aeroplane propelled just by rockets presented several risks, which would inevitably lead to a high proportion of crash landings and/or landings away from base. After a powerless descent from altitude, the chance of breaking cloud within a reasonable approach distance of the aircraft's home base was not high. The case for providing power assistance for approach and landing was overwhelming, compounded by the psychological effect on the pilot knowing that he would have full control over his choice of landing ground. Using the rocket for the approach would also cut the amount of fuel that was available for combat, which was critical since rocket motors normally ran for just a few minutes. Having a separate low-thrust turbojet in place as well would remove that problem, and it was also realised that ferrying between bases needed a jet engine. In fact, this operation would be near impossible on rocket power alone, and to transport individual aircraft by road was simply not acceptable.

After another competition with designs now adapted to take a jet engine, the winning proposals were the Avro 720 and Saro P.154 (which became the SR.53). A go-ahead was given for both types, but in 1955 the 720 was cancelled to save money. In 1952 three SR.53s were ordered with the serials XD145, XD151 and XD153. Saro's aircraft had what was essentially a delta wing but with the tips clipped to carry the armament of two Firestreak air-to-air missiles. This used a four-spar structure and had leading-edge droop together with trailing-edge ailerons and plain flaps. The fin had an all-moving tailplane on top, and the semi-monocoque fuselage was built as a single piece with frames, stringers and skins. The rear section housed a single Armstrong Siddeley Viper turbojet in the upper portion beneath the fin. A Spectre rocket was placed in the bottom of the fuselage, and all of the rest of the lower fuselage was used to hold fuel – kerosene for the jet and High Test Peroxide (HTP) for the rocket; the latter also used some kerosene, which was held separately in the wings. Two small air intakes placed just behind the canopy supplied air to the Viper, but the jet was not capable of providing enough power for the SR.53 to get airborne without the rocket running.

The mock-up of the rival Avro 720 rocket fighter project was built in metal. *Avro Heritage*

XD145 is pictured at Boscombe Down in early May 1957, almost certainly prior to its maiden flight. *Author's collection*

X-PLANES OF EUROPE

The SR.53's rear fuselage, fin and tail arrangement, with the powerplant shown to good effect. *Author's collection*

Major development

Before looking at the SR.53's career, mention must be made of a planned follow-on rocket/jet fighter that was to be a much larger aircraft. By the mid-1950s the SR.53 was no longer looked upon as a production machine for operational service – now it was seen as a type to provide experience in rocket motors and operation at high altitudes. In 1956 Specification F.177 was raised for a new supersonic mixed-powerplant fighter. The Royal Navy also produced a requirement for the same aircraft, which had to reach Mach 1.6 at 65,000 feet (19,812m) and Mach 2 for short periods. Every effort was to be made to keep the Air Force and Navy versions as close as possible, and after this the SR.53 was categorised as a lead-in aircraft for the new type.

The resulting project was the Saunders-Roe P.177, which had its fuselage powerplant arranged just like the SR.53 – one de Havilland Gyron Junior jet above (a more powerful engine than the Viper) and one de Havilland Spectre rocket below. The rocket still offered superb performance at high altitudes, but the larger jet would provide a more conventional capability and performance at lower levels. This was to be a fully operational fighter with space to carry a radar (which SR.53 did not have since it was designed for a bare minimum of equipment) and more advanced Red Top air-to-air missiles. Plans were drawn up to build twenty-seven P.177 development aircraft, starting with the initial flying shells for basic aerodynamic testing and going on to specialist airframes for the Navy and RAF. Interest was also forthcoming from West Germany, but the project was cancelled in 1957 before the first aircraft was ready to fly. This decision stemmed from that year's Government White Paper, which stated that, in the long term, manned fighters were no longer required.

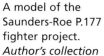

A model of the Saunders-Roe P.177 fighter project. *Author's collection*

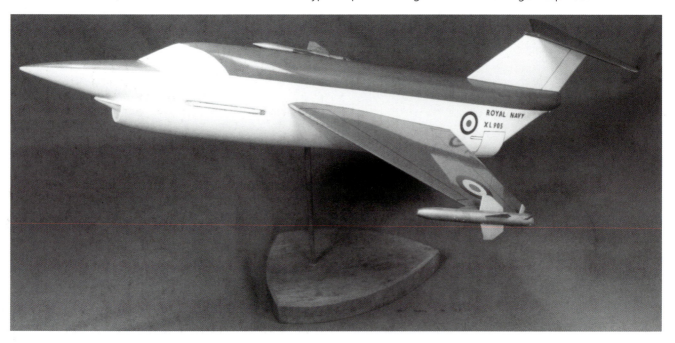

Left and below: The High Test Peroxide (HTP) fuel system is tested on XD151 in Saro's special SR.53 hangar.
Author's collection

X-PLANES OF EUROPE

Saunders-Roe SR.53 XD145 seen during a test flight. *Phil Butler collection*

Note the angle of the tailplane in this second view of XD145. *Westland Company, Isle of Wight*

Devalued flight test programme

The third SR.53, XD153, was cancelled in January 1954 and there were delays in completing the other two airframes, but the first example finally started its taxi trials on 9 May 1957. XD145 made its maiden flight on 16 May piloted by Sqn Ldr John Booth. Saro did not have an airfield of its own, so most of the flight programme was to be conducted mainly from Hurn, but this first trip (and indeed, as it proved, all SR.53 test flying) was made from the A&AEE at Boscombe Down. In September XD145 (flown in) and the near complete XD151 (brought in by road) made the type's only appearance at a Farnborough Show, and during the week the first aircraft completed six display flights.

John Booth took the second SR.53 into the air on 8 December 1957, but this machine had a relatively short career. On 5 June 1958 Booth aborted a take-off in XD151 but could not prevent the aircraft from going through the Boscombe runway boundary. It hit an approach light pole, then a concrete-and-chain fence and finally a larger marker light pole, and exploded after the fuel tanks were ruptured. The pilot was killed and several nearby houses were damaged, but the reasons behind the crash remain a mystery. The rocket motor had stopped during the take-off but no one is really sure why. XD151 had completed just eleven flights for a total of 5 hours and 15 minutes airborne, and because of this tragedy XD145 did not fly again until 23 February 1959.

The still incomplete second SR.53, XD151, was displayed statically at the 1957 Farnborough Show. *Author's collection*

Here, XD145 demonstrates the SR.53's clipped delta wing. *Author's collection*

A spectacular flyby by XD145 at Farnborough. The first SR.53 flights were made 'clean', but dummy wingtip Firestreak missiles were added, which, during early sorties, carried cameras to film the rocket plume. *Westland Company, Isle of Wight*

X-PLANES OF EUROPE

Another fighter to employ a mixed jet/rocket powerplant was the Republic XF-91, flown in America in May 1949. This picture shows the first XF-91 (46-680) after the original nose intake had been replaced by a radar nose. It is seen on the ramp at Edwards South Base in 1953. *Mike Machat collection*

Previously, on 15 May 1958, XD145 had been flown supersonic for the first time, in the process reaching Mach 1.14 (the previous best had been around Mach 0.98). However, after the accident to XD151 new restrictions on SR.53 operations limited the amount of flying that could be made – basically the aircraft was only allowed to operate from one Boscombe runway in one direction because this particular surface had a barrier at one end. Mach 1.26 was attained in July 1959, and on 13 September the eventual maximum of Mach 1.48 was achieved, together with an altitude of 56,750 feet (17,297m). The second of these flights was sortie number fifty-five, and the climb to 56,750 feet was made in 3 minutes 56 seconds. During what proved to be XD145's last flight (on 20 October 1959), an attempt to reach a maximum altitude through a vertical climb achieved a figure of 56,900 feet (17,343m).

After the abandonment of the P.177 programme the Air Staff was not really sure what to do with the SR.53. In August 1958 the programme was reappraised and it was planned to keep the aircraft flying since even in its present form it could fly higher than, and at the same Mach numbers as, any aircraft currently available in the UK. On 2 February 1959 a set of plans was drawn up for a limited programme of research to be carried out after some modifications had been introduced to the airframe. However, XD145's flying career eventually closed at forty-six flights (17 hours 45 minutes), fifteen of which came after XD151's loss. Including the trips to Farnborough, at no time did either SR.53 travel beyond a radius of 60 miles (96km) from its Boscombe base. Other pilots to fly the type were Lt Cdr Jack Overbury and Lt Cdr Peter Lamb, both of whom were Saunders-Roe test pilots. After the end of its flying, the first SR.53 was used by the Rocket Propulsion Establishment at Westcott (an offshoot of the RAE) for a period of ground testing, which started on 16 December 1960. In flight the aircraft was found to be very pleasant to fly with well-harmonised controls, satisfactory longitudinal stability characteristics, and a fast rate of roll.

The Sanders-Roe SR.53 was a fine aeroplane and, indeed, a fine achievement by what was a relatively small company, not least because the HTP fuel it used was an unstable and most unpleasant chemical to handle. However, the aircraft arrived in an environment where it was thought that manned fighters were no longer required. In addition, the expected high-flying bombers that would need rocket interceptors to counter them were soon afterwards forced to fly at low level to avoid defensive surface-to-air missiles (over just a short period of time the quality and capability of this type of weapon had improved dramatically). Finally, the need to boost a fighter's altitude performance with a rocket became no longer necessary once more modern and far more powerful jet engines appeared. These could be equipped with substantial reheat, which gave new jet fighters a much improved altitude performance. The concept of a mixed powerplant was made to work by Saunders-Roe, but the SR.53/P.177 family remains a great 'might have been' of British aviation history.

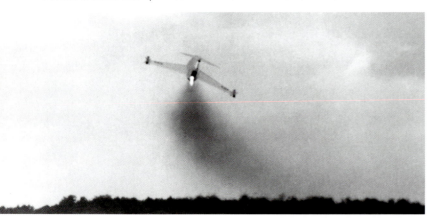

This photograph, scanned from a very small snapshot print, shows the SR.53 after making a pass across the Farnborough Show display area with the rocket motor running. A spectacular sight! *Author's collection*

A picture of XD145 taken very early in its career. *Author's collection*

XD145 makes a fast pass with its Spectre rocket in operation. *Author's collection*

The same aircraft pictured flying at quite low level during a test sortie.

29 Short S.C.1 (1957)

Short S.C.1

Span: 23ft 6in (7.16m)
Length: 29ft 10in (9.09m) with probe
Gross wing area: 211.5sq ft (19.67sq m)
Gross weight: Rolling VTO: 8,050lb (3,651kg); VTO: 7,700lb (3,493kg)
Powerplant: 5 x RR RB.108, 2,130lb (9.5kN)
Max speed: 265mph (426km/h); maximum dive speed 345mph (556km/h)
Ceiling: 20,000ft (6,096m)

The first jet-powered vertical-take-off aircraft that was also capable of forward flight was the British Short S.C.1. This aeroplane resulted from a design competition to find a specialised research type – it was never intended for production. However, it did much to chart the way forward in the development of VTOL aviation, not only in what the aircraft achieved but also perhaps in showing what should not be done to produce a successful design. Today, the S.C.1 would be described as a technology demonstrator.

Design competition

Britain's first jet-powered 'aircraft' to be capable of a vertical take-off and landing was the Rolls-Royce 'Flying Bedstead' (qv). By September 1953 the data coming from the Bedstead and from experiments with models undertaken by RAE Farnborough had indicated that jet lift and control was likely to be satisfactory for the vertical flight phase. It was now time to investigate the transition from vertical to horizontal flight, something that the Bedstead could not do, and a tender design competition was held against Specification ER.143T (T for Tender). This called for a small aircraft that would investigate the general problems associated with VTOL and the transition to and from horizontal flight at heights up to 5,000 feet (1,524m). Its powerplant was to be based on the small Rolls-Royce RB.108 jet engine with 2,100lb (9.3kN) thrust, which had been specifically designed for VTOL applications; this light engine had a thrust/weight ratio of 8.7:1 (very high for its day) and first ran in July 1955.

The Air Staff supported the new programme and in a March 1954 document it emphasised the need to halt the ever-increasing cost of airfield development as performance requirements advanced. This noted how the increasing take-off and landing distances of all types of service aircraft were now posing a severe operational and financial burden. Not only was it difficult to find suitable airfield sites in the areas where such aircraft were required, but also the cost of building hard runways at such sites had risen a great deal. For example, the high tyre pressures of modern aircraft required very thick concrete together with a high degree of surface finish to enable the aircraft to operate successfully and to allow the field itself to withstand normal operations without excessive maintenance and repair. The arrival of aircraft with even higher performance would exacerbate this situation further – the time had arrived to look for a completely new solution to the problem.

Designs were submitted against ER.143T by Avro (a project based on the 707B – qv), Fairey (a Delta 1 [qv] variant), Percival, and Short Brothers & Harland. Shorts was the only company to submit a completely new design. This was called the P.D.11 and was described by the review team as outstanding since it was also the only proposal that provided independent

This early photograph of XG900 possibly shows the engine running before the first flight and without the lift jets fitted. Note the fixed 'bare' undercarriage and the 'puffer pipe' under the nose. *Short Brothers & Harland Ltd*

The first S.C.1 is seen on the ramp at Farnborough. Modified 'covered' undercarriage legs are now fitted, and the picture shows how the springs just above the wheels have absorbed the aircraft's weight. The grill over the lift jets is well shown, and also the open 'frill' just forward of the grill, which was used to guide air into the lift units when the S.C.1 was moving forward. *Author's collection*

X-PLANES OF EUROPE

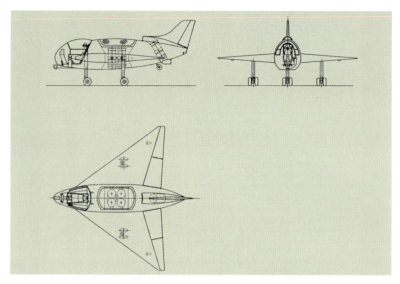

The Short & Harland P.D.11 project as first proposed in February 1954. In this form it had a span of 23ft 6in (7.16m) and a length of 24 feet (7.32m). *British National Archives, (AVIA 53 – 487)*

control of thrust and lift. It also fulfilled the requirements of the specification with a generous margin. The P.D.11 was delta-winged and had a battery of four RB.108s mounted vertically in the centre section with a fifth engine mounted in the rear of the fuselage to give horizontal thrust for normal cruising. This arrangement meant that the initial flights could be made with normal take-off and landing techniques and without using jet lift. Vertical take-off could then be performed on the lifting engines only, the transition to horizontal flight being made by opening up the thrusting engine, in which case the control of horizontal and vertical thrust would be completely separate and independent. In general the aircraft was kept as simple as possible.

The RAE had framed the original specification and the only project that came close to meeting the requirements was the P.D.11, which was quickly declared the winner. After initially carrying out its work on the transition from vertical to horizontal flight, it was envisaged that the P.D.11 would become a flying test bed for control and stabilising systems and possible later operational types using lift engines. Unlike some 'fighter type' possibilities, it also had a good view downwards for the pilot (comparable, in fact, to a helicopter). Two prototypes (serials XG900 and XG905) were ordered, and in October 1954 Specification ER.143D (D for Development) was raised to cover them. By the time this pair had been built, the P.D.11 had been re-titled S.C.1, and its appearance had been altered in some respects from the original proposal.

The all-metal S.C.1's delta wing was swept 54° on the leading edge and a non-retracting undercarriage was fitted, the length of the legs giving what the designers believed was adequate clearance between the main jet nozzles and the ground. It also had a wide track to keep the wheels well away from the jet efflux. The vertical engines could swivel through a range of 35° in pitch, which allowed them to provide assistance in accelerating and decelerating transitions. In conventional flight, elevators, ailerons and rudder controlled the S.C.1, and in jet-borne flight the control was provided by jet nozzles or 'puffer pipes' positioned under the nose and tail (for pitch) and under each wingtip (for roll). The fore-and-aft nozzles were also connected to the pilot's rudder control and could swivel differentially to provide yaw control. This system of air jets had been incorporated to provide control during a vertical ascent or descent and also in the transition period to normal forward flight. All five engines provided bleed air for the system.

XG900 uses the brake parachute stored above the tail jetpipe to slow down after making a conventional landing. The photo was taken in either April or May 1957 and the aircraft still has the original undercarriage. *Short Brothers & Harland Ltd*

SHORT S.C.1 (1957)

Testing times

Ground handling trials with the first S.C.1, XG900, began at Sydenham in December 1956, and the aircraft made its first flight from Boscombe Down without the lift engines fitted on 2 April 1957. Tom Brooke-Smith piloted the aircraft. In March 1958 XG900 flew with dummy lift engines in place, and on 2 May it arrived at RAE Bedford. By the end of the month the aircraft was performing tests to check the airflow characteristics through the lift engine bay, tests that were aimed at providing a suitable airflow to windmill the lifting engines in readiness to start them up. The testing of XG900's aerodynamic qualities was concluded during autumn 1957, and the airframe had its lift jets installed in the winter of 1958/59. In March 1961 XG900 was allocated to RAE Bedford's Aero Flight.

From May 1958 XG905, complete with a full set of lift engines, was used for gantry testing over a grid. A special hovering control gantry had been built at Belfast, which featured a raised platform and a grid floor that deflected the hot gasses away from the aircraft to prevent re-ingestion. The second aircraft also had loose tethers to ensure that it made no uncontrolled movements during the hover. XG905 had originally been due to make its first flight the

XG900 pictured in front of the wind tunnel at Boscombe Down during its conventional flight trials. With the aid of the tunnel, the jettisoning of the pilot's cockpit canopy was successfully tested (an essential trial for any new aircraft fitted with ejector seats). *Ministry of Defence*

X-PLANES OF EUROPE

SHORT S.C.1 (1957)

Short S.C.1 XG900 is on display at a Farnborough Show, standing over a ramp with a grid floor. *Author's collection*

Below: XG905 pulls into a climb after performing a vertical take-off at Bedford. *Phil Butler collection*

Opposite above and below: The S.C.1's main task was to research vertical take-offs and landings. The aircraft is seen here in the hover. Note the exhausts for the four lift jets protruding beneath the fuselage, and how the undercarriage is now extended after the weight of the aircraft has been removed. *Short Brothers & Harland Ltd*

X-PLANES OF EUROPE

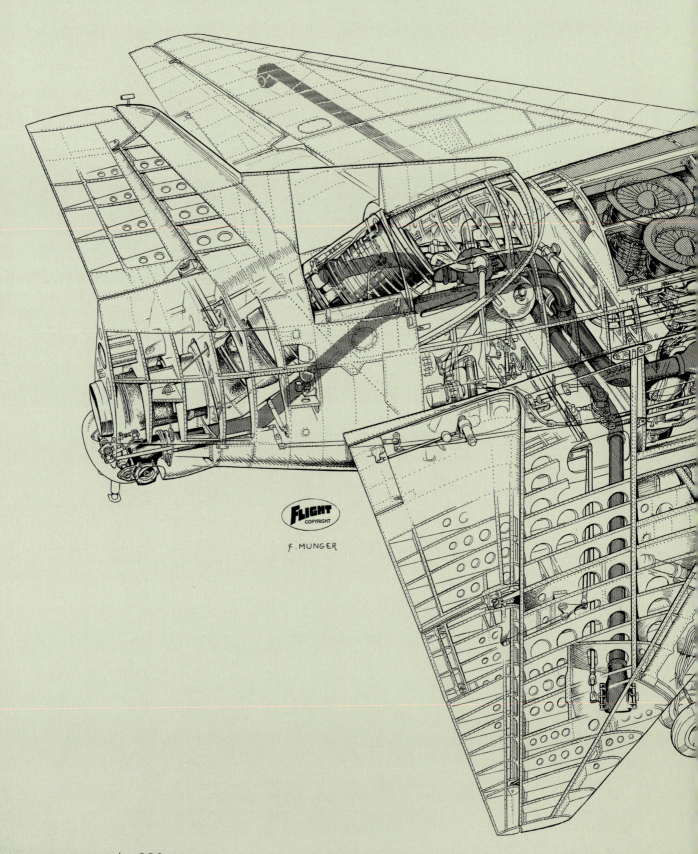

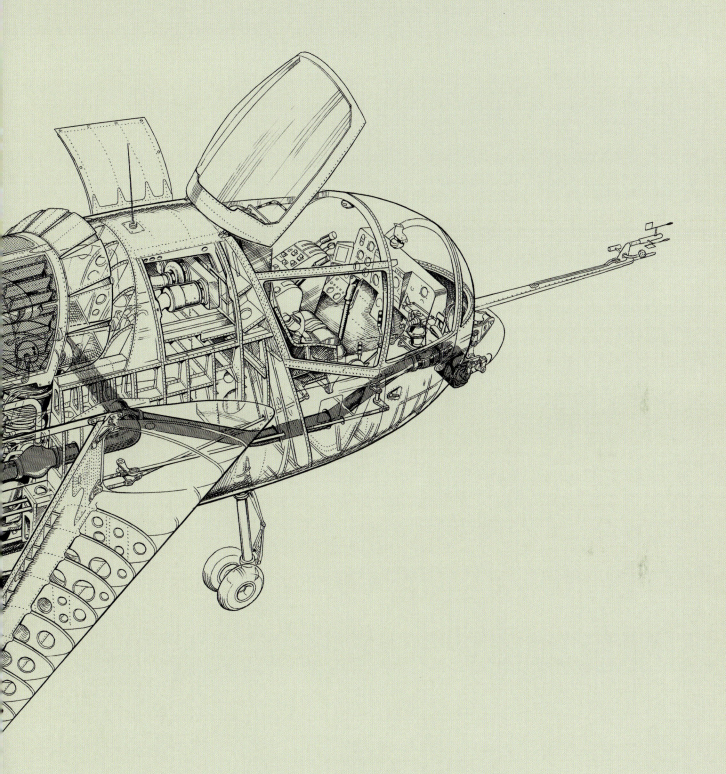

This is the four-seat Short S.C.8 project from artwork dated November 1960. In fact, single- and two-seat S.C.8 proposals were first assessed by the Air Staff and the RAE from January 1960 as a replacement for the S.C.1. One of the S.C.1s would be rebuilt with a lengthened centre fuselage as the S.C.8. The two-seat version would probably have been used for blind landing VTOL trials, but in June 1960 the decision was taken not to go ahead with the S.C.8 in this form, in part because neither S.C.1 could be spared. However, suggestions were made to install Boulton Paul lift fans, which would provide far more lift than the RB.108s, and it is possible that this four-seat arrangement resulted from that idea. *RAF Museum, Hendon*

previous January, but during the later stages of its engine tests debris entered the intakes, which stripped two of the lifting engines. After repair a further incident occurred on 12 March when a rivet entered the engine, but since then modifications to the intake guards had been introduced and new engines installed.

Brooke-Smith piloted XG905 on its first restricted gantry flight on 23 May 1958; the first free hover over the grid with the tethers off was made on 25 October. He described the work as a 'most exhilarating business' because he was both 'professor and pupil' at the same time. One objective was to ensure that all four lift engines would start together, sustain 'idle' running in a satisfactory manner, then accelerate or decelerate correctly to ensure that a crisp response was available (which was vital in the hover). On 6 April 1960 the first double transitions (VTO to forward flight, then stop to make vertical landing) were achieved at Bedford, the first occasion on which this had been achieved by a jet-powered fixed-wing aircraft anywhere in the world. Prior to this momentous event the two aeroplanes had steadily closed the gap in the flight envelope between wing-borne flight and jet-borne operation to the point where the transition needed to be made. It was found that the lowest possible wing-borne speed was 154mph (248km/h).

XG905 went to the September 1959 Farnborough Show, but Brooke-Smith was forced to end his first performance rather abruptly when cuttings from freshly mown grass clogged the wire mesh intake guard placed over the lift jets on the upper fuselage. The guard did prevent the grass from entering the engine, but the layer covering the wire mesh effectively starved the RB.108 of air. XG900 made its Farnborough Show debut in September 1958 (as a static exhibit), its second appearance in September 1960 (where it was joined by XG905), and its third in 1961; it also fitted in a display at the June 1961 Paris Show. At the 1960 Farnborough Show, where it was described as the 'world's first practical jet-propelled vertical-take-off and landing aeroplane', the S.C.1 was labelled 'the Star of the Show'.

This is thought to be XG905, seen in a hover but moving forward with the 'frill' deployed. The nose 'puffer pipe' has been modified and enlarged. *Author's collection*

Tom Brooke-Smith retired as a test pilot at the end of 1960, and Alex Roberts took over as S.C.1 project pilot. The culmination of Roberts's work in the 1960s was a successful demonstration of a transition by the S.C.1 using a full electrically signalled control system – specially designed by Shorts – as opposed to the mechanically signalled system used earlier.

Although having a maximum vertical-take-off weight of 7,700lb (3,493kg), the S.C.1 was capable of performing a new manoeuvre called a 'rolling VTO', which pushed the take-off weight above 8,000lb (3,629kg). Here the aircraft would build up enough forward speed to reduce the possible effects of problems such as hot gas ingestion but without reaching a speed that provided any noteworthy lift (which was the case with an STO – short take-off). The S.C.1 was a demanding aircraft to operate, in part because it had five engines and four of them had to be shut down during conventional flight (primarily because they would very quickly use up the available fuel supply). This meant, of course, that they all had to be started again when preparing to land, which gave the pilot a high workload in the circuit. Although the S.C.1 was never intended for production or operational service, Shorts did look at some developments, which included the S.C.8 from late 1959. This was to have six RB.108 lift jets and one RB.145 propulsion unit and was to be converted from an S.C.1 airframe.

On 2 October 1963 XG905 suffered a failure of the gyro input to the autostabiliser. The fault made the aircraft uncontrollable and it turned over and crashed. Despite so much attention having been given to making the systems safe, the pilot, J. R. Green from the RAE (who was on loan to Shorts), was killed in this crash. XG905 was not repaired until May 1966, and when it first began hovering again on 17 June it was re-tethered to ensure that the modifications made to the gyros could be checked out safely. During the period of repair XG900 had been grounded. In June 1967 XG905 spent nearly two weeks at A&AEE Boscombe Down, then on the 16th of the month it returned to RAE Bedford to join XG900 for employment in VTOL control and instrument research with the Blind Landing & Experimental Unit. This work examined the techniques that would be required to perform VTOL operations both in bad weather and at night. XG905 was released from service in April 1971. XG900 continued its trials flying until September 1968, but in March 1969, after a period in store, it was allocated to ground running operations only.

In most respects the two S.C.1s were simple aircraft to fly (as in steer through the sky), but in forward flight their performance was fairly mundane since this stocky airframe was not designed for high performance. Much of their active life was spent in the hands of RAE Bedford on control development, and both examples are now preserved. They contributed a great deal to VTOL research in

> It is easy to get the various control systems tried in the 1950s to the 1970s confused. As well as the traditional connections of rods or cables between the pilot and the control surfaces or engines, there were experiments with electrical signalling. Here pilot inputs were converted into an electrical signal that was fed along wires and turned back into mechanical movement near the control surface or engine – it being easier to thread wires round an aeroplane than mechanical control runs! However, this electrical signalling had nothing to do with what today is called 'fly-by-wire' (FBW). With FBW the pilot sends his desire for a manoeuvre to a computer, which then decides what type of control surface, system or engine needs to be adjusted to achieve the pilot's request. FBW also ensures that the aircraft is stable when there are no pilot inputs made. Before FBW, help with making any aircraft stable used autostabilisers, which were electrical/mechanical devices that continually adjusted the control surfaces without pilot input to make the aircraft appear steady to the pilot and reduce his control workload. Such autostabilisers sometimes provided rate stabilisation (of roll, pitch or yaw), others attitude stabilisation (of roll, pitch or yaw), and some offered a combination of both, as in the S.C.1.

XG900 is seen during an 'outdoor' exercise away from base, a scene that was to become very common once the Harrier entered service. *Author's collection*

X-PLANES OF EUROPE

The Shorts S.C.1 photographed on static display at Farnborough in September 1961. The relatively large amount of cockpit glazing on the aircraft could not have been shown better.
Roy Bonser-KEC

general and were important contributors to the 'jet V/STOL crusade', so politically they helped the P.1127 and Harrier programmes even though those aircraft used a different system for both lift and control (i.e. vectored thrust and no reliance on autostabilisers – qv). The successful development of the vectored thrust principle on those Hawker aeroplanes confirmed that dedicated lift engines like the RB.108s used in the S.C.1 were a burden when the aircraft was in forward flight because they were dead weight. It would, however, be quite wrong to compare S.C.1 unfavourably against the P.1127/Harrier since Hawker's aircraft was started as a possible combat aircraft while S.C.1 (which represented the RAE's VTOL ideas) was only ever intended for research. The Short S.C.1 trials aeroplanes were indeed a great success, although their story is marred by XG905's fatal accident in 1963.

Groundbreaking aircraft and pilot seen together at Bedford! The second S.C.1, XG905 (left), with test pilot Tom Brooke-Smith, stands alongside the Rolls-Royce 'Flying Bedstead'. In the background are an early English Electric Lightning and WW598, a Hawker Hunter F Mk 6. *Short Brothers & Harland Ltd*

224

30 Hawker P.1127 (1960)

Hawker P.1127

Span: XP831: 24ft 4in (7.42m); XP984: 22ft 10in (6.96m)

Length: 49ft 6in (115.09m) with probe

Gross wing area: XP831: 185.0sq ft (17.21sq m); XP984: 186.0sq ft (17.30sq m)

Gross weight: XP831: 15,115lb (6,856kg) with full fuel; XP984: 19,000lb (84.4kg)

Powerplant: initially 1 x BS Pegasus 2, 11,200lb (49.8kN); later 1 x BS Pegasus 3, 13,500lb (60.0kN)

Max speed/height: c720mph (1,158km/h) at sea level, Mach 1.2 in dive

Ceiling: XP831: c50,000ft (15,240m); XP984: 55,000ft (16,764m)

The aircraft covered in this book include several efforts to produce a fixed-wing vertical take-off and landing (VTOL) or vertical and short take-off and landing (V/STOL) aeroplane, either for research or with an eventual service type in mind. However, at the time of writing in early 2011 the only truly successful combat aircraft to be capable of doing this has been the British Hawker Harrier, which used the inspired method of having vectoring nozzles on the fuselage sides to provide vertical thrust for lift. The Harrier story begins with the Hawker P.1127 research prototypes, first envisaged in the late 1950s. The Kestrel service trials aircraft and then the Harrier followed these. Although P.1127 was designed right from the start as a potential combat aircraft, the six examples to be built were all used purely for development, then research.

A novel concept

An idea for lift/cruise based on the principle of vectored thrust appeared in a project by Frenchman Michel Wibault, drawn in 1954. This showed a design for a ground attack aircraft called the Gyroptere, and was enough to prompt Bristol Engines in 1956 to devise a new lift/thrust engine concept based on the principle of vectored thrust. The outcome was an engine called the BE.53, with jet nozzles on its sides. Hawker Aircraft's ideas for a V/STOL aircraft came together in mid-1957 when designer Ralph Hooper completed a project called the P.1127 powered by a single centrally mounted BE.53. In fact, the aircraft was designed around the new engine, and over the next two years the BE.53 and the P.1127 were refined to the point where the combination had four rotating nozzles on the fuselage sides and no jetpipe. These nozzles would face vertically downwards to provide lift and could be rotated (vectored) rearwards to provide forward thrust. The front nozzles would take cold air from the engine fan while the rear pair would split the hot exhaust gasses. The value in having a new combat aircraft that could take off vertically or from just a short run was that it might not have to rely on a large airbase and a long runway, facilities that were becoming ever more vulnerable to enemy attack.

Discussions with Supreme Headquarters Allied Powers, Europe (SHAPE), and NATO representatives indicated that the P.1127 held promise as a possible light attack aircraft, but it would need to have more equipment. In June 1960 the British Ministry of Aviation issued a contract for the development and manufacture of two P.1127 prototypes for research into V/STOL flight under Specification ER (for Experimental Research) 204D, although Hawker

X-PLANES OF EUROPE

P.1127 XP831 is seen in the summer of 1960 prior to its first flight. In appears as built with no markings or serial applied. *Author's collection*

had for some time been working on its own and had started construction of the first P.1127 in May 1959 as a private venture. The BE.53 was subsequently named Pegasus and the engine had its first bench run in September 1959, rated at 11,000lb (48.9kN). A second batch of four P.1127s, described as development aircraft for military research and development, was ordered in November 1960 and the six aeroplanes were given the serials XP831, XP836, XP972, XP976, XP980 and XP984.

The P.1127's layout was closely related to the engine installation. High wing and tail surfaces were necessary to clear the engine efflux in all nozzle positions, while the high engine mass flow demanded large intakes to keep the static losses small. Hovering control was provided by compressor air ducted to nose, tail and wingtip reaction control valves. There was an all-moving tailplane and a small dorsal fin, but the original delta-type swept wing was altered several times across the six airframes. The P.1127 used

The first Hawker P.1127, XP831, undergoes pre-flight testing in 1960. The engine cover has been removed. Note the rather bulbous rubber intake lips, which were used until they began to disintegrate during high-speed flight testing. *BAE Systems*

This nose angle of one of the early P.1127s reveals how large the air intakes had to be to supply the Pegasus engine. This aircraft is now fitted with metal intake lips. *Author's collection*

predominantly conventional light alloy construction but with some parts built in steel or titanium. With its big side intakes, bicycle undercarriage and wingtip outriggers (the bicycle arrangement saved weight) it presented a somewhat unusual appearance against the sleek supersonic fighters that had appeared all over the world during the 1950s. However, the basics for a very practical subsonic attack aircraft were now in place.

Groundbreaking research

The first P.1127, XP831, arrived at Hawker's flight test facility at Dunsfold on 15 July 1960, having been moved by road from its Kingston birthplace. Fitted with a Pegasus 2, an initial engine run was made on 22 September with the aircraft placed over a grid platform to minimise any re-ingestion of hot gasses. Tethered hovering flights began on 21 October and continued for nearly a month, while the first taxiing tests with XP831 were made on 9 and 10 November. On 15 November the aircraft achieved a brief hover over solid ground and revealed handling characteristics that were better than had been predicted, then on the 19th it completed an untethered 'free' hovering flight over the grid platform. This was a major step forward, and the work was shared between Hawker test pilots Bill Bedford and Hugh Merewether. The objective of these early trials was to establish the piloting techniques required to hold the P.1127 in the hover.

The next step was to take XP831 to RAE Bedford, and on 13 March 1961 it made a satisfactory conventional first flight from there in the hands of Bill Bedford. Subsequent flight testing showed that the flying characteristics were generally as expected, but the aircraft lacked performance and really needed a more powerful engine. The outcome was the eventual Pegasus 5, which supplied 18,000lb (80.0kN) of thrust and was first flown in P.1127 XP984 on 13 February 1963 (albeit on that occasion in a de-rated condition). Nevertheless, on 13 June 1961 an initial step towards transition (vertical to/from forward flight) was made when XP831 took off from the grid and moved forward along the runway at about 50 feet (15m) above the ground. A top speed of around 58mph (93km/h) was recorded.

The second P.1127, XP836, made its first conventional take-off from Dunsfold on 7 July 1961. On 8 and 9 September test flights using both prototypes included translations from the hover at speeds up to 109mph (175km/h) by XP831, and forward flight with jets deflected from conventional flight down to the same speed by XP836, which meant that the full speed range from hovering to fully wing-borne flight had now been covered. (A 'translation' has the aircraft still partly jet-borne, whereas a 'transition' implies fully wing-borne flight.) On 12 September 1961 the P.1127 was successfully taken through a series of transitions in both directions, then on the 18th the complete transition sequence from VTO to wing-borne flight and back for a vertical landing. The concept of a workable VTOL combat aircraft had been achieved. To celebrate,

X-PLANES OF EUROPE

XP831 is in hover with the nozzles rotated to the vertical position and the undercarriage and outriggers lowered. *Author's collection*

This is the original P.1127 wing shape as used on XP831. The nozzles are facing rearwards so the aircraft was in forward motion when the picture was taken. *Author's collection*

on 12 December XP836 achieved supersonic speed in a dive and became the first V/STOL aircraft in the world to pass that landmark.

The progress was spoiled, however, when XP836 was written off on 14 December after one of its lightweight fibreglass cold-engine nozzles failed due to a manufacturing defect and became detached. The aircraft crashed on the approach to Yeovilton after Bedford had been forced to eject. These fibreglass nozzles were subsequently replaced by a steel version similar to the hot-gas nozzles. Initial flying had taken place using fixed metal intake lips of rounded (XP831) and sharp (XP836) cross-section. Later P.1127s were fitted with rubber intake lips of compromise cross-section that were designed to inflate during V/STOL operation and deflate after the transition to normal flight, but flight at high speeds left them badly damaged and fixed metal lips eventually took their place.

XP972, the third aircraft, first flew on 5 April 1962 with a new wing. In all, the P.1127s flew with four different wing forms. XP831 and XP836 had begun with protruding outrigger fairings; XP972 (and XP980) introduced curved tips and extended leading edges; the fourth aircraft (XP976), which flew on 12 July 1962, had a kinked leading edge with protruding outrigger fairings; and XP984 was fitted with a swept wing. These changes were made to improve the type's conventional flight handling characteristics, and the XP984 wing was really quite different from the shape on XP831. In fact, the last P.1127 was essentially built to Kestrel configuration (see below) with a Pegasus 5 engine. XP980 was used to assess the techniques required to make the P.1127 perform slow landings and steep descents and transitions.

The first non-Hawker pilot to sample the aircraft was Sqn Ldr Jack Henderson of the RAE, who took XP831 into the air on his first evaluation flight on 8 November 1961. Two American pilots from NASA also flew in the first P.1127 during June 1962, while Hawker Siddeley's Duncan Simpson joined the test team when he flew XP976 on 25 August. The first public performance by a P.1127 was XP831's appearance at Upavon on 16 June 1962. The SBAC Show at Farnborough in September saw both XP831 and XP972 on display, which left such a mark that the press were full of praise for this 'revolutionary' aircraft, but XP972 was written off at Tangmere on 30 October when it crash-landed after suffering a fire in the engine. The wreck was scrapped.

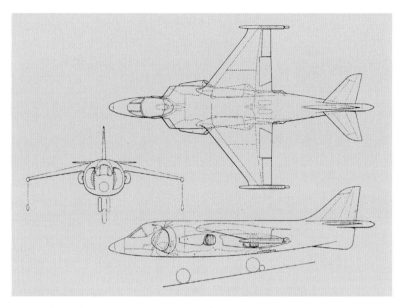

An early P.1127 three-view drawing. *Author's collection*

Within the UK the winter of 1962/63 proved to be one of the worst in living memory. As a result P.1127 carrier trials aboard HMS *Ark Royal* were delayed until 8 February 1963 when Bill Bedford flew XP831 out to the ship while it was steaming in the English Channel. Despite neither pilot having any carrier experience, Bedford and Merewether were able to perform a series of short and vertical take-offs and vertical landings without trouble, and they found no major problems in operating the aircraft from a deck. On 16 June XP831 crashed at the Paris Air Show at Le Bourget. During a hover, which formed part of Bedford's demonstration, the nozzles suddenly rotated partially aft through a problem with a jammed nozzle drive motor valve. The aircraft lost its lift and immediately dropped to make what might be described as a heavy 'landing'. The pilot was uninjured, but XP831 was not ready to fly again until 13 October 1964.

On 22 May 1964 XP984 reached Mach 1.15 indicated during a dive starting from 43,000 feet (13,106m). Five days later this aircraft was flown again after the tips of its tailplane had been extended, and these, coupled with a bob weight that had been introduced in the longitudinal control circuit, improved the stick force and tailplane angle per 'g' quite substantially. On 12 June XP984 reached 683mph (1,099km/h) IAS, the highest achieved so far by any P.1127.

Follow-on developments

The superb results recorded by the P.1127s in their effort to get V/STOL capability accepted by the armed services was followed by a 1962 order for nine more development aircraft. This new

To display the versatility of the P.1127-type aircraft, during February 1963 XP831 was taken out to the aircraft carrier HMS *Ark Royal* where it performed a series of successful deck trials. *BAE Systems*

version was named the Hawker Siddeley Kestrel and the first example, XS688, made its first flight on 7 March 1964. In due course the Kestrels were used to form a Tripartite Evaluation Squadron, where pilots from Britain, America and West Germany flew them. These were essentially 'in-service' aeroplanes with a UK military designation, so fall outside the parameters of this book, but the unit did cover (very successfully) an astonishing amount of ground in the V/STOL operation of such aircraft, particularly away from normal air bases. Afterwards six of the Kestrels went to America and, with the designation XV-6A, were used for further trials work. The Tripartite Squadron led to the ordering of the Harrier attack aircraft for the RAF, the first of which flew in August 1966. In the meantime, however, an ambitious supersonic V/STOL development called the P.1154 had appeared in 1961, and this was ordered for both the RAF and Royal Navy, but the project was cancelled in early 1965.

Meanwhile, in February 1965 P.1127 XP831 joined RAE Bedford's Aerodynamics Flight, where it was used for research until its final flight on 10 October 1972. From July 1965 XP976 was employed on cockpit head-up display (HUD) testing at RAE Bedford. The return to Dunsfold on 5 November 1965 was its last flight, but before being scrapped XP976 was used for a variety of ground duties (including battle damage repair training) lasting through the 1970s. XP980 went to Boscombe Down in 1966 and continued flying until 1968. After that the airframe was employed in several roles including crash barrier trials and ground handling, and in early 1981 was still capable of taxiing. In 1966

This image from 1963 shows the three P.1127s that were then on flight test. Left to right, they are XP831, XP976 and XP980. Two of the series had by then been lost, and XP984 was still to fly. *BAE Systems*

In February 1965 XP831 became a member of the Aerodynamics Flight ('Aero Flight') at RAE Bedford, for which it received appropriate identification on its nose.

XP984 was fitted with a Harrier wing for aerodynamic development at Dunsfold. Its trials work for RAE Bedford included flights in mid-June 1966 to and from the carrier HMS *Bulwark* operating in the English Channel, and during the next nine years the aircraft spent time at Bedford, Farnborough and Dunsfold. However, on 31 October 1975, as the last flying P.1127, XP984 was badly damaged in a landing accident at Bedford. It was repaired and went on to be used for ground instruction. Three of the six P.1127s survive today.

The Hawker P.1127 has proved to be a landmark in British and world aviation history. Although numerous vertical-take-off research aeroplanes were tested during the 1950s and 1960s, the vectored thrust concept adopted by the P.1127 was for many years the only really successful method of providing vertical thrust, and it proved reliable and relatively easy to operate. As a result, this pioneer design from Hawker was turned into the immensely successful Harrier, which, since its entry into RAF service in 1969, has racked up an outstanding record in several conflicts and with several air arms. Of course, today's Harrier represents a great advance over the earlier aircraft, but only now, in 2011, is a replacement on its way in the form of the Lockheed Martin F-35 Lightning II, designed and developed with major BAE Systems collaboration. This new aeroplane replaces the old vectored thrust nozzles with a lift system consisting of a lift fan and driveshaft, two round 'roll posts', and what is termed the 'three bearing swivel module' at the tail of the aircraft, all provided by Rolls-Royce. The latter is a large thrust vectoring nozzle, which can deflect the main engine exhaust downwards while the lift fan just to the rear of the cockpit provides a counter-balancing thrust. Fully supersonic, the F-35 should form an excellent replacement for the long-serving Harrier.

XP972 was the first of the second batch of P.1127s to be built, and made its maiden flight in April 1962. *Author's collection*

X-PLANES OF EUROPE

Here we see the 'developed' shape of Hawker Siddeley Kestrel XS695 in flight. The wing pylon carries a rocket pod. *BAE Systems*

The first of these images (right) shows the original P.1127, XP831, hovering at Hawker Siddeley's airfield at Dunsfold. As a comparison, an early Harrier is seen in a similar pose (below). This may be serial XV277, which was the second Harrier to be built and was used by Hawker Siddeley for various clearance trials and displays. In fact, it never joined the RAF. *BAE Systems*

P1127 XP831 was first of the type built. Powered by Bristol Siddeley Pegasus and currently on display at The Science Museum, London, UK. *Chris Sandham-Bailey www.inkworm.com*

Kestrel XS688 was the first of 9 Hawker Siddeley Kestrels produced, shown in Tripartite Evaluation Squadron markings. Sent to USA and renumbered 64-18262.
Chris Sandham-Bailey www.inkworm.com

P1127 XP980 in Royal Navy colours to represent the later Sea Harrier FRS1. Later fitted with Harrier GR1 wing and currently on display at the Fleet Air Arm Museum, Yeovilton, UK. *Chris Sandham-Bailey www.inkworm.com*

Kestrel 64-18262 (formerly XS688) was sent to the US Air Force for trials, currently on display at the National Museum of the United States Air Force at Wright Patterson AFB, Ohio, United States.
Chris Sandham-Bailey www.inkworm.com

31 Handley Page HP.115 (1961)

Handley Page HP.115

Span: 20ft 0in (6.10m)
Length: 50ft 4in (15.34m) with probe
Gross wing area: 432.5sq ft (40.22sq m)
Gross weight: 5,600lb (2,540kg)
Powerplant: 1 x AS Viper A.S.V.9, 1,850lb (8.2kN)
Max speed: 201mph (323km/h)
Ceiling: Unknown

Investigations made in 1958 by the Supersonic Transport Aircraft Committee showed that the configuration most likely to give the required lift/drag ratio at approximately Mach 2 was a fully integrated design using a narrow delta, gothic or ogee planform, but the final choice would need plenty of research to confirm it was the right one. This was, of course, the start of the Anglo-French Concorde programme, and the ogee wing was generally regarded as being the most practicable. It was considered that some intermediate trials aircraft, particularly for the wing shape, would be essential before the final full-size airliner could be built. Consequently, a Fairey Delta 2 (qv) was rebuilt as the BAC.221 (qv) to look at the ogee wing's behaviour at high speeds, but some time before the 221 was ready, Handley Page had built the much simpler HP.115 research machine to assess slender aircraft low-speed characteristics.

Low-speed test vehicle

The original plans made in 1958 called for a glider, and a design competition was held in early 1959 against Specification X.197T. However, the HP.115 was built from the start as a powered aeroplane because it was decided that such a type would make a more practical proposition. Consequently, ER.197D of 21 December 1959 was raised to cover the single HP.115 to be built (which was ordered in 1960 and received the military serial XP841). The BAC.221 was, by its very nature, a complex aircraft and took a long time to complete. In contrast, the HP.115 was to be assembled cheaply and quickly; to minimise costs the contractor was to incorporate existing components as much as possible. The specification stated that it was required to operate close to its base airfield in daylight conditions only and at heights up to 15,000 feet (4,572m) above sea level.

The HP.115 was built almost wholly in light alloys, early plans for a wooden structure having been abandoned for various reasons (including the fact that wood gave a heavier airframe). The aircraft adopted a pure delta wing rather than the supersonic airliner's 'gothic' wing and had the leading edge swept at a constant 74° 42' (except for the curved tips). Parts of the wing could be detached, however, to allow three other leading edge shapes to be fitted, thereby permitting other wingforms to be investigated. In the end none of them were ever needed as the basic configuration handled so well. The engine was mounted in a nacelle on the upper rear fuselage and the fin was placed on top; this

Opposite: The extremely high angle of sweep on the HP.115's wing leading edge is shown superbly by this image, together with the engine nacelle and cockpit detail. *Phil Butler collection*

X-PLANES OF EUROPE

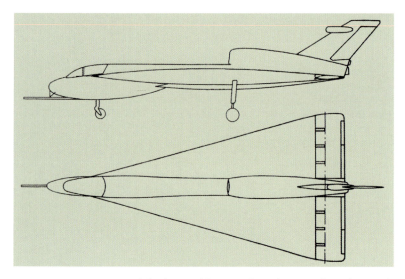

HP.115 general arrangement. *Phil Butler collection*

A fine research aircraft

The HP.115 was built at Radlett and on completion was taken by road to RAE Bedford. There, following a prolonged period of taxi trials, it made its maiden flight on 17 August 1961 piloted by Sqn Ldr Jack Henderson. Conditions for the first flight needed to be relatively calm, although the object of investigating the low-speed slender shape was that it was expected to be a handful in turbulence. On 23 October XP941 officially became a member of Bedford's Aerodynamics (Aero) Flight, and in due course many pilots, including the American astronaut Neil Armstrong, flew it. The only major problem experienced with the HP.115 in more than a decade of flying happened on 20 November 1964; this was a port-side main undercarriage failure that occurred as XP941 was just about to climb away after making a rolling landing. The problem was a fatigue failure, which left the leg broken and hanging at an angle. The pilot (Henderson) burned off most of his fuel, and when he finally landed he kept the port wing from dropping for as long as possible. When it did hit the ground XP941 left the runway, but the resulting damage was not severe, although the repairs took until May 1965.

left the multi-spar wing clean and uncluttered. Large fabric-covered elevons were attached along the wing trailing edge and both elevons and rudder were manually operated. Three tanks in the fuselage and inner wings held 140 gallons (637 litres) of fuel. The aircraft was single-seat, there was a fixed tricycle undercarriage (using a nose leg from the Percival Jet Provost and the main legs from the Piston Provost), and it was powered by an Armstrong Siddeley Viper ASV.9 jet. Only two examples of this particular Viper variant were built and both were used by the HP.115. The aircraft's installed test equipment was required to measure time, indicated speed, height, angles of flying control surfaces, angles of incidence and side slip, rates of pitch, roll and yaw, normal and lateral accelerations, and elevator stick forces. The airflow over the wing was to be observed by injecting smoke into the core of the vortex.

Flying at low speeds, the HP.115 airframe experienced relatively gentle stresses, but the engine(s) had to run for long periods at maximum power, which brought more extreme rates of wear for the powerplant and more frequent servicing. In the air XP941's longitudinal stability and handling were excellent, and when flying at speeds as low as 70mph (113km/h), with an angle of incidence in

This Handley Page photograph of HP.115 XP941 was probably taken very soon after the aircraft had been completed. *Phil Butler collection*

the region of 30°, control was easy. Lateral control was very good but would deteriorate with loss of speed or in turbulence. Here the HP.115 would experience a phenomenon called Dutch roll (a simultaneous oscillation in both the rolling and yawing planes). This could give bank oscillations of +/-60°, but recovery was achieved simply by reducing the angle of attack.

Low-speed flight with a high angle of attack was necessary if the unflapped slender delta that was to become Concorde was to have a manageable touchdown speed. Consequently, much of the HP.115's work involved a close analysis of vortices and it proved to be an ideal 'classroom' to do this. The work involved using smoke released from generators placed on the inner wing leading edges (the smoke also added to the engine deterioration due to compressor blade contamination), and from spring 1966 microphones and strain gauges were attached at strategic points to measure vortex noise. After the latter had been fitted, the aircraft returned to the air on 18 May. In September XP941 had some pressure-plotting transducers installed together with a parachute on the wingtip, and flew again on 22 February 1967. Practically all of XP941's flying was spent on research, with only a few sorties for other purposes; these, however, did include displays at the 1961, 1962 and 1964 SBAC Farnborough Shows and the 1965 Paris Salon.

XP941 was also displayed at an Open Day held at RAE Bedford on 29 and 30 May 1964. Lt Cdr Paul Millett (by then Aero Flight's HP.115 project pilot) showed how the aircraft's violent natural Dutch-roll characteristics at such high incidence could be stopped immediately using the manual controls (and unaided by an autostabiliser). XP841 continued to fly until August 1973, by which time the second of the two Viper 9s was showing its age. The last flight was a delivery trip to RAF Colerne in readiness for preservation. In all, the aircraft made at least 1,060 flights.

Prior to the HP.115's first flight some scientists took the view that the aircraft would be very hard to handle in roll, especially after this showed up badly in a fixed base simulation. Jack Henderson, however, was adamant that the real-life motion cues available to the pilot would make all the difference. They did. XP941 handled very well, and a frequent comment from the sixty-one pilots who flew it was 'they should make them all like that'. The HP.115 did much to clear and secure the low end of the supersonic transport's flight envelope and was arguably one of the most cost-effective UK research aircraft ever.

In 1964 the Handley Page HP.115 visited the Farnborough Show where it is seen performing a flyover. *Graham Hopkin*

32 Bristol 188 (1962)

Bristol 188
Span: 35ft 1in (10.70m)
Length: 77ft 8in (23.67m) with probe
Gross wing area: 396.25sq ft (36.85sq m)
Gross weight: Unknown; 1953 proposal was 30,000lb (13,608kg)
Powerplant: 2 x DH Gyron Junior PS.50 (D.G.J.10RkN), 10,000lb (44.4kN) dry, 14,000lb (62.2kN) afterburner; 20,000lb (88.9kN) at Mach 2/36,000ft (10,973m)
Max speed: Mach 1.88 at 36,000ft (10,973m)
Ceiling: Unknown

The Bristol 188 is an aeroplane that, in Britain today, is generally not remembered with much affection. It never achieved its full objectives and overall was an expensive machine, but it was also a groundbreaker. Its trials programme was one of the first occasions where recording data was achieved using real-time telemetry, and the airframe was built in stainless steel, a brand-new material for the UK's aircraft industry to work with. Unfortunately, this material became the source of many delays to the programme and Sir George Edwards, head of BAC, is quoted as saying, 'We learned how not to build aircraft with the 188.' However, the 188 had a spectacular appearance and was a fascinating aircraft.

Mach 2 research programme

In the late 1940s and through the 1950s the increases in maximum speed year on year were quite extraordinary. By 1952 it was clear to everyone that fighters capable of supersonic speeds were the way forward, but during that year the Ministry of Supply raised the level even higher when it issued Specification ER.134T, which described a Research Aircraft for Mach Number 2. To allow the problems of travelling at such speeds to be examined, particularly the build-up of kinetic heat through air friction, this document requested a machine capable of flying at a sustained Mach 2 on the level for a full 10 minutes. RAE Farnborough advised that a thin 'straight-winged' aircraft with engines in nacelles mounted centrally on the wing was the most suitable configuration, and in general Bristol's Type 188 submission followed that pattern. Powered by two Rolls-Royce Avon RA.24 engines, the 188 won the ER.134T design competition, and at that stage had a wing with a moderately swept leading edge and a straight trailing edge.

A contract for two Bristol 188 prototypes together with a non-flying structural-test airframe was placed in February 1953, and a mock-up was inspected in November 1954. However, a top speed of Mach 2 was soon considered insufficient and the ER.134D development specification now requested Mach 2.5. This resulted in studies into eight possible engine installations because the Avon's performance would deteriorate above Mach 2.1 at 50,000 feet (15,240m). There were also plans for extra aircraft, in part to test an Armstrong Siddeley engine to be used by the forthcoming Avro 730 Mach 3 bomber. In 1955 the order was increased to five aeroplanes, but in the end just the two originally contracted 188s, serials XF923 and XF926, were built due to the cutbacks in defence announced in 1957 (the Avro 730 was one of the projects abandoned). Finding a suitable engine that could provide reasonable durations of flight time at the required speeds proved to be problematical, but in 1957 the de Havilland Gyron Junior was finally selected. Particular emphasis was placed on supersonic intake design, and the PS.50 Gyron Junior was specifically designed for sustained supersonic flight. The two units would have fully variable afterburning and their massive nacelles would dwarf the 188's relatively small wing.

It was the problem of kinetic heat, and the all-stainless-steel structure developed to cope with it, that provided the greatest obstacles in the development phase. The strength of aluminium alloys falls off rapidly with temperature, and the advantage of their lightness therefore decreases as the thickness of the materials has to be increased to maintain the strength and rigidity of the structure – the economical limit for the use of aluminium alloys was about Mach 2.2. Only stainless steel could handle what the aviation press called the 'Thermal Thicket', but the search for a suitable alloy that could be produced as sheet proved to be difficult. Eventually, the Firth-Vickers Rex 448 was selected and a considerable development programme was undertaken in cooperation with the Sheffield-based manufacturer. However, finding a process that could provide the required standards of surface flatness, finish and thickness tolerance took two years, and adapting that for the puddle welding process (argon-arc fusion spot welding) required more time for new skills to be learned. Suitable methods had to be found to fabricate, weld and join components using special bolts, rivets and fasteners. Nevertheless, the resulting finish was one of the smoothest yet seen on any aircraft.

The steel construction would delay the aircraft, but the research was kept ahead of development and also gained valuable experience in steel design and manufacture. The 188's structure was designed to cope with speeds of Mach 1.2 at sea level and Mach 2.5-plus above 35,000 feet (10,668m). An extensive arrangement of instrumentation (including paper and magnetic tape recording) and continuous telemetry to ground receiving equipment was built into each airframe. There were strain gauges and

Both 188s are seen in the hangar at Filton on 24 October 1963. A Vickers Valiant bomber, de Havilland Heron airliner and Hawker Hunter fighter are visible in the background. *David Charlton, British Aerospace*

X-PLANES OF EUROPE

several hundred transducers, and these would provide a rapid supply of data from both engine and airframe to study the aircraft's aerodynamic behaviour, stability, turbulence, structure loads, distortion and kinetic heating. Special transparent materials were also used for the small cockpit windows, and the 188 had a powerful refrigeration system to protect the pilot and the extensive instrumentation from the build-up of heat. To assess the aircraft's flutter characteristics, models of the 188 were tested on rockets fired from RAE Aberporth. The static test airframe was delivered to RAE Farnborough in May 1960, then in 1961 it was moved to RAE Bedford.

As built, the Type 188's inner wing was straight, but it had triangular leading edge strakes at each end to help counteract the 'long bubble' type of airflows that tunnel tests had indicated were separating from the inboard wing's leading edge. Plain trailing edge flaps with a maximum depression of 55° were fitted to the inner wing. Outboard of the nacelles the wings were swept 38° with the outer portions set at 64°. The tip was formed by the balance area of the aileron forward of its hinge, which, in effect, gave all-moving wingtips. The wing box was formed by front and rear spars with intermediate spars made from corrugated webs. The fuselage was oval in cross-section and used a conventional structure of stressed skin covering stringers and frames. It contained five fuel tanks, while the nose was home to a pressurised section that housed the test instruments. The main undercarriage gears folded into the inner wing, with the wheels themselves lodged in the fuselage. Cascade-type air brakes were fitted to each side of the rear fuselage and an all-moving T-tail was used to keep the horizontal surface well clear of the jet efflux, tunnel testing having established that a low tailplane would give instability and pitch-up at moderate angles of attack. The tail was hinged to the top of the forward part of the 65°-sweep vertical fin. Beneath the tail, ahead of its hinge, was a vertical blade that moved inside a slot at the top of the fin. The tail also employed a multi-spar structure, the fin used multiple framing fixed to the rear fuselage, and the rudder had no aerodynamic balance.

Flight test

A consequence of the delays brought about by the problems in designing and building the aircraft was a regular postponement of the first flight. XF923 was rolled out on 26 April 1961, but it was almost another year before it flew. This latest delay was caused by engine surge and afterburner problems experienced during bench testing and ground running, for which the air intakes had to be modified. On 14 April 1962 XF923 finally took off from its Filton birthplace to travel to A&AEE Boscombe Down for low-speed handling trials. The pilot for the first flight was Godfrey Auty, Bristol's chief test pilot, and by this time the national press had alerted the British public to this new 'hot' machine, which had been christened the 'Flaming Pencil'. Displays at the Farnborough Show in September enhanced the feeling, with the Gyron Junior afterburners contributing a tremendous noise. By the end of November XF923 had completed nineteen flights, but on 15 November it returned to Filton to begin a series of ground resonance tests.

In fact, the first aircraft never flew again because it was eventually grounded to save money. The maximum speed achieved by XF923, on its final flight, was Mach 0.86, since it was intended that it should operate only in the subsonic regime and at moderate altitudes.

XF923 ready for flight. *Author's collection*

240

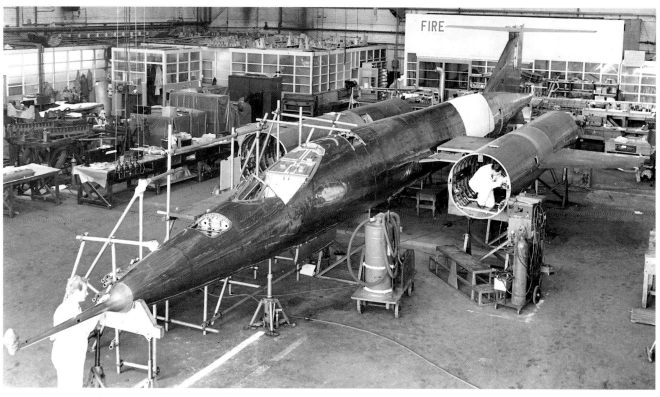

XF923 is seen under construction on 22 July 1960. *David Charlton, British Aerospace*

XF923's engines undergo ground testing on 13 December 1961. By then, fire extinguisher fairings had been added to the upper forward nacelles, but they did not appear on XF926 – a key distinguishing feature. *David Charlton, British Aerospace*

The first Bristol 188, XF923, is ready for taxi trials on 3 April 1962. *David Charlton, British Aerospace*

Engine and afterburning troubles, double flameouts and the unscheduled removal of the two engines on two occasions, together with other problems and bad weather, meant that the Boscombe Down portion of the test programme was not completed. However, within the flight envelope that was explored the aircraft's flight characteristics proved to be very good and the engineering systems worked well. In general, no troubles were experienced with trimming, and in the climb there was no marked change in stability with change in centre of gravity. Overall Auty reported that the 188 was easy and pleasant to fly in instrument meteorological conditions. For visibility in rain where no windscreen wiper was fitted this was the best aircraft he had ever flown, and the machine's asymmetric handling was good, both in the air and on the ground. With the resonance tests completed, XF923 was assigned to storage at Filton without its engines.

In the meantime further problems were experienced on the bench with the Gyron Junior, including a mechanical failure. The remedial action and design alterations required to solve them resulted in a reduced performance. It was now expected that flight at Mach 2 would not be cleared until spring 1964, and then for just 3 minutes. Any possibility of fitting advanced intakes capable of Mach 2.2 (which had been planned) was fading fast; indeed, the value of the programme as a whole was questioned during the autumn of 1962. For the time being, however, it was allowed to continue.

This photo may have been taken during XF923's performances at the September 1962 Farnborough Air Show. *Author's collection*

Shots of both XF923 (undercarriage down) and XF926 (undercarriage up) taken from nearly the same angle suggest no differences between the two airframes. However, XF926 has some lines marked on the underside of the tailplane and, when the photo was taken on 31 July 1963, it appears not to have the drag chute housing fitted to the port side of the rear fuselage (the intention had been to house the chute in the tail). The suction relief doors (or flaps) circling the forward nacelle are open on XF923 as it prepares to land – during high-speed flight these were closed. *David Charlton, British Aerospace*

X-PLANES OF EUROPE

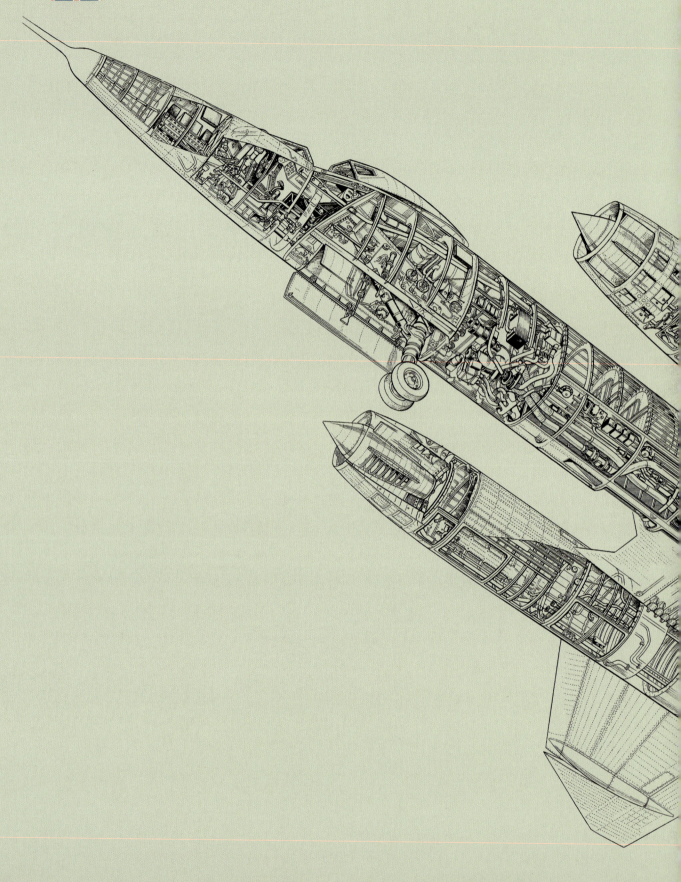

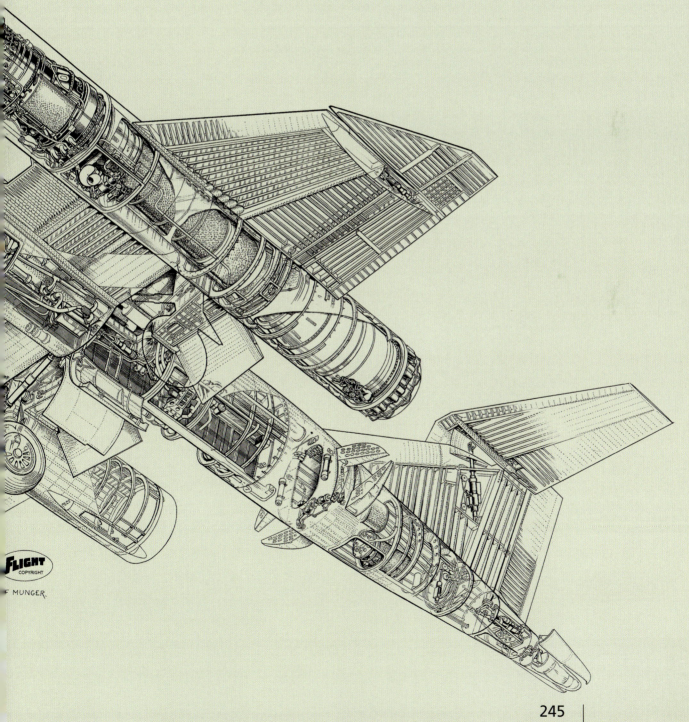

This extraordinary view of XF926 (now with its drag chute housing) shows that the engine nacelles were not much smaller in diameter than the fuselage. *Courtesy of the late Jim Oughton*

This side-on view of the second Bristol 188, XF926, reveals very clearly why the aircraft was known as the 'Flaming Pencil'. *Author's collection*

In 1963, with XF923 grounded, the flying programme switched to XF926, which made its maiden flight on 29 April using the engines removed from the first machine. Thanks to the engine troubles this flight had been postponed from August 1962. The second aircraft was specially instrumented for research, and by early June it had completed fourteen sorties, ten of them supersonic. The maximum speed achieved so far was Mach 1.63 above 40,000 feet (12,192m), and on four occasions it had proved to be possible to fly twice in a day. The aircraft did not make any high-speed manoeuvres except for a 3g turn at 25,000 feet (7,620m) while flying at Mach 0.9, but handling proved to be fine.

Unfortunately, a defective reheat nozzle system, which caused fluctuations in the nozzle position above about Mach 1.5, limited the progress that was made. Two unsuccessful engine relights on Flight 11 prompted a decision to suspend the high-speed programme to permit an engine change. In truth, the PS.50 Gyron Junior was not reliable or developed enough. It showed a tendency to surge outside a narrow range of incidences, while blade vibration problems required considerable modifications. The 188 was the only aircraft using the PS.50, and the pressure of work on de Havilland from other orders prevented a rapid solution to some of the problems. In August 1963 it was proposed that the project be run down and closed within the current financial year, although a limited but intensive flight programme up to December 1963 was drawn up for XF926. It was hoped that this would supply as much useful data as possible.

Up to late June a further twenty-one flights were made. Flutter testing was restricted by the fact that the engines burned fuel at a much higher rate than had been predicted and, indeed, there would never be enough on board to provide flight at sustained high speeds. Twelve supersonic flights were made in June and July, however, and Mach 1.83 was achieved in July on one of the final flights before the engines were changed. Reheat malfunctions were still a problem, but an operating technique had been worked out using a method of careful selection and adjustment, which appeared to make the afterburners work better.

With the opportunity for further testing still available, Mach 2-capable Gyron Juniors were installed during August and September – the original units had been limited to Mach 1.6 operation. Flying resumed on 4 October, but by mid-December just eleven flights had been made because the operation of the inlet guide vanes now gave considerable trouble, and the starboard power unit surged supersonically half a dozen times and had to be modified. However, there were no other major worries because the cause of the afterburner problems had at last been cured. Flight 47 in mid-November saw XF926 achieve Mach 1.88 at 36,000 feet (10,973m), the fastest speed achieved so far and indeed the highest that the aircraft attained during its career. Right through the flight programme the 188 had given low figures for drag, and estimates indicated that it would be capable of 1½ minutes at Mach 2 and a

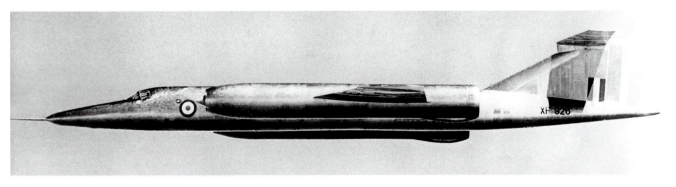

Above and right: A model of the Type 188N. *Courtesy of the late Jim Oughton*

maximum of Mach 2.2, but there was no longer enough time to undertake the pressure-plotting, kinetic heating and digital recording programme that had been outlined when the new engines were installed. Bad weather delayed the last four flights until January 1964, the final sortie being made on the 16th. A further sixty-flight programme proposed by Bristol to assist with Concorde development was not taken up.

Both airframes were now placed in store, XF926 joining XF923 in March 1964. On 7 November 1966 they were Struck Off Charge and were subsequently sent to the Proof & Experimental Establishment at Shoeburyness to serve as gunnery targets. XF926 survived and in November 1974 was recovered and taken to what today is the RAF Museum at Cosford. As such it was given ground instruction airframe number 8368M and has been on display there ever since.

The 188 proved to be the only jet-powered aircraft to be built and flown by the Bristol Aircraft Company before it became part of the British Aircraft Corporation. It was an expensive project, but a good percentage of its funding covered basic research that benefited other aircraft and programmes. The introduction of real-time telemetry, where data could be assessed as it happened, was an important breakthrough, but there was never enough internal fuel to provide long flights – 25 minutes was standard, although on one occasion 48 minutes was achieved. With the Americans already having flown the X-series of research aircraft to Mach 3 and beyond, the case for the 188 might be questioned, but the data it supplied did help the Concorde supersonic transport programme and the concurrent BAC TSR.2 strike aircraft. It is understood that an important reason why the 188 performed so badly, and failed to reach Mach 2, was the arrangement for the airflow passing through the nacelles, which did not match up very well. The reason behind this was successive changes to the type of engine to be fitted in the aircraft, and in the end the powerplant formed the biggest restriction to the value and potential of the Bristol 188 as a research vehicle.

De Havilland Engines fitted Gloster Javelin Mk.1 fighter XA552 with two Gyron Juniors, the same powerplant as the Bristol 188. 188 test pilot Godfrey Auty flew this aircraft many times, which was painted in a deep blue colour scheme. *Author's collection*

X-PLANES OF EUROPE

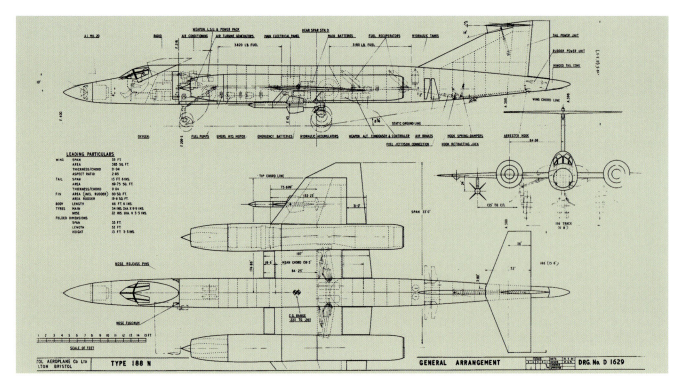

There were proposals for some 188 developments. This drawing shows the Bristol 188N single-seat fighter, possibly for naval use. There are subtle differences from the standard research aircraft's airframe and it carries an AI Mk 20 radar in the nose and two air-to-air missiles beneath the wings. The non-structural end of the rear fuselage could fold downwards while the nose section with the pilot's cockpit folded to port. There was no need for wing folding and two fuselage tanks held 3,820lb (1,733kg) and 3,180lb (1,442kg) of fuel respectively. The span was 35 feet (10.67m), the wing area 383sq ft (35.62sq m), and the powerplant was two de Havilland Gyron Juniors. The drawing is dated 31 March 1955. *The late Jim Oughton*

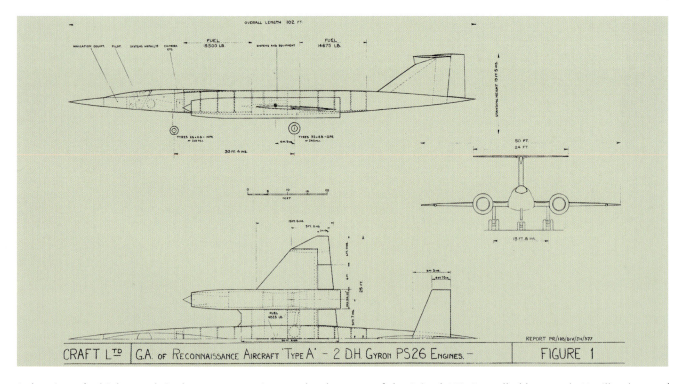

A drawing of a high-speed single-seat reconnaissance development of the Bristol 188. Propelled by two de Havilland Gyron PS.26 engines, more powerful than the Gyron Junior, this August 1957 idea had a span of 50 feet (15.24m) and an overall length of 102 feet (31.09m). Cameras were placed behind the nose gear, fuselage tanks held 15,500lb (7,031kg) and 14,675lb (6,657kg) of fuel, and there was a tank with a 4,825lb (2,189kg) capacity in each inner wing. This design was larger than the 188 and perhaps could be compared to the Lockheed SR-71. *The late Jim Oughton*

XDF923 makes a pass during its performance on 8 September 1962. *Roy Bonser-KEC*

The first Bristol 188 XDF923 retracts its undercarriage at the start of its display at the Farnborough Air Show on 8 September 1962. *Roy Bonser-KEC*

A little story to finish the 188 chapter, and a story well known in the test pilot world, is that on 31 July 1963 RAE test pilot Paul Millet was in XF926 when he experienced a double-flameout while flying at more than 1,000mph (1,609km/h) at 47,000 feet (14,325m). He was able to land safely but the event meant that after this single flight Millet was now able to wear a 1,000mph (1,609km/h) tie for the first time, and also a Gliding Badge because for a period the 188 had been flying as a glider.

33 Dassault Balzac (1962)

Dassault Balzac V

Span: 24ft 0in (7.32m)
Length: 43ft 0in (13.1m)
Wing area: 292.5sq ft (27.2sq m)
Max gross take-off weight: 15,432lb (7,000kg)
Powerplant: 1 x BS Orpheus BOr.3 cruise turbojet engine, 4,850lb (21.6kN)
8 x RR RB.108A lift turbojet engines, 2,210lb (9.6kN)
Max speed/height: 686mph (1,104km/h) at sea level

The Marcel Dassault Company started working on the concept of vertical take-off and landing (VTOL) aircraft in the early 1960s, and for its early flight research decided to rebuild the original Mirage III prototype into a research aeroplane. The aircraft's single French Atar 101 turbojet was replaced by a Bristol Siddeley Orpheus 3 engine with 5,000lb (22.2kN) thrust for forward propulsion, while a battery of eight smaller 2,200lb (9.8kN) Rolls-Royce RB.108 turbojets was installed to provide vertical lift. The main engine and separate lift engines were not integrated and acted independently of each other. Air was fed to each of the smaller lift engines by retractable air intake grilles (Rolls-Royce had designed the lift engine intakes and tested them extensively), and during normal forward flight their exhausts were covered by flush-fitting retractable fairings. By selecting this route the French thus adopted a somewhat different approach to jet-powered vertical flight from that taken by the British with their experimental Hawker P.1127 VTOL aircraft (qv). The latter was powered by a single turbojet augmented by four large louvred lift fans – by comparison, the Balzac's propulsion and lift thrust system was rather more complicated with its nine separate independent components.

The Balzac was built using the airframe of the Mirage III fighter prototype 001, and in its new form it was renamed Balzac V 001, the 'V' of course reflecting VTOL operation (at times it was called the Balzac V). Balzac was actually the nickname given to the Mirage III 001 even before it became a VTOL prototype and the nickname should be 'Balzac 001' rather than just 'Balzac', but almost everyone shortens the name to 'Balzac'. It was Dassault practice to number its prototypes from 001, and development aircraft from 01. At the time 'Jean Mineur Publicité' was a famous advertising company in cinemas and its telephone number was BALZAC001. This number was, therefore, known to everybody and so the name Balzac was given to the prototype initially just for fun, but in due course it became official.

In truth the only surviving parts from the original were the wings and fin, and although the main fuselage frames and cockpit section were retained the overall structure was entirely new and was built by Sud. The forward propulsion powerplant was the single Orpheus 3 turbojet mounted in the fuselage tail, and the ducts from the small side intakes (with fixed shock cones) that supplied air to it were arranged to unite and pass between the two rows of four RB.108 lift jets. The latter were disposed in pairs fore and aft of the mainwheel bays and their presence forced a widening of the fuselage, which automatically eliminated the original aircraft's area-rule shaping at that point. Nevertheless the Orpheus was sufficiently powerful to provide high-subsonic speeds on the level. There was almost no alteration to the original nose contours, except that the pilot had a slightly better downward view.

The Balzac used a control jet system designed by SNECMA and based on the experience and work done on the Coléoptère (Chapter 35). It used 11% lift-jet air bleed that was taken into a common system of ducting, which featured twin ducts at the nose, tail and wingtips together with (for low-speed yaw control) single ducts in the sides of the rear fuselage. During operation one of each pair of ducts or 'puffer pipes' would run continuously at full thrust, and the total thrust and volume from all four corners would remain constant. Asymmetric thrust (as required for attitude control) was supplied by reducing the flow to the main duct on one side while producing additional flow through the second duct on the other, while the yaw jets were controlled by a single valve linked by cable with the normal rudder controls. As long as the lift jets were supplying power, the elevons and jet system would operate together. The Balzac's total fuel capacity was 363 gallons (1,650 litres) and sufficient of this was held back in a main tank to achieve a vertical landing. When all of the lift engines were running together the fuel supply allowed a total of 12 minutes of hovering.

Work progressed rapidly and the Balzac made its first ground runs on 31 July 1962. It began tethered hover testing at Melun-Villaroche on 12 October 1962 with Dassault's chief test pilot René Bigand at the controls. As part of his preparations Bigand had flown the Short S.C.1 (qv) on eight occasions. (Bigand died on 18 May 1967 when the first Mirage F.1 prototype he was testing broke up in flight due to flutter.) After two more tethered flights, the first free-flight hover was achieved on the 18th (almost two months earlier than had been projected), and for its third free flight on 25 October the Balzac continued to hover for more than 2 minutes. On 6 November the aircraft was displayed to the press (rather unusually early, since only eight test flights had been made) in hovering flight over the Melun-Villaroche test pit – the ninth flight was the public display.

At the start the aircraft had a fixed, strut-braced undercarriage with an exceptionally long-levered suspension for its twin-wheel main units (this was instrumented for landing loads), but after the trials programme had moved sufficiently forward a complex retractable Messier undercarriage was fitted at Dassault's experimental shops at St Cloud during the hard winter of 1962/63 so that the aircraft could undertake forward flight at higher speeds. After a short hop the previous day, Bigand took the Balzac on its first conventional flight on 2 March 1963, and the aeroplane's first successful transition from vertical take-off to horizontal flight was achieved on 18 March 1963 during its seventeenth test flight (the aircraft made a conventional landing). On 28 March a decelerating transition from wing-borne flight to a vertical landing was made, while a full double transition (VTO to forward flight to vertical landing) was achieved the very next day. Flight evaluation by CEV began on 10 April, and subsequent flight tests proved that the aircraft was able to survive the failure of any one or two of its RB.108 engines. Then during the winter of 1963/64 it was fitted with lift-jet deflector doors specifically for ground running and to perform short, forward running take-offs. These were made at a lift speed of 60 knots (111km/h), the doors allowing their thrust to be vectored aft at angles up to a maximum of 45° from the vertical.

The Dassault Balzac on the ramp, showing the lift engine intakes in the open extended position. *Copyright Musée de l'Air et de l'Espace, Paris/Le Bourget*

X-PLANES OF EUROPE

The Dassault Balzac is seen in low-altitude hover. Note the aircraft's novel 'trailing arm' nose and main landing gear designed for maximum shock absorption to mitigate impact loads during vertical landings. *Musée de l'Air et de l'Espace, Paris/Le Bourget*

The test programme progressed well until 10 January 1964 when the Balzac crashed at Melun-Villaroche from a low-altitude hover at about 325 feet (100m), fatally injuring its pilot, Jacques Pinier. The accident scenario was described as starting with a slow vertical descent during which the aircraft began to experience divergent lateral wing oscillations that grew in intensity until they became uncontrollable. The left wing eventually struck the ground at a fairly steep angle, and the aircraft continued to roll over due to the continuous emission of lift engine thrust. The ultimate loss of control was attributed to the control authority of the three-axis autostabilisation system being exceeded during roll pulse testing. Pinier suffered fatal injuries when the aircraft rolled over onto its back, trapping him inside the cockpit. Unfortunately, prior to the impact he had been unable to eject because he was at such a low altitude and the aircraft was in a steep bank.

The extensively damaged Balzac was rebuilt and resumed flight testing on 2 February 1965. A new flying programme was planned to establish flying techniques and any aerodynamic alterations that might be required to improve the machine's transversal handling. After several evaluation flights by CEV, a trial take-off from a clearing in a wood (on 15 June), and a flying display at that year's Paris Show in June, the Balzac suffered another fatal accident on 8 September 1965, once again while flying in a low-altitude hover. This time it was being evaluated as part of a Franco-American exchange programme on VTOL technology. US Air Force Major P. E. Neale ejected from the aircraft but not within the seat's operating envelope, and was killed on impact. Although the findings of the French accident investigation board were never made public, it was widely speculated that excessive use of the lift engines caused by hydraulic control system problems resulted in fuel starvation and subsequent flameout of both the main Orpheus 3 turbojet and, unbelievably, all eight RB.108 lift engines at once. The aircraft was destroyed, but by now the development of the improved Dassault Mirage IIIV prototype was under way.

The curious crouched attitude of the Balzac on the ground is well shown in this photograph.

X-PLANES OF EUROPE

These images of the Balzac were taken before first flight and just before ground running began. In due course the nose was painted black to simulate a radar nose and to avoid glare for the pilot, and the main undercarriage doors were fitted.

An independent view

A visit was made by RAE Farnborough representatives on 3 and 4 December 1963 to see the Balzac in France, and some fascinating background information on the aircraft is available from the resulting report. The Balzac was approximately a 0.87 linear scale model of the forthcoming Mirage IIIV tactical strike VTOL aircraft and roughly half of the weight. Since the 5,000lb (22.2kN) thrust of the Orpheus 3 alone would result in a lower propulsive thrust/weight ratio than that of the Mirage IIIV, the acceleration during an accelerating transition in a level attitude would suffer. Therefore the Balzac's lift engines were fixed at 7° nose up, whereas the Mirage IIIV was to be more nearly horizontal. The wing, a 60° delta, had a thickness/chord ratio of 5% and carried split elevon controls. The wing was somewhat thicker than that of the Mirage IIIV to allow more space for the air jet ducting and to increase the fuel capacity of the integral wing tanks.

The aircraft was 'rolled out' in July 1962, and by the end of October had made three tethered and six free hover flights. Tethered flight was found to be very difficult and of somewhat limited value for anything other than gaining a very restricted idea of whether or not the characteristics were satisfactory for free hover. The aircraft was then grounded for modifications including an increase in roll control power (by moving the nozzles nearer

It is sometimes forgotten that the Balzac still used the delta wing which featured so strongly with many of Dassault's series of Mirage fighters and bombers.

to the wingtips), the fitting of the retractable undercarriage, and the installation of a brake parachute. It flew again in March 1963 and the first public demonstration of a double transition was made on 8 April 1963.

Following the Paris Air Show in 1963, several flights were made to study control problems with one engine stopped. First a vertical take-off was done on seven engines, followed by a partial accelerating transition to about 40 knots (74km/h). Then, after a conventional take-off, seven lift engines were started and the aircraft decelerated to about 100 knots (185km/h), and the results were much better than expected. Some slow rolling and vertical take-offs from the 'solid' were also done in July 1963, following lift engine starting over the flush pit at Melun-Villaroche. All VTOL flying had so far been done from this pit, except for the 1963 Paris Show displays where a 'portable' platform was used (for which the pilots had a strong dislike). In July the aircraft was grounded for further modifications.

Another French VTOL design submitted to NBMR.3 in 1961 was the Sud Aviation X-600 project which featured a cranked 'double-delta' wing and had a span of 7.255m (23ft 10inc) and length 14.600m (47ft 11inc). It was to be powered by six Rolls-Royce RB.162 lift jets set in three pairs in the centre fuselage and either a single RB.168 or Pratt & Whitney JTF-10 propulsion unit. Top speed was expected to be in the region of Mach 1.8. There was also a version with a pure delta wing swept at 78° on the leading edge.

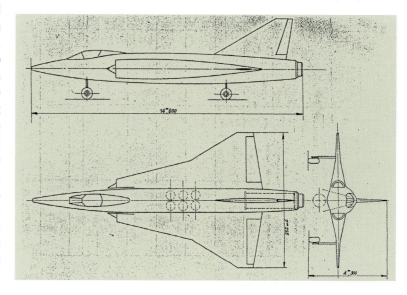

Dassault Balzac, powered by eight Rolls-Royce RB108-1A lift turbojets and one Bristol Siddeley Orpheus BOr 3 Cruise turbojet. *Chris Sandham-Bailey www.inkworm.com*

Although the upper image of the Dassault Balzac has the undercarriage up, in both pictures the aircraft is in fact in the hover.

For accelerating transitions a VTO was performed in the 7° nose-up ground attitude using full power on all lift engines. The propulsion engine thrust was increased more slowly after take-off, then, to increase forward acceleration, a small nose-down attitude change was made, which was soon followed by a sharp rotation to about 12° nose up to produce aerodynamic lift as the speed increased through 80 knots (148km/h). In spite of this, the aircraft only gained height by virtue of the initial rate of climb developed at lift-off. The transition would end, typically, after 50 seconds with the aircraft at 180 knots (333km/h) and 500 feet (150m), having in the process covered 10,000 feet (3,050m) horizontally.

On decelerating transitions the lift engines were normally lit at about 200 knots (370km/h) and 1,500 feet (460m) on a downwind leg when opposite the up-wind end of the runway. The light-up was accompanied by a moderate nose-up trim change, but with no appreciable changes in control characteristics, and the 'finals' turn was made in a descent at 170 to 180 knots (315 to 333km/h) with the aircraft more or less lined up with the landing direction at 170 knots (315km/h) and 500 feet (150m), keeping height in hand. Attitude was held constant at the normal 7° nose-up during a deceleration (i.e. with the lift engines vertical). Rate of descent was controlled with the lift engines, a sharp increase to almost full power being required as the speed fell towards 100 knots (185km/h). The normal deceleration rate was 4 knots per second (7.5km/h per sec) with a little power kept on the Orpheus engine to allow for adjustment. The lateral behaviour of the Balzac was such that, while an approach might be started across-wind, the pilots would probably tend to fly a curved or spiral path so that the aircraft ended up into wind, such was the sensitivity to crosswinds. One criticism made of the Balzac by the RAE team was the field of view from the cockpit – the downwards view ahead was seriously obstructed by the nose, and aggravated by the aircraft's nose-up attitude.

The Balzac was subsequently followed by the Dassault Mirage IIIV prototypes. The IIIV was originally proposed against the NBMR.3 requirement (NATO Basic Military Requirement 3) for an all-weather supersonic VTO strike, reconnaissance and tactical support aircraft, which was circulated to European industry in June 1961. The first of two prototypes, rather

DASSAULT BALZAC (1962)

Here the Balzac is mounted on the special 'portable' take-off platform used to display the aircraft at the 1963 Paris Show. *David Hedge*

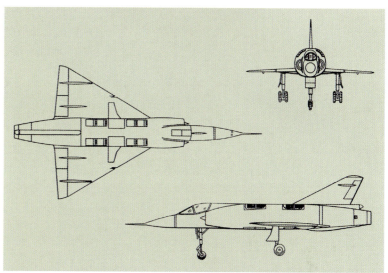

Drawing of the Dassault Balzac.

bigger than the Balzac of course, made its first hovering flight in 1965. The Balzac and the Mirage IIIV were impressive aircraft that showed evidence of considerable design ingenuity and attention to detail. Flight testing revealed a wealth of data, but in December 1965 the Mirage IIIV production programme was postponed, then cancelled in 1966, in part due to the very high cost of the weapon system and in part from the fact that development of the airframe was in advance of its propulsion system. In addition, the expensive lift jets did not provide enough thrust while the aircraft itself had a limited weapon load and range.

The Balzac was followed by the larger Mirage IIIV which was submitted against the NATO NBMR.3 requirement. This picture of the second aircraft was taken in 1966 and shows the open doors on top of the fuselage which provided air to the lift engines.

34 EWR VJ 101C (1963)

EWR VJ 101C

Span: 21ft 6in (6.55m)
Length: 56ft 9in (17.30m) with probe
Gross wing area: 200.2sq ft (18.62sq m)
Gross weight: 18,000lb (8,165kg)
Powerplant: 6 x RR RB.145, 2,750lb (12.2kN); X2 afterburner on wing units, 3,750lb (16.7kN)
Max speed/height: X1: 771mph (1,240km/h) at 19,685ft (6,000m); X2: 820mph (1,320km/h) at 19,685ft (6,000m)
Ceiling: Unknown

The EWR VJ 101C 'tiltjet' aircraft project was the first of two high-performance VTOL aircraft to come out of West Germany during the 1960s (the second is discussed later in this book). In its early life the VJ 101C was intended to serve as a prototype platform for an interceptor, but this later aircraft did not go ahead. During its career the VJ 101C became the first VTOL aircraft to fly at supersonic speed on the level, and it was another project to use a trials hover rig to test the concept (in fact, in this case, two of them). The VJ initials stood for Versuchsjäger ('Experimental Fighter'), although prior to the type's unveiling at Manching in May 1963 it had been dubbed by the popular press as the Traumjäger ('Dream Fighter').

An entirely new concept

In the late 1950s Bölkow, Heinkel and Messerschmitt all submitted designs to meet a requirement for a new fighter. It was intended that the new type should have VTOL capability, and in early 1959 the three organisations founded a joint venture subsidiary company in Munich, Entwicklungsrind Süd (EWR), to build the resulting airframe. It was called the VJ 101C and merged some of the characteristics of the earlier proposals into a very sleek aeroplane with a high wing and swivelling engine nacelles mounted at the tips. The wingtip nacelles, or pods, each housed a pair of engines for lift and for forward cruise propulsion. For hovering flight they were complemented by a pair of vertically mounted lift jets placed just behind the cockpit with a door that opened when these units were running. The six engines were all Rolls-Royce RB.145s, and during forward flight the two lift jets shut down. This particular configuration was not unique because Bell in America had previously produced its D-188 project as a potential fighter for both the US Air Force and Navy, and this too had engines in rotating wingtip nacelles. However, that programme was abandoned in 1961 having progressed little further than a full-size mock-up. By then work on the VJ 101C was under way, and Bell Aerosystems was to provide a good deal of support to the EWR project.

For control during flight the 101C did not employ compressor bleed air with 'puffer pipes', a feature of many early VTOL aircraft, but used variations of thrust from the wing nacelle engines. To do this the engines needed to make fast responses to thrust change commands from the pilot. The idea was first tried in June 1960 on a contraption called the Wippe ('seesaw'), which was built at EWR but assembled by Rolls-Royce at Hucknall in England. The Wippe used a horizontal beam with a transverse horizontal pivot at one end and a rudimentary cockpit on the other. Mounted vertically in the centre at a

This early view of X1 shows its fixed undercarriage and the swivelling engine pods almost in the vertical position. The lift engine door is closed. *VFW-Fokker*

suitable distance from the axis of oscillation was a Rolls RB.108 lift jet. At the cockpit end the 'free' arm could go up and down and the pilot could control this movement by using the engine throttle. The arm could move 15° either up or down and required 80% of the available thrust to stay on the level – opening and closing the throttle made it rise or fall like a seesaw. The Wippe made 146 'flights' at Hucknall before the programme ended there in November 1960, and another sixty-one after it returned to Manching.

This effort was followed by a special hover rig flying platform assembled as a skeletal fuselage of the VJ 101C and laid out to the same configuration. A frame of tubular steel was fitted with outriggers, and three 2,100lb (9.3kN) Rolls-Royce RB.108 lift engines were placed in the approximate positions of the VJ 101C, each of them equidistant from the centre of gravity. One was mounted behind the pilot, the others at the wingtips, and the machine had a span of 33 feet (10.06m) and a length of 35 feet (10.67m). The first tests made with this rig, in March 1961, saw it mounted on a telescopic pole with a universal joint, which gave 4° of freedom – pitch (via differential throttling), roll, yaw (by outer engine swivelling) and altitude. The pole trials lasted for some time and it was not until 13 March 1962 that the rig, with an undercarriage now in place, performed its first free flight in the hands of George Bright,

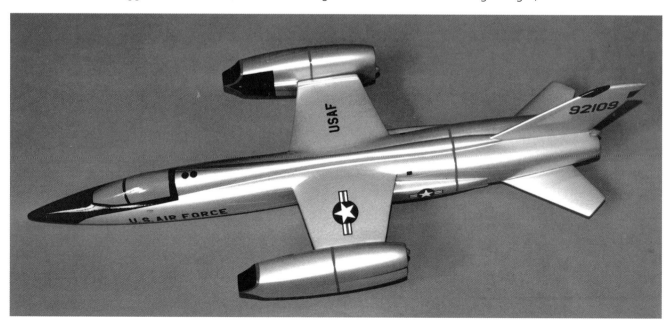

A model of the Bell D-188 project, which had a great deal in common with the VJ 101C. *George Cox*

The EWR hover rig had three RB.108 lift jets and was designed to simulate the hover aspects of the VJ 101C. *Author's collection*

EWR's American test pilot. It went on to make 126 free flights in all. Subsequent trials were made with a simulated wing and fuselage skin covering made of cloth, which showed that the rig exhibited superb control in all types of weather conditions – hot, cold, wet and windy – either with the automatic flight system operating or in manual control.

In the meantime work had progressed on the VJ 101C. Its very thin swept wings were built as a one-piece structure and contained some fuel. The entire airframe was built primarily in light alloy, although some titanium and steel were employed in the hot areas near the engines. There was a small horizontal tailplane and a larger fin, and the aircraft used a narrow-track tricycle undercarriage that retracted into the fuselage. Telemetry

The Wippe test platform was built in the UK *Thomas Mueller collection*

VJ 101C X1 is seen during early ground tests mounted on top of a pedestal. *VFW-Fokker*

equipment was carried in the nose. The development and construction of the complete swivelling wingtip pod installation was the task of Rolls-Royce at Hucknall, which also built a fifth pod specially for testing in the company's wind tunnel. These pods had a central shock cone and swivelled on a hollow shaft through which passed the control lines (for engine operation) and the fuel and oil lines.

A unique intake system was used on the pod, which was capable of supplying air to the engines through all phases of operation – during a vertical lift-off, the swivelling of the pod during transition to forward flight or back, and normal flight. When the 101C was moving forward horizontally at slow speeds the intake cowlings moved forward to expose additional intake area. Everything was packed in tight to give the pod the lowest possible frontal area and they could rotate through 94° to provide a component of reverse thrust when the 101C was slowing for landing. One benefit of the swivelling pod was that all of the installed thrust was available for VTOL, with no thrust losses such as would arise with jet deflection. In forward flight a single throttle could operate all engines, but each unit had its own throttle for individual operation. For roll, the thrust from two engines on one side was reduced while the opposite side had theirs increased. For pitch the forward lift units had the thrust either reduced or increased as required while both sets of pod engines did the opposite. For yaw the two pods could tilt in opposing directions. The VJ 101C became purely a research aircraft and carried no weapons; it was the follow-on VJ 101D that was now expected to serve as a fighter.

This photograph, dated 16 October 1963, shows X1 with the engine pods in the forward-flight position, almost as if it is about to make a conventional take-off. Considering that two RB.145s are in each nacelle, the powerplant was very compact. *VFW-Fokker*

In flight

Two prototype VJ 101Cs were built, labelled X1 and X2 and carrying German serials D-9517 and D-9518 respectively. VJ 101C X1's role was to serve as a low-speed aircraft to explore the VTOL characteristics and the flight envelope up to about Mach 0.45 maximum, so to begin with it had a fixed undercarriage. Ground running tests began in late December 1962 (or January 1963), the aircraft made its first hovering flight (again piloted by Bright) on 9 April, and on 10 May it was unveiled to the public at EWR's test facility at the Manching airfield near Munich. The first conventional take-off followed on 31 August to begin the evaluation of the aircraft's low-speed behaviour. A small degree of Dutch roll experienced early on was cured by the application of the X1's automatic damping system. The first transition from hovering flight to aerodynamic flight was achieved by Bright on 20 September, but this was only a partial transition (from vertical to forward flight). The first full double transition (vertical take-off, transition to forward flight, back to the hover, then vertical land) was not long in coming, however, and was achieved on 8 October 1963. On 3 May 1964 the first VJ 101C was displayed at the Hanover Air Show.

Despite having been earmarked for slow-speed research, on 29 July 1964 VJ 101C X1 reached a speed of Mach 1.04 in level flight. This was without having reheat available, making the aircraft the first VTOL type in the world to achieve this mark. In fact, X1 went supersonic on several occasions during a brief

A model of the proposed VJ 101D fighter project. *Author's collection*

high-speed flight programme held in August. On 14 September 1964, at the start of its 132nd flight, VJ 101C X1 crashed after making a conventional take-off. The powerful pitch autostabiliser unit had not been correctly installed and this produced a rapid divergent pitch oscillation. The airframe was wrecked and, despite managing to eject, Bright was injured. In all, the aircraft had accumulated nearly 15.5 hours of free flight.

X2 was chosen to perform the high-speed portion of the test programme. Afterburners were introduced to the wingtip pods to take the speed through to what was hoped would be about Mach 1.1. X2 also featured a new autopilot and Bright took it on its first hovering flight at Manching on 27 October 1964. The first conventional flight was made on 12 July 1965. A first vertical take-off with afterburning was performed on 12 October (which must have been something to see and hear), then X2 made a first successful double transition using the afterburners on 22 October.

The proposed Mach 2-capable VJ 101D interceptor, with the engines mounted in the fuselage and not in swivelling pods, was never built. However, part of X2's flight programme covered basic VTOL research as well as testing for the Advanced Vertical Strike Fighter (AVS), a 1960s proposal for a V/STOL fighter programme between West Germany and the United States that would use lift engines that swung out from the sides of the fuselage; this too was never built. In this role X2 completed a first rolling vertical take-off from a conventional runway using reheat on 19 September 1968. It went supersonic (Mach 1.14) for the first time on 21 April 1969, and it is understood that at a later date it achieved a top speed of Mach 1.2. Towards the end of its career VJ 101C X2 found employment in the testing of avionics and fly-by-wire systems for the Panavia MRCA Tornado. It continued to operate until the last flight (No 325) was made on 27 May 1971.

A former member of the Harrier development team has said that he was astonished that the VJ 101C's designers had put all of the engines and their thrust at the wingtips. Consider the effect of an engine failure in the hover – the aircraft would turn over almost instantly! At least the Harrier would crash flat, giving the pilot a chance to escape. Also consider the complexity of the engineering needed to get the plumbing and services from the fixed wing to the moving engines, and the auto control necessary to keep all of the engines working in unison and to try to compensate for engine failures. It is worth commenting that the next version (the unbuilt VJ 101D) put the engines back into the fuselage. Consequently, it would be wrong to describe the VJ 101C as a success. It was a fascinating experiment, which flew supersonically and continued to fly for eight years, but to employ a configuration where the engines were so far apart was surely a mistake for a vertical-take-off aeroplane.

X1 is photographed in the hover, or maybe more accurately moving slowly forward, since the engine pods are angled slightly. *Author's collection*

The first VJ 101C X1 at altitude in clean condition for maximum forward speed. *VFW-Fokker/Thomas Mueller*

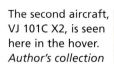

X-PLANES OF EUROPE

The second aircraft, VJ 101C X2, is seen here in the hover. *Author's collection*

The VJ 101C hovers with the wing nacelles set fully in the vertical position. Note the exhaust pipes for the forward fuselage lift jets, and that all six engines are numbered – 1 and 2 and 5 and 6 in nacelles, 3 and 4 in the fuselage.

Two early pictures taken in 1963 showing the first VJ 101C, without any identity applied, on the ground and just entering the hover. The large size of the engine nacelles comes over well in these views. Note the cover for the fuselage engines just behind the cockpit canopy.

EWR VJ 101C, powered by six Rolls-Royce RB145 turbojets. Currently on display at Deutsches Museum in Munich, Germany. *Chris Sandham-Bailey www.inkworm.com*

35 Hunting H.126 (1963)

Hunting H.126

Span: 45ft 4.5in (13.83m) with 4° dihedral
Length: 50ft 2in (15.29m) with probe
Gross wing area: 217.0sq ft (20.18sq m)
Gross weight: 10,740lb (4,872kg)
Powerplant: 1 x BS Orpheus 805, 4,850lb (21.6kN)
Max speed: 288mph (463km/h)
Ceiling: Unknown

First thoughts

The idea for a 'jet flap' wing dates back to at least 1938 when the German aerodynamicists Hagedorn and Ruden in Hanover were working on boundary-layer control, in the course of which the effect of large quantities of ejected air at the wing trailing edge became apparent. Unfortunately, their report did not become available in Britain until 1945. The UK's research into the concept began in November 1952 at the British National Gas Turbine Establishment (NGTE), and the first project for a research aircraft was submitted by Hunting Percival Ltd in 1955 with a proposed conversion of a de Havilland (Canada) Otter utility transport. Specification ER.175D covered this but, once the engineering problems of jet flap had been studied in detail, in July 1956 the Otter project was turned down. However, there was strong support at RAE Farnborough that flight experiment with a jet flap aircraft should proceed and plans now turned to an all-new design. Hunting Percival received a contract to investigate possible layouts for a small jet flap aircraft, and in September the firm completed a report that described twelve preliminary designs, the most promising of which was the JFR.12 powered by two fuselage-mounted Armstrong Siddeley Viper jets (this came under Hunting Percival's H.121/6 project number). The JFR.12 was expected to be capable of 19 minutes of flying time in full jet flap operation, or 46 minutes on cruise. Further studies were made for a 60° delta-wing design, but these were rejected due to the high power that would be required to give a useful increase in lift coefficient.

Eventually the work came together in the company's H.126 design, and on 30 April 1958 a purchase requisition was made for two examples. Detailed design was under way by July

The unusual Hunting H.126 was designed to explore the low-speed handling characteristics of an aircraft fitted with the 'jet flap' wing from the point of view of providing propulsion and additional lift. The objective was to blow air out through the back of the full span of the wing so fast that the oncoming air considered it to be one large mechanical flap; in effect this would artificially increase the wing area. In the 1950s the application of jet flap was still not clearly defined, but its use in improving the airfield performance of a high-subsonic-speed aircraft such as a transport showed great promise. If such a type could fly more slowly when taking off and landing it would not require such a long runway. Hunting Percival Aircraft (the Percival part of the name disappeared in 1957) became involved in this research through some earlier work in the field of hot gas ducting in helicopters with tip-driven rotors. The resulting H.126's rather basic – even archaic-looking – appearance belied the fact that it was an advanced and unique aircraft.

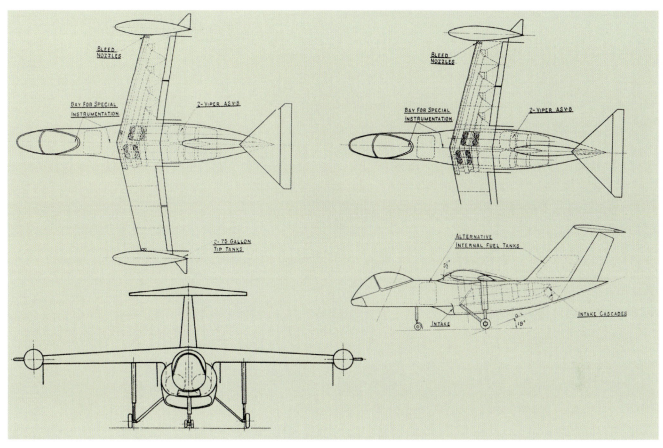

The Hunting Percival JFR.12 design with two Viper ASV-8 jets in the centre fuselage had a span (without tip tanks) of 26 feet (7.92m), a length of 37ft 3in (11.35m), and a gross wing area of 111 square feet (10.32sq m). The estimated all-up weight was 5,000lb (2,268kg). The drawing is dated 25 September 1956. *British National Archives (AVIA 65 – 610)*

XN714 is towed from the hangar at Luton in August 1962 prior to receiving its yellow paint scheme. The cockpit and intake are masked and ready for the painters. *Phil Butler collection*

X-PLANES OF EUROPE

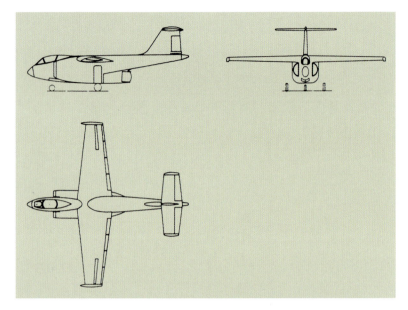

This is the Avro 746 jet flap research aircraft proposal of August 1957. The Ministry rejected this design because of its cost, since it could not sponsor a special engine development such as a version of the Bristol BE.53 used here while there was any chance of obtaining a powerplant using engines already available. For this particular project, which was to test high lift coefficients, the Ministry preferred a twin-engine layout. Using the BE.53 made it a fairly large aircraft anyway, and doubling the powerplant would make it even bigger. The 746 was 43 feet (13.11 m) long, had a span of 42ft 5in (12.92 m), and a wing area of 300 square feet (27.90sq m). The BE.53 was at the time a new development for the P.1127 (qv), and air for the 746 was to be bled from the compressor to feed the wing's jet flap system, while a conventional jetpipe exhausted underneath the fuselage. *Avro Heritage, Woodford*

XN714 was the only Hunting H.126 research aircraft to be completed. Here the aircraft has wool tufts all over its airframe and the pilot has part of the canopy behind him screened off, presumably to give some shade. *Author's collection*

1959, by which time the two Vipers had been replaced by a single Bristol Orpheus jet engine. The airframes were XN714 and XN719 and were covered by a new Specification, ER.189D, which expected the aircraft to carry sufficient fuel to achieve an endurance of not less than 15 minutes flying time at 10,000 feet (3,048m) with the engine operating in all conditions up to maximum continuous power. In the meantime, during 1957 Avro had presented its own brochure for a jet flap aircraft called the Type 746, but this was turned down in 1958.

The main aerodynamic features of the H.126 were a high-set wing to reduce the adverse effects of ground interference, a high-set tailplane to avoid the jet 'sheet' (and to avoid the most intense region of downwash), and a thick wing to avoid leading-edge separations and (from a practical point of view) to accommodate the wing ducting. Because of the high lift coefficients attainable by the wing, a powerful pitching control was required. This was achieved by combining a conventional manually operated elevator with a variable-incidence power-operated tailplane and a geared pitch jet. The moving tailplane was necessary to cope with the very large change of downwash near the ground, while a large fin would maintain weathercock stability.

The single de-rated Orpheus was installed in the nose beneath the cockpit. In the first instance all of the exhaust passed through a diffuser and was collected in what was termed the 'dustbin' – a vertical distribution manifold.

From here 60% of the jet efflux was fed into the wing ducts and exhausts, making the wing in essence a large jetpipe. There were three ducts in each wing, the aft pair supplying six fishtail nozzles and the front feeding two fishtails and a roll reaction-control jet (which took 5% of the thrust, leaving 55% for the wing itself). The jet sheet coming from the fishtails in full-span trailing-edge slots passed over highly cambered flaps and stainless steel power-controlled ailerons. Of the remaining exhaust, 30% went to the bifurcated jetpipe, which was placed low on the fuselage just to the rear of the wings, and the rest was used to feed reaction jets placed in the tail and exiting through a nozzle aft of the fin. The reaction jets in the wingtips were used for roll control and were controlled solely by an autostabiliser, while the yaw and pitch control jets in the tail were controlled directly by the stick in parallel with the normal flying controls. The fuselage jetpipes provided a nose-up moment to approximately counter the nose-down moment of the jet flap efflux.

Having hot exhaust gasses passing through so much of the airframe posed many design problems, but the use of heat-reflection shields actually permitted the majority of the H.126's structure to be built in light alloy. The aircraft had a fixed tricycle undercarriage and the second H.126, XN719, was to have featured 8° of dihedral on the wings (XN714 had just 4°). However, its construction was suspended on 8 May 1962, and the incomplete airframe was eventually destroyed.

Low-speed flying

XN714 began its ground running and taxi trials in August 1962 at Hunting's Luton factory where it was built. It was then dismantled and despatched to RAE Bedford in December, but severe winter weather prevented further taxiing until 19 March 1963 (when a few hops were also made). The aircraft sported a rather dazzling yellow colour scheme and the first flight was made on 26 March, piloted by Hunting chief test pilot Stanley B. Oliver. The second flight to assess the handling was made on 16 May at an all-up weight of 10,643lb (4,828kg). Oliver reported that the take-off was straightforward with adequate rudder control available. He experienced a little trouble in getting the aeroplane in trim

The H.126's heavy fixed undercarriage and thick wing are shown to good effect at this angle. *Author's collection*

Photographic evidence suggests that the H.126's characteristic nose-down flight attitude was not always visible, but it is well shown by this view, which also reveals how narrow the wing was. *Author's collection*

The Hunting H.126 and the Handley Page HP.115 (behind) low speed research aircraft photographed making their way across the English Channel on 9 June 1965 during their flight to the Paris Air Show at Le Bourget. *Clive Rustin*

longitudinally, and there was a slight directional wander in straight climbing flight. At 8,000 feet (2,438m) there was no sign of airframe buffet and no other problems were encountered. He noted that the trim change for application of power was nose-up, and for reduction of power nose-down, while putting the flaps down gave a nose-up trim change with the reverse when the flaps were raised. When the H.126 was airborne it flew at a most distinctive nose-down attitude.

Oliver made the fifteenth flight on 11 July 1963, and on 25, 26 and 31 July XN714 was flown by RAE Bedford pilot Flt Lt I. H. Keppie. His report stated that the aircraft was subject to a slight Dutch-rolling oscillation of 2° or 3° amplitude in both yaw and roll, but this was not particularly uncomfortable. The maximum EAS with flaps up was given as 250 knots (288mph/463km/h), although during this period XN714 was only flown to 225 knots (259mph/417km/h), and with 20° of flap 124 knots (143mph/230km/h). The aircraft was found to be almost neutrally stable from the stall up to 210 knots (242mph/389km/h). The tailplane and aileron controls were powerful and sensitive, but the rudder felt sluggish and insensitive by comparison. It was found that the stall was violent with flaps down and power on, and there was no stall warning, but the aircraft did not appear to be in danger of auto-rotation, even during a violent stall. Recovery was rapid. The H.126 was also found to be vulnerable to crosswinds during take-off and landing, and in particular the latter.

XN714 is seen at RAE Bedford, probably in May 1963, around the time of its first flight. Wool tufts can be seen fixed to the wings and the fuselage to permit the airflow to be viewed and photographed. *Phil Butler collection*

XN714 visited the Paris Air Show in June 1965, flying to Le Bourget via a long list of stops to refuel and including a night stop – in fact, the H.126's limited range made this trip quite an operation. The pilot for the show was D. G. Addicott, who had replaced Oliver when he moved to the BAC One-Eleven airliner programme. The H.126's range restrictions meant that it rarely travelled beyond Bedford's reach, although it did fly to Cranwell in September 1965 and up to Gaydon for a Battle of Britain display in September 1966. The close proximity of its Luton birthplace also allowed XN714 to return there during the early years of its flying career.

After a period spent at Boscombe Down from mid-October 1964, where it was used for canopy jettison trials, the H.126 joined RAE Bedford's Aero Flight on 18 March 1966. However, the British Aircraft Corporation, into which Hunting had by then been amalgamated, did most of the maintenance work. While in RAE service, XN714 was flown by John Farley, who was the RAE project pilot for the aircraft. Trials into high-lift flight continued for another 18 months before XN714's flying came to an end towards the close of 1967, when it was found that the wheel brakes were worn out. The aircraft was taken to the Hawker Siddeley facility at Holme-on-Spalding-Moor to be serviced and was then dismantled and carried across the Atlantic on 3 April 1969 by a Short Belfast transport aircraft. In America XN714 was tested in a large wind tunnel at the NASA Ames Center, but it did not fly. It arrived back in the UK on 14 May 1970, was Struck Off Charge in June 1972, and passed into preservation in 1974.

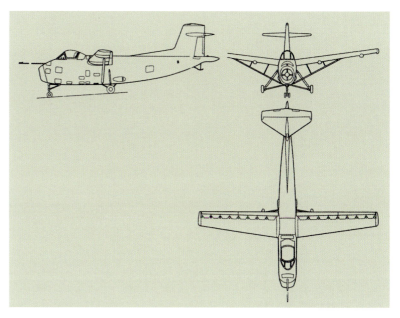

A three-view of the Hunting H.126. *Phil Butler collection*

Although based with the RAE for much of its career, the research performed by the H.126 was carried out primarily for the NGTE. XN714 proved to be successful in highlighting the problems and qualities of the jet flap and its operation, although the concept has never been adopted, since having a thick wing (and the potential fire risk of the hot ducting inside) is not good practice for transport aircraft. In addition, the take-off distance of modern airliners is no longer a problem thanks to their very effective and far simpler leading edge/trailing edge flap system. The lift coefficients demonstrated by the H.126 were remarkable, a figure in the region of 7 far exceeding the standard 1.5 for that time, and XN714 also demonstrated a minimum speed of 44 knots (51mph/82km/h). During its life the aircraft received hardly any modifications.

XN714 is just about to land at the end of a test flight during the early part of its career. Stanley Oliver is the pilot. *Author's collection*

36 BAC.221 (1964)

BAC 221

Span: 25ft 0in (7.62m)
Length: 57ft 7.5in (17.56m) with probe
Gross wing area: 504.0sq ft (46.87sq m)
Gross weight: c15,000lb (6,804kg)
Powerplant: 1 x RR Avon RA28R, 10,150lb (45.1kN) dry, 14,000lb (62.2kN) afterburner
Max speed: Mach 1.6 (drag limit)
Ceiling: Unknown

The Fairey Delta 2 high-speed research aircraft was described earlier in this book. The first Delta 2 airframe was eventually rebuilt into the British Aircraft Corporation (BAC) Type 221 for employment as a high-speed test aircraft for the forthcoming Concorde supersonic transport. The new design presented so many changes from the original Delta 2 that it demands a small section to itself. In its new role the very attractive 221 was complemented by the Handley Page HP.115 (qv), which primarily looked at the low-speed end of the Concorde research programme.

Ogee wing

In 1958 explorations into the possibilities of a supersonic transport had shown that the wingform most likely to give the required lift/drag ratio at Mach 2, the speed at which the airliner would operate, was the ogee wing. Building an aircraft like this, which would not only travel at Mach 2 but would do so for far longer periods than normally achieved by supersonic military types, would of course be a huge step forward. The wing shape in particular would need to be evaluated by a research vehicle before the full-size aeroplane was built, and in mid-1958 the Delta 2 was considered a possible candidate to assess the wing's high-speed qualities. However, the Delta 2's own wing would not suffice – the airframe would have to be rebuilt with the full ogee wing.

Talks with Fairey eventually led to the issue of a brochure in September 1958, which outlined the replacement of the delta with an ogee wing. In its most simple form the proposal showed the substitution of one set of wings by a new set, but wings of such a different form and characteristics would also necessitate some modifications to the forward fuselage, intakes and undercarriage. To keep the fuselage changes to a minimum it was essential that the trailing edge and the hinge line of the new wing's control surfaces were located in the same relative positions on the fuselage as the original wing. This would then enable the main spars to mate with the existing attachment points. Compared to the Delta 2, the elevators and ailerons would have more area.

For the rebuild, the fuselage from the engine face aft, the fin, rudder, air brakes and reheat installation were all unaltered, but an additional 6 feet (1.8m) of fuselage was inserted between the engine and cockpit. Both the pressurised cockpit and the droop nose were retained, but the nose cone was substituted by a nosepiece built as an integral part of the new wing. The droop nose itself could also now provide intermediate angles of 5° and 8°, which were selected on the ground before flight. The original 1958 proposals showed the intakes extending through to the wing upper surface, but the conversion featured modified intakes extended forward and swept downwards to a position on the wing underside, which allowed the wing leading edge to be unbroken, an important feature. They were designed for a maximum of about Mach 1.6, although some sources indicate that the 221 did reach Mach 1.8 during its career. Finally, at times the Delta 2's endurance had been somewhat marginal, but the ogee provided more space for fuel.

The go-ahead was given in 1959, and on 31 December Specification ER.193D was issued to cover the project. In July 1961 this was replaced by ER.221D. Then in 1960 Fairey's aircraft and helicopter interests became part of Westland, and on 7 April the latter made the decision to end all of its fixed-wing activity. As a result it would not be responsible for the ogee wing project, and for a short period the main contract was put in the hands of Hunting Aircraft at Luton. On 9 September 1960 it was switched to Bristol Aircraft, where the design was given the designation Type 221 (both firms were now part of the newly formed BAC). The aircraft would investigate the subsonic and supersonic behaviour of the new slender ogee wing with its sharp leading edge and 'streamwise tips', and it would also be equipped for landing stability trials and other slow-speed tests.

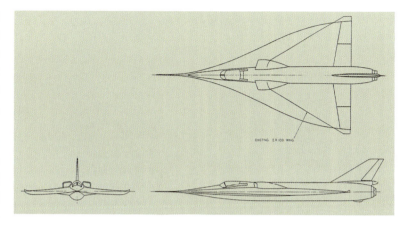

This is the original September 1958 proposal to have the Delta 2 fitted with an ogee wing. Note the overwing intake position, and that the old delta wing is also outlined on the plan view. This design had a span of 24ft 8.5in (7.53m), an overall length of 54ft 7.5in (16.65m), and a wing area of 540 square feet (50.22sq m). *RAF Museum*

Rebuild

WG774 arrived at Filton for its conversion on 5 September 1960, but the work took far longer to complete than had been estimated, and it was not finished until 7 July 1963. For reasons of economy there had also been no prior ground testing of equipment, so the ground clearance work for the aircraft itself took the

This photograph was taken on the day of the BAC.221's rollout in July 1963. *Phil Butler collection*

The very impressive BAC.221 is seen during a test flight after it had been painted in its dark blue scheme. *BAE Systems*

These photographs of WG774 were taken at roughly the same angle, first in its Fairey Delta 2 form (top), then for comparison as the BAC.221. *Author's collection*

This shot was most probably taken shortly before WG774's first flight in its rebuilt form on 1 May 1964. The aircraft is still primarily in bare metal. *Phil Butler collection*

The BAC.221 is seen taking off from Filton on its first flight, which lasted for 23 minutes. *BAE Systems*

X-PLANES OF EUROPE

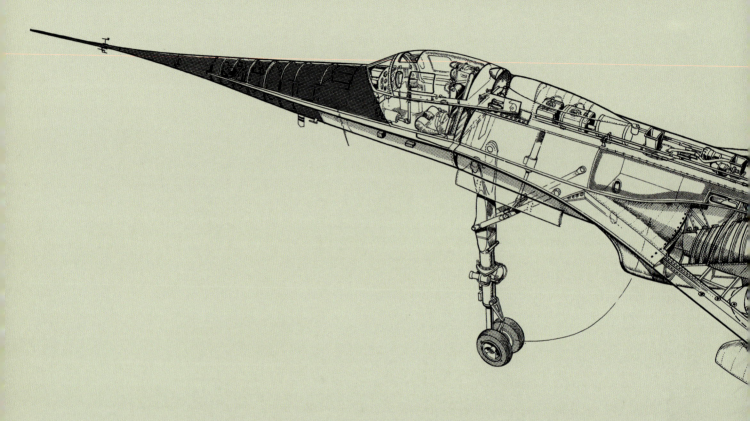

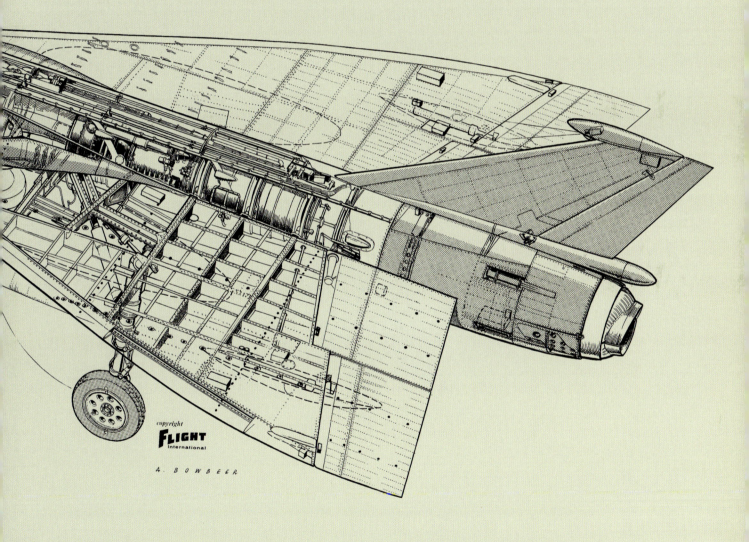

X-PLANES OF EUROPE

WG774 at Bedford in May 1966. Note the spindly undercarriage – the Delta 2 had quite a long undercarriage, but the 221's was longer. The main legs were new but were based on the existing English Electric Lightning fighter undercarriage, while the nose leg was a modified Fairey Gannet unit. *Phil Butler collection*

best part of another year before WG774 made its second maiden flight on 1 May 1964. The pilot was Godfrey Auty, who described the trip as 'absolutely first class'. In the respect of detail shape and thickness (twist and camber, etc) the Type 221's wing was not the same as Concorde's, so it was not possible to assess the high-speed characteristics of the airliner's wing in full. The late arrival of the 221 also reduced its value to the airliner programme, so WG774 spent much of its Filton-based time studying the approach and landing phase and on the development of an auto-throttle system for approach speed stability.

So many air-to-air shots of the Delta 2 and the 221 present these aircraft banking away from the photographer, so it is good to see a view of the aircraft flying below camera level to provide some upper-surface detail. *Phil Butler collection*

278

However, over the first two years WG774 was still able to perform some extensive flight testing for the manufacturer. The new longer nose brought with it a reduction in the aircraft's directional stability, which was cured by an 8-inch (20.3cm) extension to the fin. On the top of the fin was a bullet fairing for a cine camera, which was used to record airflow patterns over the wing, and that too had to be modified. The data collected from each test flight was always analysed against the equivalent readings taken in the wind tunnel and/or calculated theoretically.

In May 1966 WG774 rejoined the Aero Flight at RAE Bedford and continued its successful flying career right through to retirement in June 1973. Today it forms part of the Concorde display at the Fleet Air Arm Museum at Yeovilton. As either Fairey Delta 2 or BAC.221, the airframe just got on with what it was asked to do reliably and with very little trouble. Over the years there has been controversy that the World Speed Record holder WG774 was the airframe chosen to be rebuilt as the Type 221, rather than WG777. However, it is understood that when the decision was made WG777 still had much to do as part of its flying programme at RAE Bedford, while WG774 had pretty well finished its flight testing. And at that time preservation was perhaps not considered to be as important as it is today.

The surviving Fairey Delta WG777 accompanies the BAC.221 WG774 on a photographic sortie to demonstrate the different wing shapes of the two aircraft. *Clive Rustin*

The BAC.221 pictured on static display at Farnborough on 10 September 1966. *Roy Bonser-KEC*

37 Dassault Mirage G (1967)

Dassault Mirage G

Span: 45ft 11in (14.0m) forward, 23ft 11.5in (7.3m) swept
Length: 55ft 1.5in (16.8m)
Wing area: 268.8sq ft (25sq m)
Max gross take-off weight: 33,113lb (15,020kg)
Powerplant: 1 x P & W/SNECMA TF-306E, 20,500lb (91.1kN) with afterburner
Max speed/height: Mach 2.15 at altitude (some early sources state Mach 2.5)
Ceiling: Not available

The Dassault Mirage G qualifies for this book because it was the first French jet to have variable-geometry swing wings. Although originally thought of as a fighter prototype, well before the end of its flying career the G had been classed as a purely experimental demonstrator aircraft. It was financed throughout by the French government.

After the end of the vertical take-off programme represented by the Balzac (qv) and the Mirage IIIV, the French Ministry of Armed Forces turned instead towards the concept of a new conventional take-off fighter aircraft fitted with either swing wings or with fixed swept wings coupled with high lift devices. The resulting project for the latter was a single prototype called the F2, which first flew on 12 June 1966 but which never progressed beyond the prototype stage. In 1964 the Ministry requested the development of a variable-sweep-wing aircraft to operate with both the Air Force and the Navy, and in February 1965 the Dassault design team of Jean-Jacques Samin and Jean-Paul Emoré proposed the Mirage IIIG. A scale model of the IIIG was presented at that year's Paris Air Show, and on 18 October 1965 an order was placed for one two-seat Mirage G prototype.

The G shared an identical fuselage and engine configuration to the F2 and was similar in size, thereby enabling a comparative assessment of the two wing arrangements to be made, but finding the best position for the wing movement mechanism presented some major problems. However, by the autumn of 1965 it had been established that having the wing pivot position slightly flush to the fuselage was the best solution. With the pivots mounted inside the fuselage it was found that there were large centre-of-pressure position changes relative to the c.g. because all of the effective wing area came outside the pivots. Unless some complex fuel management systems were employed, the result of this situation was large trim forces and therefore high drag. Moving the pivot further out into the wing itself reduced the shift of c.g. but also reduced the effectiveness of the variable-geometry layout, thereby giving problems of pitch-up at low speeds. It also required a movable 'glove' to preserve the smooth contouring around the wing/body.

The construction of the sole prototype began at Saint-Cloud in January 1966, and on 27 May 1967 the substantially complete airframe was put on static display at the Paris Air Show. Also displayed at that Show was a model of the single-seat single-engine Mirage G3M project for the Navy, which was very similar to the G. The G itself was to be powered by a single Pratt & Whitney/SNECMA TF-306 turbofan fed by a bifurcated air intake arrangement with a two-position centre-body in each intake, the engine being described as more powerful and more economic to use than France's own Atar. The wings were to be set at 20° when fully forward, then moved back to an angle of 70° when fully aft, and selections could also be made for 30° and 55°. The wing also featured full-span double-slotted trailing-edge Fowler flaps and two-position leading-edge slats, and there were spoilers and tailerons to provide lateral control while a low tail position was chosen to reduce interference from the wing. A taileron is a tailplane in which both sides are used as primary control surfaces in both pitch and roll. The halves of the split all-flying tailplane would move in unison to provide pitch control, then (when the wings were fully swept) in opposition for roll control (when the ailerons became inactive).

Into the air

When the Mirage G was rolled out in early June 1967 the expectation was that it would fly for the first time in late July. However, due to a long series of vibration tests and extensive modifications to the hydraulic system this was postponed, the loss of the Mirage F1 prototype on 18 May 1967 having prompted a re-examination of the strength of the G's tailplane and of its flutter characteristics. The F1 was a smaller version of the F2 produced by Dassault as a private venture, and eventually won major production orders. The prototype was lost while flying at high speed and low level.

On 18 October 1967 the Mirage G made a short hop at Melun-Villaroche (some sources report an unofficial full circuit of the airfield). Soon afterwards it was dismantled and taken to Istres for its first flight, which it achieved on

| The single Mirage G prototype seen probably during final assembly. Note the fixed forward portion of the wing root.

X-PLANES OF EUROPE

The G stands on the runway at Melun-Villaroche on 18 October 1967 ready to take off on its first 'airborne hop'. *Dassault Aviation Publicity*

The Mirage G pictured on its first official flight on 18 November 1967. Although this was a two-seat aircraft, during some of the early test flights only the pilot was on board. *Dassault Aviation Publicity*

18 November piloted by Jean Coureau. Throughout the flight the wing was set in the fully forward position, and in reaching this landmark the Mirage G had become the first European swing-wing aircraft to fly.

During Flight 5 on 24 November the wing was pushed back to 55° and the aircraft was taken to Mach 1.15. The next day during Flight 7 the G reached a speed of Mach 1.5 at 36,000 feet (10,973m), then on 8 December Coureau took the aircraft to Mach 2.1 with the wings at their maximum 70° sweepback setting. The progress made with the flight test programme was swift and the fiftieth flight was achieved on 7 May 1968, these flights having been completed in two stages with grounding after Flight 28 to permit an extensive inspection to be made. The first set of flights had embraced sorties at speeds between 98 knots (182km/h) and Mach 2.15, which at the time *Flight* magazine described as a 'remarkable speed range', and heights between low level and 50,000 feet (15,240m). Dassault claimed that the G had remarkable manoeuvrability at both subsonic and supersonic speeds, while the handling characteristics were described as well harmonised, regardless of the wing-sweep angle. Results from the flying programme also showed that the Mirage G had a better performance at the high and low ends of the profile over the Mirage F2, but in the middle of the range it was similar to the fixed-wing aircraft.

By April the aircraft had been flown by both Coureau and by Jean-Marie Saget of Dassault, and by Cdr Bernard Ziegler from the French Flight Test Centre. Later many overseas pilots would fly the aircraft, and in due course LTV in America signed a contract with Dassault to acquire knowledge of the French company's experience with swing wings. This was to help LTV produce a variable-geometry fighter aircraft project for the US Navy, but that particular competition was won eventually by the design from Grumman, which became the F-14 Tomcat.

DASSAULT MIRAGE G (1967)

A photo taken from the chase plane's cockpit through the canopy glass (hence the curved lines). It shows the wings in the forward position, the deployed airbrakes in the lower rear fuselage and the single jetpipe. *Dassault Aviation Publicity*

Here the aircraft is seen on its fifth flight with the wings set at 55°. *Dassault Aviation Publicity*

And a similar view taken on the seventh flight with the wings now swept at their 70° maximum angle. *Dassault Aviation Publicity*

X-PLANES OF EUROPE

This view was made during Flight 8 on 28 November 1967 with the wings again at 70°. A speed of Mach 1.83 was recorded on this sortie. *Dassault Aviation Publicity*

The Mirage G makes its 50th take-off at Istres on 7 May 1968. Note the leading edge slat. *Dassault Aviation Publicity*

Despite the relatively successful flight trials no Service orders for the type followed, and plans for a Mirage G production programme were cancelled in 1968. It was reported that the reasons behind the abandonment of series manufacture were that the Air Force wanted two engines for an aircraft of this sort of weight, the engine itself was American when it was desired to establish a proper aircraft engine industry in France, and there was an overall shortage of funding. However, test flying with the aircraft continued until 13 January 1971, when the single prototype was lost in a crash near Istres, Jean Coureau ejecting safely. This had been its first flight since 4 December 1970, the latest period of grounding having been used to carry out some scheduled modifications. At the time of its loss the Mirage G had completed 316 flights for a total flight time of 400 hours.

In 1968 a contract was issued for two twin-engine, variable-geometry two-seat nuclear strike fighters designated Mirage G4, but while these were under construction the operational requirements were modified and trhey were converted into dedicated interceptors. As such the first two-seat Mirage G4-01, after being redesignated G8-01, first flew on 8 May 1971. The second machine, G4-02, was converted into a single-seat aircraft as the G8-02 and made its maiden flight on 13 July 1972. Once again, however, no production orders were placed for this bigger and much heavier aeroplane.

Colour photo of the single-engine Mirage G, again with just the pilot aboard. Note the glove filling the space in the fuselage left when the wing was in the fully forward position, and the all-moving tailplane with a separate moving portion on its trailing edge. *Dassault Aviation*

The two-seat Mirage G8 prototype 01 first flew in May 1971. *Dassault Aviation*

38 VFW VAK 191B (1971)

VFW VAK 191B

Span: 20ft 2.5in (6.16m)

Length: 53ft 7in (16.33m) with probe

Gross wing area: 134.5sq ft (12.51sq m)

Gross weight: 19,841lb (9,000kg)

Powerplant: 1 x RR/MTU RB.193-12, 10,163lb (45.2kN); 2 x RR RB.162-81, 5,577lb (24.8kN)

Max speed: 684mph (1,100km/h)

Ceiling: 49,210ft (15,000m)

Concept

In August 1961 the need to replace the Fiat G.91 attack aircraft spawned a NATO competition for a VTOL successor with the generic designation VAK 191 (Vertikal startendes Aufklarungs-und-Kampfflugzeug – vertical take-off and landing fighter aircraft – with 191 indicating a G.91 successor). Work on the Focke-Wulf's FW 1262 began in September 1961, and in the summer of 1963 it was declared the winner. West Germany and Italy agreed to develop the aircraft jointly as the VAK 191B, and for military purposes it was expected to carry a 1,250lb (567kg) weapon load over a distance of 180 nautical miles (333km).

Three single-seat aircraft were to be built by Vereinigte Flugtechnische Werke (VFW) at Bremen, and three of a two-seat version by Fiat in Turin; the German firm was to build the centre fuselages and wing centre sections, with the wings, tails and fuselages coming from Italy. VFW had been formed in 1963 by the merger of Focke-Wulf and Weser-Flugzeugbau, and in 1964 Heinkel was also absorbed into VFW. In 1969 VFW merged with Fokker of the Netherlands to become VFW-Fokker.

As discussed earlier, the most famous and only successful vertical-take-off type of combat aircraft has to be the Harrier. However, from the mid-1950s to the mid-1970s there were many other attempts to produce a viable VTOL aircraft. After the VJ 101C, a second project in this category to come out of Germany was the VAK 191B 'lift-plus-lift/cruise' project, which began as a full-combat aircraft programme but eventually became a pure research type.

The SG 1262 hovering test rig was used to assess systems that were to be fitted on the VAK 191B. *Author's collection*

This side view of the VAK 191B mock-up, in Luftwaffe markings, shows open entry and exit doors over the two lift jets. *VFW-Fokker*

A first flight was expected in 1968 and the VAK 191B was to serve as a close air support aircraft and nuclear strike fighter with good low-level penetration. However, NATO's policy of massive retaliation in a war with the Soviets was now succeeded by one of graduated response. With a new emphasis on battlefield manoeuvrability and tactical performance, the 191B could not be adapted to Germany's change of strategy, so by 1968 the aircraft had no place in the country's military scheme. Consequently, a decision was made to go no further than prototype evaluation. In late 1966 the two-seater was abandoned to save money, the airframes being replaced by three more single-seaters, then in August 1967 Italy formally withdrew. Fiat stayed as a sub-contractor responsible for the previously agreed portions of the airframe, but the second batch of three was cancelled. In 1968 the VAK 191B was reclassified as a research aircraft, in part as a test bed for the MRCA programme (later the Tornado).

The Rolls-Royce/ MTU RB.193-12 cruise engine. The intake diameter was 33.3 inches (84.5 cm), overall length was 101.4 inches (257.6cm), basic weight 1,742lb (790 kg), and installed weight 2,315lb (1,050 kg). *Rolls-Royce*

The three VAK 191Bs (from front to back, serials D-9563, D-9564 and D-9565) are lined up at Bremen on 11 April 1972. Note the different settings for the lift engine intakes – D-9565 has the ingestion guards used for early engine running. D-9563 also has its RB.193 forward nozzles set to vertical, while D-9564 has them set fully aft. Each aeroplane has the VFW-Fokker logo on its fin. *VFW-Fokker*

From certain angles the VAK 191B was impressive. Here the pilot is about to board D-9564, possibly for a pre-first-flight taxi, on 1 February 1971. A nose probe has still to be fitted. *VFW-Fokker*

Features

A combination of twin lift engines and a rotating-nozzle bypass engine provided the VTOL capability, with the lift jets supplying about 50% of the total VTOL thrust. Rolls-Royce's light 5,577lb (24.8kN) RB.162-81 was chosen for the lift unit and a new cruise engine, the Rolls-Royce/MTU (Motoren-und-Turbinen-Union) RB.193-12, was specially sized for the 191B – a development contract was awarded in December 1965. The lift units were placed symmetrically fore and aft of the cruise unit, which was housed in the centre of the fuselage at the 191B's centre of gravity. It was thought that when the vectoring nozzles were directed backwards, enough thrust would be available for low-level cruise at near sonic speed. This powerplant combination had given the lowest lift-off weight of the three original competitors, and during normal flight both lift units would have their intake and outlet doors closed.

The RB.193 had contra-rotating low-pressure and high-pressure rotors to minimise the gyroscopic effects. Despite using the same vectored-thrust concept as the Bristol Pegasus engine in the P.1127, the RB.193-12 was rather smaller, giving 10,163lb (45.2kN) of thrust. As with the Pegasus, rated thrust was based upon a mean-bleed mass flow, and an increase in this would result in the engine running hotter. The nozzles could be rotated through about 100° and the engine was loaded into the 191B from beneath the fuselage. The space under the RB.193 was to have formed a bay for weapons, equipment or auxiliary fuel, but on the prototypes this was filled with data acquisition and transmission equipment. Both RB.162s were set with their thrust axes inclined rearwards at an angle of 12.5° from the vertical to provide a small component of forward thrust. With both exhaust doors extended at 45°, thereby directing the exhaust through 90° to the rear to provide forward thrust, it was hoped that the lift engines would get the machine home if the RB.193 failed. The RB.162s reached their rated thrust just seconds after start-up. Should one fail, the fuel to the other was cut off immediately to prevent a dangerous thrust imbalance, which would cause pitching. However, the aircraft would then descend rapidly.

VAK 191B V1 in the hover with lift unit doors open.
Author's collection

A 1970 study of D-9564, the second VAK 191B.
EADS Archive Ottobrunn/Thomas Mueller

X-PLANES OF EUROPE

The jet efflux produced by the VAK 191B in the hover is well illustrated by this view. One can easily imagine the noise! *VFW-Fokker*

For the 191B VTOL strike aircraft it was argued that a large vectored thrust engine alone was too heavy and uneconomical since, because of the high thrust, it was oversize for cruising and had to be throttled back for the larger part of a mission, thereby wasting fuel. The philosophy was that it would be better to use a smaller cruise engine that operated at an economised power setting in normal flight and supplement the V/STOL thrust with lift engines, which, despite being deadweight when in flight, were expected to give a lighter solution. Indeed, the combined weight of the three engines was less than the current Pegasus, but the installations were more complex and the 191B's structure weight was as heavy as a Harrier's. VAK 191B had a long fuselage and a diminutive wing with bicycle undercarriage and outrigger wheels. The VAK 191B's maximum VTO weight was expected to be around 19,841lb (9,000kg). In level flight the aircraft would have been subsonic – it was not intended to be supersonic at altitude.

Orthodox aluminium alloy construction was used, and the cantilever shoulder-wing was built in one piece as a multi-spar structure. VAK 191B had both ailerons and trailing-edge flaps and a one-piece all-moving tailplane. The forward exhaust door of the rear lift engine could be extended to act as an air brake at high speed. Stabilisation around all three axes in the hover was achieved by using controllable nose, tail and wingtip 'puffer' nozzles with the air blown through them bled from all three engines.

The highly autostabilised flight-control system made use of electrical signalling and was refined using the SG 1262 hover rig, a sort of 'Flying Bedstead' (qv), which was powered by five Rolls-Royce RB.108 lift jets and first flew in August 1966. This test vehicle was displayed at the April 1968 Hanover Show, and its five engines could be made to simulate the functions of the single vectored-thrust RB.193 and the two RB.162s. Engines Nos 1 and 5 on the rig represented the two lift jets, No 2 the 'cold' efflux of the RB.193, and Nos 3 and 4 the propulsion and 'hot' jets respectively. It was flown by VFW pilot Ludwig Obermeier, who sat on rather than in this machine, and was taken up to several hundred feet altitude during the Hanover displays. In fact, the SG 1262 itself provided a programme of some magnitude, gathering data for a wide variety of engineering subjects. It weighed 7,700lb (3,493kg) and had an endurance of 12 minutes.

Unveiling

The rollout of V1, the first prototype, took place during the Hanover Air Show on 24 April 1970, but untethered hovering did not start until 10 September 1971. The 1970-71 period was taken up with extensive pre-first-flight engine runs, tethered hovers and ground tests. The pilot for the first hovering flight on 10 September was Obermeier. He took off vertically and made a 3-minute circuit over the airfield at about 115 feet (35m), and well below transition speed, before ending with a vertical landing. V1 was joined in the air by the second prototype V2 on 2 October 1971.

Progress was slow, but in January 1972 Obermeier achieved a forward speed of 92mph (148km/h) and reported that the aircraft handled

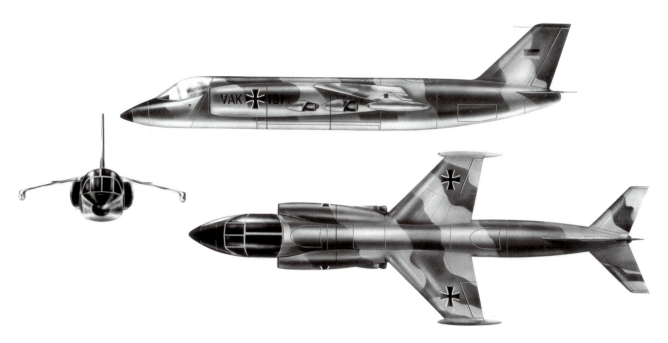

A drawing showing the planned two-seat version of the VAK 191B. *Author's collection*

well, and that control in the hover, particularly about the roll and yaw axes, was excellent. All the taxiing and hover trials were made at Bremen and were completed by April 1972 to end the programme's 'first phase'. Bremen was unsuitable for making full-transition flights, so V1 was taken by a Sikorsky S-64 helicopter to the Luftwaffe's test airfield at Manching. Transition between jet-borne and wing-borne flight and clearance of an agreed flight envelope was covered by the 'second phase', and the first full cycle of vertical take-off into normal horizontal flight followed by a return to the hover for a vertical landing was made on 26 October 1972. The transition speed was about 207mph (333km/h) and on this flight V1 reached a top speed of 276mph (444km/h). Also, the RB.162s were shut down and restarted in flight for the first time. All three 191Bs had now entered flight test.

VFW VAK 191B. One example is on display at the Deutsches Museum Flugwerft Schleissheim at Oberschleißheim near Munich, a second at Wehrtechnische Studiensammlung (Military technical collection) at Koblenz, both in Germany. *Chris Sandham-Bailey www.inkworm.com*

What might have been: VFR VAK as it might have been painted in the Luftwaffe NATO scheme of the 1960s. *Chris Sandham-Bailey www.inkworm.com*

'Phase three', testing specific items for the MRCA, was due to begin in late 1973, but on 31 December 1972 work was halted following a German government decision to stop funding the VAK 191B after that date. The flight envelope had been extended to 345mph (555km/h) forward speed and to 30° per second yaw. Rate of climb at ground level is believed to have been 115 feet per second (35m/sec). It was found that the autostabilisers completely eliminated any tendency to pilot-induced oscillations, and the lift engines had been relit when flying at 253mph (407km/h). The three aircraft were all stored at Manching, having completed thirty-one flights in all.

Return to flight

During 1973, however, new interest was forthcoming from the US Navy, and the German government stated its readiness to contribute to the cost of a flight investigation of the mixed lift and cruise propulsion principle, which for America held interest for its planned Sea Control Ship programme (a small aircraft carrier with specially designed V/STOL aircraft aboard). A joint agreement was signed in mid-1974 to use the 191B to conduct trials to 'generate technology and predict techniques' for future V/STOL designs. VFW-Fokker would conduct the flight tests and the German government would provide the aircraft for a programme that would last until May 1975.

The US Navy financed the rest. Flight testing resumed on 1 June 1974 using V1 and V2, and on 27 November Obermeier made the 191B's fiftieth flight. Besides Obermeier, government pilot Horst Philipp was assigned to the 191B, then after May 1975 the flight test team was joined by Lt Col Jacob Evert Iles USMC as the first non-German pilot to fly the 191B. His normal mount was the AV-8A Harrier.

All flights were monitored over a telemetry link and V1 was primarily concerned with investigating the effects of jet efflux on the aircraft and its surroundings. The first aircraft was also responsible for examining hot-gas reingestion when operating in low-speed jet-borne flight. It was found that even during prolonged hovering in crosswinds only minor hot-gas reingestion was experienced and the aircraft could be landed easily. The first prototype was also fitted with roll bleed nozzles of larger area to increase the roll-control power by about 20%, and flight tests demonstrated a considerable improvement in handling about the longitudinal axis. V2 was used mainly to explore the higher speed range of the jet-borne flight envelope and to determine the optimum combination of speed, nozzle and power settings, and angle of attack for the transition to and from wing-borne flight. When the programme ended the VAK 191Bs had accumulated ninety-one flights, totalling just 12 hours flight time.

39 The Musée de l'Air et de l'Espace, Paris le Bourget

Originally founded in 1919 and inaugurated in its present form in 1975 on the historical Le Bourget Airfield near Paris, the Musée de l'Air et de l'Espace is considered to be the world's first true air museum. This colourful facility currently houses the oldest and richest collection of pioneering flying machines, with more than 400 authentic aircraft. Visitors can relive many significant first steps of aviation and space history through the comprehensive displays, which show:

- Aircraft of the milestone early record flights.
- Military aviation history with aircraft from the French Air Force and Naval Aviation plus legendary Warbirds.
- Vertical flight pioneers, a technology born in France more than a century ago.
- The Hall of Prototypes, displaying post-war French aviation projects that paved the way for many of today's successful aircraft, including the Triton, France's first jet-powered aircraft designed in 1943; the prototype Mystère IV, the first to fly Mach 1 in a dive in 1953; the Leduc 010, the first aircraft to fly on thermopropulsive (ramjet) power; the Griffon, the first French aircraft to reach Mach 2 in 1958; the Trident, the first aircraft to fly with the integral combination of turbojet and rocket power; the vertical-take-off Mirage III Balzac; and the variable-sweep-wing Mirage G 8.
- Two Concorde supersonic airliners, including the prototype and the unique Air France Boeing 747 mock-up that allows visitors to walk through a section of the aircraft via a cutaway display from the passenger cabin to the cargo hold, showing all the complex internal structure.
- Space Hall, showing the discovery of the universe with the Planetarium.
- For young visitors, a fun new area called Planète Pilote, opened in 2010, a great first glimpse at all aspects of aviation and space.

The Museum also hosts year-long exhibits, festivals, fly-ins and special evening programmes.

Its brand-new restaurant, l'Hélice ('The Propeller'), offers a gorgeous panoramic view of the legendary Le Bourget tarmac.

Musée de l'Air et de l'Espace
Aéroport de Paris Le Bourget – BP173
F-93352 Le Bourget Cedex, France

Tel +33 1 49 92 70 00
Restaurant: +33 (0)1 48 35 30 49
www.museeairespace.fr
(Also on Facebook, Twitter, YouTube and DailyMotion)

Located only 10 minutes from Paris and Roissy Charles de Gaulle Airport.

Free access to the permanent display.
Planète Pilote: €6
Special displays (Concorde, B747, DC 3 and Super Frelon Helicopter): €7

Open Tuesday to Sunday:
10.00am to 6.00pm,
1 April to 30 September
10.00am to 5.00pm,
1 October to 31 March
Closed Mondays,
25 December and 1 January

Surviving airframes

Avro 707	WD280: RAAF Museum, Point Cook, Australia WZ736: Manchester Museum of Science and Industry, England WZ744: RAF Museum, Cosford, England
Boulton Paul P.111A	Midland Air Museum, Baginton, England
Bristol 188	Aerospace Museum Cosford, England
EWR VJ 101C	X2: Deutsches Museum, Munich, Germany
FAF (F + W) N-20-2 Arbalète	Verkehrshaus der Schweiz (Swiss Transport Museum), Lucerne, Switzerland
Fairey Delta 2/BAC.221	WG774: Fleet Air Arm Museum, Yeovilton, England WG777: RAF Museum, Cosford, England
Handley Page HP.115	Fleet Air Arm Museum, Yeovilton, England
Hawker P.1127	XP831: Science Museum, London, England XP980: Fleet Air Arm Museum, Yeovilton, England XP984: Brooklands Museum, Weybridge, England
Hunting H.126	RAF Museum, Cosford, England
Leduc 010	Musée de l'Air et de l'Espace at Le Bourget Airport, Paris, France
Leduc 022	Musée de l'Air et de l'Espace at Le Bourget Airport, Paris, France
Nord 1500 Griffon	Musée de l'Air et de l'Espace at Le Bourget Airport, Paris, France
ONERA Deltaviex	Ailes Anciennes Toulouse (Association of Ancient Wings Museum), Toulouse, France
Payen PA 49	Musée de l'Air et de l'Espace at Le Bourget Airport, Paris, France
Rolls-Royce 'Flying Bedstead'	XJ314: Science Museum, London, England
Saunders-Roe SR.A/1	TG263: Solent Sky Museum, Southampton, England
Saunders-Roe SR.53	RAF Museum, Cosford, England
Short S.B.5	RAF Museum, Cosford, England (with the spare rear fuselage fitted with the T-tail)
Short S.B.4 Sherpa	Fuselage property of the Ulster Aviation Society, Lisburn, Northern Ireland
Short S.C.1	XG900: Science Museum, London, England XG905: Ulster Folk and Transport Museum, Cultra, Northern Ireland.
SNECMA C.400 Atar Volant	Musée de l'Air et de l'Espace at Le Bourget Airport, Paris, France
Sud-Ouest SO 6000 Triton	Aircraft 3: Musée de l'Air et de l'Espace at Le Bourget Airport, Paris, France
Sud-Ouest SO 9000 Trident I	Musée de l'Air et de l'Espace at Le Bourget Airport, Paris, France
VFW VAK 191B	V1 (and SG 1262 hover rig): Wehrtechnische Studiensammlung ('Military Collection'), Koblenz, Germany V2: Deutsches Museum, Schleißheim, near Munich, Germany V3: Airbus, Bremen, Germany (former VFW-Fokker facility)

Glossary

A&AEE	Aeroplane & Armament Experimental Establishment, Boscombe Down
Anhedral	Downwards slope of wing from root to tip
Angle of attack	Angle at which wing is inclined relative to the airflow
Angle of incidence	Angle between chord line of wing and fore and aft datum line of fuselage
Area rule	Principal aerodynamic law for keeping transonic drag to a minimum. States that cross-section areas of an aeroplane plotted from nose to tail on a graph should form a smooth curve
ASM	Air-to-surface missile
Aspect ratio	Ratio of wingspan to mean chord, calculated by dividing square of span by wing area.
ATAR	Atelier Aéronautiques de Reichenbach, aeronautical workshop in city of Reichenbach, Germany
AVM	Air Vice Marshal
AWA	Armstrong Whitworth Aviation
BAC	British Aircraft Corporation
C(A)	Controller of Aircraft (UK MoS post)
Capt	Captain
CAS	Chief of the Air Staff (UK Air Ministry post)
Cdr	Commander
CEMH	Centre d'Essais des Moteurs et des Hélices
CEV	Centre d'Essais en Vol
CinC	Commander in Chief
Chord	Distance between centres of curvature of wing leading and trailing edges when measured parallel to longitudinal axis
c.g.	Centre of gravity
Critical Mach Number	Mach number at which an aircraft's controllability is first affected by compressibility, i.e. point at which shock waves first appear
CTOL	Conventional Take-Off and Landing
Dihedral	Upwards slope of wing from root to tip
DMARD	Director of Military Aircraft Research and Development (UK MoS post)
DTIA	Direction Technique et Industrielle de l'Aéronautique de Secrétariat d'Etat à l'Air
Dutch Roll	Combined yawing and rolling motion of an aircraft
EAS	Equivalent airspeed (rectified airspeed with a compressibility correction)
ETPS	Empire Test Pilots' School, Farnborough (UK)
Flt Lt	Flight Lieutenant
Flutter	High-frequency oscillation of an aircraft's structure induced by both aerodynamic and aeroelastic forces
Fly-by-wire	Flight control system using electronic links between the pilot's controls and the control surface actuators
Gp	Group
Gross weight	Usually signifies maximum weight with internal fuel plus all equipment/weapons aboard, but not external drop tanks
HSA	Hawker Siddeley Aviation Ltd
HTP	High Test Peroxide
Hypersonic	Speed range above Mach 5
IAS	Indicated air speed
ICBM	Intercontinental ballistic missile
IFR	In-flight refuelling (UK)
IFR	Instrument flight rules (US)
IMN	Indicated Mach number
JATO	Jet-assisted take-off
Lt	Lieutenant
Mach number	Ratio of an aeroplane's speed to that of sound in the surrounding medium, expressed as a decimal
MAE	Musée de l'Air et de l'Espace
MoD	Ministry of Defence; created in the late 1940s to coordinate policy of three British Armed Services. In April 1964 it was reconstituted to absorb functions of Air Ministry, Admiralty and War Office; Air Ministry (civilian body that had governed RAF) ceased to exist
MoS	Ministry of Supply (UK); provided stores for RAF from 1946 onwards. Disbanded and reconstituted as Ministry of Aviation in 1959
NATO	North Atlantic Treaty Organisation

NGTE	National Gas Turbine Establishment (UK)	STTA	Service Technique de Télécommunication de l'Air
nm	nautical mile	Subsonic	Speed range slightly below Mach 1, or the speed of sound
ONERA	Office Nationale d'Étude et de Recherches Aéronautiques	Supersonic	Speed range above Mach 1
OR	Operational Requirement	t/c	thickness/chord ratio
PDTD(A)	Principal Director of Technical Development Air (UK MoS post)	TMR	Thrust Measuring Rig (Rolls-Royce 'Flying Bedstead')
RAAF	Royal Australian Air Force	Transonic	Speed range either side of Mach 1 where an aircraft has both subsonic and supersonic airflow passing over it at same time
RAE	Royal Aircraft Establishment, Bedford and Farnborough (UK)		
RAeS	Royal Aeronautical Society (UK)		
RAF	Royal Air Force	TRE	Telecommunications Research Establishment, Malvern (became RRE) (UK)
RATO	Rocket-assisted take-off (replaced JATO when rockets permanently adopted to give extra take-off thrust)		
		vg	variable geometry
		V/STOL	Vertical/short take-off and landing
RATOG	Rocket-assisted take-off gear	VTOL	Vertical take-off and landing
RNAS	Royal Naval Air Station (UK)	VTO	Vertical take-off
RRE	Royal Radar Establishment (UK)	USAF	United States Air Force
SAUF	Société Anonyme des Usines Farman	USMC	United States Marine Corps
		USN	United States Navy
SBAC	Society of British Aircraft Constructors; now Society of British Aerospace Companies (UK)	Wg Cdr	Wing Commander
SFECMAS	Société Française d'Étude et de Construction de Matériels Aéronautiques Special		
SHAPE	Supreme Headquarters Allied Powers, Europe		
SMPA	Service de Marchés et de la Production Aéronautique		
SNCAC	Société Nationale de Constructions Aéronautiques du Centre (Aérocentre)		
SNCAN	Société Nationale de Constructions Aéronautiques du Nord		
SNCASE	Société Nationale de Constructions Aéronautiques du Sud-Est		
SNCASO	Société Nationale de Constructions Aéronautiques du Sud-Ouest		
SNECMA	Société Nationale d'Étude et de Construction de Moteurs d'Aviation		
Sqn Ldr	Squadron Leader		
SST	Supersonic Transport		
STA	Service Technique de l'Aéronautique		
STOL	Short take-off and landing		
STOVL	Short take-off and vertical landing		

Bibliography and Source Notes

Although the coverage of each individual type in a book like this is really the equivalent of a magazine article, a good deal of primary source material still needs to be consulted, namely original documents held by National Archives and in Museums and Company Heritage Centres. The archive collections of numerous individuals listed in the Acknowledgments were also an important source.

Special thanks go to Sylvie Lallement and the Archives Department Staff of the Musée de l'Air in Paris, who facilitated access to the excellent museum archives and arranged for copies of the photos to be made available to the author. Thanks also to Paul Marais-Hayer, noted French aviation photographer, who assisted with the selection of the material used for this book. Co-author Tony Buttler also contributed photographs of noted French research aircraft. Material used with the kind permission of the Musée de l'Air of Le Bourget, Paris, France, is noted in the photo credits of those captions.

Contemporary issues of the British *Flight*, *Aeroplane* and other magazines were consulted, Phil Butler's recent series of articles on British jet prototypes in Air-Britain's *Aeromilitaria* magazine also filled important gaps, and the most important secondary sources were as follows:

Bateson, Richard P. *Saro A/1 Fighter Flying Boat* (ISO Publications, 1996)

Beamont, Roland *Testing Years* (Ian Allan, 1980)

Birch, David 'The Süd VJ 101C' (*Archive* [Journal of the Rolls-Royce Heritage Trust] No 80, April 2009)

Buttler, Tony 'Control at the Tips: Aero-Isoclinics and Their Influence on Design' (*Air Enthusiast* 81, May/June 1999)

Farley, John *A View from the Hover* (Flyer Books, 2008)

Foster, David and Matthews, Henry 'Handley Page HP.88' (*World X-Planes*, Volume 1, 2005)

Hygate, Barry *British Experimental Jet Aircraft* (Argus Books, 1990)

Jones, Barry *British Experimental Turbojet Aircraft* (Crowood Press, 2003)

Matthews, Henry 'Hawker P.1127 & Kestrel' (*Aeroplane*, November 2002)

'Vertical Explorers' (*X-Planes Profile 8*, 2003)

Matthews, Henry and Wood, Allan 'The Saga of SR.53' (*X-Planes Profile 2*, 2001)

Meekcoms, K. J. and Morgan, E. B. *The British Aircraft Specifications File* (Air-Britain, 1994)

Middleton, Don *Test Pilots: The Story of British Test Flying 1903-1984* (Collins Willow, 1985)

Sturtivant, Ray *British Research and Development Aircraft* (Haynes Publishing, 1990)

Williams, Ray 'A Tale of No Tails' (*Air Enthusiast* 17, December 1981/March 1982)

Other published material

'Atar Volant' (*Aviation*, 2 February 1956)

Berliner, Don (ed) *Paris Air Show* (MBI Publishing, 2000)

de Narbonne, Roland 'Grognard' (*Fana de l'Aviation*, November-December 2006)

'Triton' (*Fana de l'Aviation*, 1979)

de Uphaugh, Johnny 'French Experimental Jets' (*Aeroplane*, July 2004)

Fana de l'Aviation, June 2009 – Paris Le Bourget Hors serie

Fayer, Jean Claude *Prototypes de l'Aviation Française 1945-1960* (E-T-A-I, 2002)

'France's Atar Volant' (*Aeroplane* 7 June 1957)

Francillon, René J. 'Baroudeur' (*Air International*, June 1995)

Fricker, John 'Mirage Might Have Beens 2 Balzac' (*Air International*, November 1993)

Godfrey, David W. H. 'Resurgent French Industry' (*Aeroplane*, 24 May 1957)

Goujon, Charles (ed) *Trident* (France Empire, 1956)

Hay Stevens, James 'The Baroudeurs Advance' (*Flight*, 6 August 1954)

'The Galtier Delta Family' (*Flight*, 13 April 1956)

'The Work of René Leduc' (*Aeroplane*, 10 June 1955)

'Towards Greater Flexibility – Le Baroudeur' (*Aeroplane*, 1 January 1954)

Kaplan, Serge and Ricco, Philippe Ricco (eds) *Gerfaut et Griffon* (Avia Editions, 2006)

King, H. F. 'A View of France' (*Flight*, 16 October 1947)

'Le Gerfaut' (*Aviation*, 15 December 1955)

'Le trident' (*Aviation*, 20 December 1956)

Lean, D. and Henderson , Sqn Ldr J. M. 'Notes on a Visit to Paris to Discuss Progress on the Balzac 001 and Mirage 3V Jet VTOL Aircraft' (RAE Technical Memorandum Aero 846, July 1964; from UK National Archives, DSIR 23-32096)

Matthews, Henry 'Dassault Balzac V' (*World X-Planes*, Issue 1, 2005)

Noetinger, Jacques *Histoire de l'Aéronautique Française 1940-1960* (Editions France-Empire, 1978)

O'Neill, Hugh 'An Afternoon with the Baroudeur' (*Aeroplane Monthly*, March 1991)

Petit, Edmond (ed) *Histoire de l'Aviation* (Hachette, 1973)

Ricco, Philippe *La Renouveau de l'Aviation Française 1945-1960* (Avia Editions, 2003)

Taylor, John W. and King, H. F. (eds) *Milestones of the Air* (Janes, 1969)

'Tout sur le Leduc' (*Aviation*, 15 December 1954)

Turcat, André (ed) *Turcat Pilote* (Cherche Midi, 2006)

'Griffon' (*Shell Aviation News*, March 1959)

Winchester, Jim (ed) *Concept Aircraft* (Thunder Bay Press, 2005)

Flight
11 January 1951
22 June 1951
26 June 1953
2 July 1954

Jane's All The World's Aircraft
Various editions

Online references
www.aviastar.org
www.mae.org
www.flightglobal.com/pdfarchive
aerostories.free.fr (in particular an article by Philippe Ricco on the Leduc story)

Index

INDEX OF AIRCRAFT

Aerocentre NC 270 56
    NC 271 56
Aerospatiale/BAC Concorde 12-14, 114, 121, 165,
                                     172-174, 194, 237,
                                       247, 272, 279
Advanced Vertical Strike Fighter (AVS) 263
Armstrong Whitworth AW-52 27-35
    AW.52G 27-31
    Whitley 28, 29
Arsenal Ars.1301 ....161-163, 185
    VG.30 161
    VG.60 52
    VG.70 ....52-54, 161
    VG.71 54
    VG.90 ....53, 54, 161
Avro 707 Family..............58-69, 104, 107, 164, 214, 294
    720   207
    730   238
    746   268
    Lancaster..29
    Vulcan..58, 63, 64, 68, 104

BAC (British Aircraft Corporation)
    One-Eleven (1-11) 271
    Type 221.................................179, 237, 272-279, 294
    Bell D-188 ....258, 259
    Bloch 160 44
    Boeing 707 21
Boulton Paul P.111 ....73-83, 85, 102, 294
    P.120..73, 82-85
Bristol 188 ....124, 238-249, 294

Chengdu J 20 9
Convair XFY-1...200

Dassault Balzac 9, 250-257, 280
    Mercure..172
    Mirage ....I 9, 13
    Mirage III 13, 14, 51, 152, 167, 172, 191, 250
    Mirage IIIV 253, 254, 256, 257, 280
    Mirage IV 14
    Mirage F1..251, 281
    Mirage F2..280-282
    Mirage G 9, 280-285
    Mirage G3M...280
    Mirage G4..284
    Mirage G8...284, 285

Mystère IV..140, 165, 167
de Havilland DH.106 Comet...................................15, 21
    DH.108 Swallow 9, 15-21
    Heron..247
    Sea Venom...13
    Vampire 15-17, 24, 49, 140
    Venom..177
de Havilland (Canada) Otter 266
Douglas DC-3...163
    DC-8   21
    F4D Skyray 167, 193

English Electric Canberra 88
    P.1 & Lightning 86, 115-117, 120, 124, 164,
                                                   224, 278, 279
EWR Hover Rig..259, 260
    VJ 101C 258-265, 286, 294
    VJ 101D 262, 263

FAF (F+W) C-3604 92
    N-20 Aiguillon 92, 93, 95-97
    N-20-1 & N-20-2 Arbalète.........................92-96, 294
Fairchild C-119 13
Fairey Delta 1 ....98-103, 174, 214
    Delta 2 ....81, 85, 102, 167, 173-183,
                                               272-274, 294
    Gannet..174, 278

Gloster Meteor 17, 49, 59, 81, 102,
                                               167, 177
    Javelin 82, 247
Grumman F-14 Tomcat...282

Handley Page HP.80 Victor 58, 104
    HP.87..104
    HP.88..9, 58, 104-110
    HP.115 ....124, 234-237,
                                                270, 272
Hawker P.1040/Sea Hawk...9, 206
    P.1052 9
    P.1072 206
    Hunter 224, 247
Hawker/Hawker Siddeley
        P.1127/Kestel/Harrier......9, 223-233, 250, 263, 286,
                                                  289, 290, 292, 294
Heinkel He 274 ....55, 56
Hunting Percival H. 126...............................266-271, 294
    JFR.12 ....266, 267

INDEX OF AIRCRAFT continued...

Leduc 010	42-46, 50, 294
016	42, 45, 46
021	42, 45-51,
022	42, 45, 46, 50, 51, 294
Lockheed F-94 Starfire	89
F-104 Starfighter	151, 193, 200
XFV-1 Salmon	200
McDonnell F-101 Voodoo	177
Messerschmitt Me 163	206
Me 262	23
Nord 1402 Gerfaut I & 1405 Gerfaut II	9, 13, 51, 161-167, 171, 184, 185
1500 Griffon I & II	50, 51, 165, 167, 184-195, 294
1600	70
1601	52, 70-72
2500 Noratlas	13, 167
North American F-86 Sabre	89
F-100 Super Sabre	176
F-107A	87
X-15	87, 153
Northrop F-89 Scorpion	89
N1M	126
XB-35	27
YB-49	27, 35
ONERA Deltaviex	168-170, 294
Panavia MRCA Tornado	263
Payen 22	171
PA 48 Mars	171
PA 49 Flechair 'Katy'	171, 174, 294
Percival Provost	236
Jet Provost	236
Rafaelyants Turbolyot	160
Republic F-84 Thunderjet	13
XF-91 Thunderceptor	212
XF-103	186
Rolls-Royce Flying Bedstead	154-160, 214, 224, 290, 294
Ryan X-13	200, 201, 205
SAAB 210	111-114
J 29	111
J 35 Draken	111-113
Saunders-Roe P.121	41
P.177	206, 208
SR.53	9, 206-213, 294
SR.45 Princess	37
SR.A/1	9, 10, 36-41, 294
Short Belfast	271
P.D.8	132
P.D.10	132, 133
S.B.1 & S.B.4 Sherpa	126-133, 294
S.B.5	115-125, 294
S.C.1	9, 157, 214-224, 251, 294
S.C.8	222
Sturgeon	127, 128
Sikorsky S-64	291
SNECMA C.400 Atar Volant	196-200, 205, 294
C.450 Coléoptère	196, 199-205, 251
Sud Aviation X-600	255
Sud-Est SE 161 Languedoc	43, 44, 46, 47, 49, 55, 56, 163, 185
SE 210 Caravelle	12, 13, 86, 172
SE 530 Mistral	24, 140
SE 2410 Grognard I & 2415 Grognard II	86-91, 167
SE 5000 Baroudeur	134-142
Sud-Ouest SO 1100 Ariel	186
SO 4000	55, 57
SO 4050 Vautour	89
SO 6000 Triton	13, 22-26, 294
SO 6020 Espadon	23
SO 9000 Trident I & SO 9050 Trident II	143-153, 165, 294
SO M1	55-57
SO M2	55-57
Sukhoi T-50	9
Supermarine 510	9, 104
553	124
Attacker	9, 106, 107
Swift	132, 133
VFW SG 1262 Test Rig	286, 290
VAK 191B	286-292, 294
Vickers Valiant	247
Westland-Hill Pterodactyl	81, 126, 127, 133

INDEX OF PEOPLE

Adams, Russell 62
Addicott, D. G. 271
Aliette, Monsieur 168
Armstrong, Neil 236
Auty, Godfrey 240, 242, 247, 278

Balmforth, Wg Cdr 61
Beamont, Wg Cdr Roland P. 117, 120
Bedford, Sqn Ldr A. W. 'Bill' 227, 229
Bigand, René 251
Bird-Wilson, Wg Cdr H. 177
Booth, Sqn Ldr John 37, 41, 210
Bratt, Erik 111
Bright, George 259, 262, 263
Brooke-Smith, Thomas 117, 120, 127, 128, 217, 222-224
Broomfield, Flt Lt Douglas 108, 110
Brown, Capt Eric 21, 40

Campbell, Donald..41
Carpentier, Roger 150, 151
Chalard, Michel 165, 167, 191
Chantemps, Claude 70
Coureau, Jean 282, 284
Cunningham, Gp Capt John 20
Curis, Bernard 191

de Havilland, Geoffrey Jnr 16-18
de Havilland, Capt Sir Geoffrey Snr 18
Derry, Sqn Ldr John 20

Edwards, Sir George 238
Elliot, Lt 76
Else, W. H. 'Bill' 31
Emoré, Jean-Paul 280
Esler, Flt Lt Eric 59, 60
Evert, Capt Jacob 292

Fairey, Sir Richard...102
Falk, Wg Cdr Roland J. 61, 64
Farley, Flt Lt John F 271
Fourquet, Robert 170
Franklin, Sqn Ldr Eric 28, 31, 33

Galtier, Jean 52, 161, 185
Genders, Sqn Ldr George 17
Gonard, Jean 44, 45

Goujon, Charles 14, 145, 148, 149
Green, J. R. 223
Griffith, Dr A. A. 154
Guignard, Jacques 55-57, 144, 145, 148-150
Gunn, Flt Lt A. E. 81-83, 85

Hanes, Col Horace A. 176
Henderson, Sqn Ldr Jack 229, 236
Hereil, Georges.......................................134, 152
Heyworth, Wg Cdr J. H. 157
Hill, Prof Geoffrey T. R. 126, 128, 133
Hubbard, Sq Ldr S. J. 157

Jakimiuk, Wsiewolod John.....................134, 136
Johnson, Major H. C. 151

Keith-Lucas, David 127, 128
Keppie, Flt Lt I. H. 270
Kincheloe, Capt Iven C. 152, 153, 193
Klinker, Olle 114

Lacerne, Jacques..134
Laderach, Major 92
Lamb, Lt Cdr Peter 212
Lancaster, Flt Lt J. O. 'Jo' 31, 32, 37
Larsen, Wg Cdr H. G. F. 159
Leduc, René 42, 43, 46, 51, 191
LeFaivre, Maj Edward N 167
Lickley, Robert L. 100
Littolf, Yvan 45, 49
Lorin, René 42, 43

MacDonald, Flt Lt A. J. 131
Major, Sqn Ldr 'Pete' 40
Maulandi, Pierre 'Tito' 136, 139, 142
Merewether, Hugh C. H. 227, 229
Midgley, Frederick...28
Millett, Lt Cdr Paul 237, 249
Morel, Auguste 199, 205
Muller-Rowland, Sqn Ldr J. S. R. 20, 21

Nadot, Pierre 88, 139
Neale, Maj P. E. 253

Obermeier, Ludwig 290, 292
Oliver, Stanley B. 269, 271
Olow, Bengt R. 112

301

Oshenbein, Tony 171
Overbury, Lt Cdr Jack 212

Parker, Flt Lt Gartrell 'Sailor' Parker 108
Payen, Roland 171, 172
Perrin, Jean 44
Philipp, Horst 292
Pinier, Jacques 253
Prickett, Flt Lt Richard B. 'Tom' 167

Rastel, Daniel 22, 23, 26, 57
Roberts, Alex 2 23
Rozanoff, Constantin 14
Rozier, Jean-Pierre 152, 153

Saget, Jean-Marie 282
Samin, Jean-Jacques 280
Sarrail, Jean 24, 45, 49
Sartre, Pierre 86
Scott-Hall, Stuart 177
Seibold, Dr W. 200
Shepherd, Capt R. T. 157
Simpson, Duncan M. S. 229
Slade, Gp Capt Gordon 99, 177, 178
Smythe, Sqn Ldr R. H. 76

Tayler, Denis 121
Taylor, D. G. 103
Turcat, André 14, 164, 165, 167, 186, 193-195
Turner-Hughes, Charles 28
Twiss, Lt Cdr L. Peter 99, 174-177, 179
Tyson, Geoffrey A. V. 37, 38

Verdin, Lt Cdr James 193
Voisin, Pierre 200
Vonner, Modeste 53

Wales, Sqn Ldr T. B. 68
Wibault, Michel 225

Ziegler, Cdr Bernard 282
Zborowski, Helmut von 196, 200

OTHER TITLES FROM HIKOKI PUBLICATIONS

Chinese Aircraft

China's aviation industry since 1951

Yefim Gordon and Dmitriy Komissarov

A unique description of China's indigenous aircraft from fighters, bombers, special mission and strike aircraft to trainers, light utility, helicopters, UAVs, airliners and transports.

312 pages, hardback, 297mm x 210mm

Over 650 b&w and colour photographs, 110 colour profiles and 100 drawings

9 781902 109046 £34.95

Courage Alone

The Italian Air Force 1940-1943

Chris Dunning

A comprehensive study of the Italian Air Force including area commands and theatres are discussed together with squadron allocations, anti-shipping operations, aircrew and details of the top fighter aces.

320 pages, hardback, 297mm x 210mm

Over 240 b&w photographs and 100 colour profiles

9 781902 109091 £34.95

Luftwaffe Eagle- from the Me109 to the Me262

Walter Schuck

A personal story of 206 combat victories flying an Me109 with an Arctic Sea fighter squadrons and the Me262 with JG 7 in WWII.

224 pages, hardback, 297mm x 210mm

Over 170 b&w photographs, drawings and maps

9 781902 109060 £29.95

MIGs Over North Vietnam

The Vietnamese People's Air Force in Combat 1965-1975

Roger Boniface

A new insight into the aerial war from the Vietnamese side.

176 pages, hardback, 297mm x 210mm

Over 150 b&w and colour photographs

9 781902 109053 £29.95

Russian Strategic Aviation Today

Yefim Gordon and Dmitriy Komissarov

The development and design of the *Blackjack*, *Bear* and *Backfire* aircraft including armament, unit badges and insignia of the units operating them.

272 pages, hardback, 297mm x 210mm

Over 500 colour photographs and colour profiles

9 781902 109131 £34.95

The Seaplane Years

A History of the Marine & Armament Experimental Establishment, 1920-1924 and the Marine Aircraft Experimental Establishment, 1924-1956

Tim Mason

240 pages, hardback, 297mm x 210mm

Over 300 b&w photographs and 20 colour profiles

9 781902 109145 £34.95

The Secret Years

Flight Testing at Boscombe Down 1939-1945

Tim Mason

Over 1,500 British, American and German aircraft were tested here.

320 pages, hardback, 297mm x 210mm

Over 500 b&w photographs and 90 colour profiles

9 781902 109145 £34.95

Soviet Strategic Aviation in the Cold War

Yefim Gordon

Aircraft development including initiatives to fit air-launched missiles to bombers, the first supersonic aircraft and the mighty 1980's Tu-160 *Blackjack*, capable of carrying 12 air-launched cruise missiles.

272 pages, hardback, 297mm x 210mm

Over 500 b&w and colour photographs and 60 colour profiles

9 781902 109084 £34.95

Soviet Tactical Aviation

Yefim Gordon and Dmitriy Komissarov

Post-war Soviet tactical aviation – aircraft, regiments and overseas combat.

356 pages, hardback, 297mm x 210mm

Over 600 b&w and colour photographs and 60 colour profiles

9 781902 109237 £34.95

Soviet and Russian Testbed Aircraft

Yefim Gordon and Dmitriy Komissarov

Soviet and Russian military aircraft, helicopter and civil airliner testbeds since the 1930s.

416 pages, hardback, 297mm x 210mm

Over 700 b&w and colour photographs and 60 colour profiles

9 781902 109183 £34.95

Vulcan's Hammer

V-Force projects and weapons since 1945

Chris Gibson

176 pages, hardback, 297mm x 210mm

Over 80 b&w and colour photographs and 140 line drawings

9 781902 109176 £29.95

Wings of the Luftwaffe

Captain Eric 'Winkle' Brown

A comprehensive description of the flying qualities from the best of the 55 individual German aircraft types which Eric Brown flew.

272 pages, hardback, 297mm x 210mm

Over 200 b&w photographs and 20 colour profiles

9 781902 109152 £34.95

Wings of the Weird and Wonderful

Captain Eric 'Winkle' Brown

Captain Brown reveals the virtues and vices of some of the more unusual aircraft types in his unique experience, including the Arado Ar 232B, and the post war swept wing de Havilland Swallow research aircraft.

288 pages, hardback, 297mm x 210mm

Over 120 b&w photographs and 20 colour drawings

9 781902 109169 £34.95